Robert Bresson

ROBERT BRESSON

A Spiritual Style in Film

Joseph Cunneen

continuum
NEW YORK • LONDON

2003

The Continuum International Publishing Group Inc
370 Lexington Avenue, New York, NY 10017

The Continuum International Publishing Group Ltd
The Tower Building, 11 York Road, London SE1 7NX

Printed in the United States of America

Library of Congress Cataloging-in-Publication Data

Cunneen, Joseph E.
    Robert Bresson : a spiritual style in film / Joseph Cunneen.
        p. cm.
    Includes bibliographical references.
    ISBN 0-8264-1471-0 (hard : alk. paper)
    1. Bresson, Robert—Criticism and interpretation.   I. Title.
    PN1998.3.B755 C86 2003
    791.43'0233'092—dc21
                                            2002152921

To Sally
who still goes to the movies with me

Contents

Film stills and photographs may be found between pages 96 and 97.

Acknowledgments

SPECIAL THANKS TO THE LIBRARIANS AT THE PERFORMING ARTS library of the City of New York; to the librarians at the Bibliothèque du film, Paris; to Mme. Mylène Bresson, for her encouragement and patient assistance in gathering the *photogrammes* from the private collection of Robert and Mylène Bresson that are used to illustrate this book; to Sam Lévin for permission to use the photograph of Robert Bresson; to Jean Collet, for sharing his bibliography on Bresson; to Paule Verdet and Sally Cassidy, for giving me a place to stay in Paris for a crucial period of research; to James Quandt, for sending his invaluable *Robert Bresson*, the hefty collection of major articles that was an undertaking of the Cinematheque Ontario in connection with the 1998 Bresson retrospective in Toronto; to Florence Delay and Pierre Étaix, who consented to be interviewed during my visit to Paris in the fall of 2001; to Kevin Doherty, who sent me material on Bresson he uses in his classes on film; to Robert Tiernan, who helped me run down some hard-to-find videos of Bresson films; to Nöel and Monique Copin, who started off as French landlords and became dear friends; to Edith Delos, who went beyond the demands of friendship in facilitating meetings in Paris; to Sam Lévin for permission to use his copyrighted photograph of Bresson; to Patrick Jordan, who edited my article on Bresson for *Commonweal*; to Justus George Lawler, my editor at Continuum, whose clear-sighted criticism helped improve my manuscript; and to the many fine commentators from whom I have learned to see better what Robert Bresson accomplished.

1

A Demanding Artist Who Respects His Audience

ALTHOUGH ROBERT BRESSON (1901–1999) IS RECOGNIZED BY distinguished critics and fellow directors as one of the greatest filmmakers of the twentieth century, he remains largely unknown to the majority of American moviegoers. This is not due to any conspiracy, but because his work does not fit in with the assumptions of the broad moviegoing audience; the result has been that his movies have never been widely distributed.

One problem is that Bresson worked in French, and the sad reality is that the market for foreign movies has sharply declined in the last thirty years. It is also true that his films are demanding; they call for one's full attention and even then need to be seen more than once. This book is intended as an argument for such viewing—and reviewing—as the way to make possible many pleasures beyond those referred to in these pages. At an exhibit of Vermeer, de La Tour, or Cézanne, we do not rush through the gallery and leave in the belief that we have exhausted the beauty and mystery of the painters' work. We realize that we have to go back and see it again. As the well-known poet and filmmaker Jean Cocteau said, Bresson was "a special figure in this terrible business of making movies. . . . By his refinement, his sense of ellipsis, his rejection of all excessive effects, his desire to give a fundamental place to construction, he is a classic."[1]

Cocteau is right in saying that Bresson is a classic, but since many readers will have had no previous opportunity to become familiar with his work, I have included plot summaries of each of his films. This may be pedestrian and even somewhat misleading, since Bresson's primary concern is hardly traditional storytelling. Without an advance outline of the narrative, however, we are in a poorer position to appreciate certain aspects of Bresson's technique: his rigorous cutting, his deliberate omissions, his frequent decision to place the effect before the cause. The material that I will provide should at least prove useful in unraveling the central themes of his films and in getting a better understanding of what Cocteau calls Bresson's "construction."

Without pretending to follow a rigid schematic outline, each of my chapters begins with a brief background treatment of the film: the source of the "story"; how the director reshaped it to his own ends; technical innovations or developments; and the place of the film in Bresson's overall work. After the summary of the narrative, emphasizing the interaction of the characters and the relation of sound and images, there is an effort to unearth the thematic significance of the film as a whole. Finally, I include responses to the work from contemporary viewers, and draw on insights from leading critics of Bresson as well as interviews he has given to editors and reviewers. My hope is that this material will motivate those who do not already know Bresson's work to seek it out for themselves. It should prepare them to appreciate stylistic habits that can at first seem unusual and should encourage those who are already enthusiasts to return to favorite films with renewed interest.

Perhaps the reader should be warned: developing a taste for Bresson's work will probably leave you less interested in the vast majority of movies released week after week. Not that Bresson's is the only method in which films should be made. When there is nothing at the local multiplex that seems worth the trip, he himself might recommend that you look for Chaplin's *City Lights* or Buster Keaton's *The Cameraman* at your local video shop. Bresson picked the former for a list of his all-time favorites, but Keaton's very "inexpressiveness" may approximate more closely certain aspects of the director's own style.

Bresson's movies are high art, which in his case does not mean something elitist or theoretical. He may well have been an intellectual but his movies are concerned with feelings, not ideas. Fortunately, the feelings he aimed at were never in the service of any ideological thesis or political remedy. Instead, he went to great extremes to avoid the easy exploitation of superficial, readily available emotions. This has led some hasty reviewers to characterize his films as "cold." For example, in *The Trial of Joan of Arc*, despite his veneration for Joan, he does not try to coerce tears from a sympathetic audience; he even minimizes images of the physical brutality practiced against her. Instead he concentrates on the intelligence and audacity of the testimony Joan actually gave during her trial before Bishop Cauchon. Such an emphasis is all the more forceful in its contrast with shots of the bishop and the Count of Warwick spying on her in her cell, or the brief sequence in which women are brought in to determine her virginity.

Even when Joan, after admitting her fear of fire, shuffles through the street to the stake that has been erected for her, Bresson does not rely on shrieks of agony or images of horror. Instead, without explanation, a little dog approaches the pyre, lingers for a moment sensing something wrong and then disappears; pigeons that were on the roof of the tribune fly away; and the chains that had held Joan are now seen to be empty. If our emotions are touched by Bresson's Joan, it is because we are caught up in the rhythm of shot and counter-shot during the many interrogations by the implacable inquisitor, convinced by the absence of special pleading in Joan's bold yet vulnerable voice, shaken by her recantation and its subsequent disavowal, and brought to a sense of closure by a final roll of drums.

An independent figure with a special sympathy for rebels, loners, and victims of an inhuman order, Bresson avoided name stars, established formulas, and slick publicity. He had a sense of the possibilities of cinematography as a genuinely new art form, speaking of the cinematographer as "making a voyage of discovery on an unknown planet."[2] Understandably, rejecting the conventions of his time made it hard for his movies to gain immediate acceptance. The result was that, though there was consistent critical praise for Bresson's films—regularly shown, for example, at the annual Lincoln Center film festival in New York—he constantly had difficulty raising money for his next project, and even his long-cherished hope of making a movie based on the book of Genesis had finally to be abandoned. Most intelligent American moviegoers have not yet had a chance to encounter Bresson for themselves; apart from brief runs in New York, Boston, San Francisco, Los Angeles, and Chicago, the only one of his thirteen movies that has been widely shown in the United States is *Diary of a Country Priest*, based on the novel by Georges Bernanos (1936).

The fact that *Diary* (1951) was Bresson's biggest U.S. success may also have made it harder for his later movies to get proper distribution. It was no help to be labeled a maker of "religious films" when industry wisdom was that religion in the movies was box-office poison. In addition, discriminating moviegoers were not apt to be attracted by a director with such a label at a time when films with religious subject matter tended to be full of sentimental clichés and/or mind-numbing sensationalism. The truth is that, although Bresson's work has a distinctly Catholic sensibility, it appeals primarily on humanistic and aesthetic grounds. As Jean Collet observes, "His ambiguity and austerity obviously do not flatter those Christians looking for easy apologetics, for an optimistic and warm-hearted religion, or for an easy harmony between the carnal and the spiritual. Placing his emphasis on the divisiveness of sin and the solitude of the sinner, Robert Bresson offers us a grave meditation of exceptional sincerity."[3] Since his heroes are always struggling for some kind of liberation or redemption, the movies uncover the deepest dimensions in human nature. Because their development is never presented in didactic or denominational terms, however, agnostics and those who consider themselves unbelievers have no reason to feel excluded.

It is clear that Bresson never aspired to make action blockbusters, and may have been constitutionally incapable of making what publicists call a "date movie."

He deliberately avoided "special effects"; Susan Sontag calls him "the master of the reflective mode" in film. She suggests a parallel between his approach and the way in which Berthold Brecht employed strategies for distancing audiences in the theater. But, she adds, "The emotional distance typical of Bresson's films seems to exist for a different reason altogether: because all identification with characters, however deeply conceived, is an impertinence—an affront to the mystery that is human action and the human heart."[4]

Bresson's failure to reach a broad audience has largely to do with his unwillingness to offer comforting illusions. His vision of reality is demanding, even tragic, but his way of examining the darker aspects of contemporary life allows one to leave the theater cleansed and strengthened. In *Mouchette*, for example, Bresson is faithful to the basic outline of Bernanos's 1937 novella *Nouvelle histoire de Mouchette*. Unflinchingly, he follows the path of his lonely fourteen-year-old heroine as she proceeds to suicide, but frames the action with deep compassion and a sense of possible liberation. The girl has grown up in a dysfunctional family in a small French village; her father and brothers are drunkards; her exhausted mother is so close to death that she is unable to care for the youngest infant. Only two images in *Mouchette* record the girl's spontaneous joy: one, when an older woman buys her a free ride on a "bumper-car" that she drives with abandon at the village fair; the other, after Arsène, a poacher who met her during a storm, has an epileptic attack in an abandoned hut. As she wipes his face with a handkerchief, Mouchette is suddenly able to sing a song of hope that she could only rasp hoarsely in school. But her fun at the fair ends quickly when her father gives her a hard slap after she smiles at a boy in another car, and Arsène rapes her after recovering from his seizure. The morning after her night in the woods Mouchette has no chance to tell her dying mother what has happened, and the idea of death remains with her as she wanders through the village. After coming to a hill overlooking a pond, the girl makes a kind of game of rolling down the hill. Twice she is stopped by a bush next to the pond; the third time her body disappears.

I will take up *Mouchette* in detail in chapter 8; here I want to suggest only how Bresson's view of the human condition shows a clear-minded honesty about life and an emotional identification with its victims. What is important to realize is how he uses his skill as a director to express this understanding, one that is compatible with both a strong sense of evil and a hint of transcendence. His biggest difficulty, Bresson himself said, "was to make *Mouchette* bearable without softening it."[5] He does not shrink from showing the pressures of village life that all but crushed Mouchette's sense of possibility, but he frames the action, both during the opening credits and after her disappearance, with the triumphal music of Monteverdi's "Magnificat," drawn from the latter's *Vespers for the Blessed Virgin.*

Despite her limited resources to combat the repression of village life, Bresson does not depict Mouchette as a purely passive figure. Though society may look on her last act simply as suicide, she remains a rebel; even at the end she struggles desperately for liberation, perhaps to be joined with her mother. Indeed, one of the major themes of the present book is to suggest that, though his films do not pretend to offer solutions to human problems, Bresson's willingness to face up to the collapse of traditional ideals, to examine the lack of communication among men and women and the corrupting effect of money on society as a whole, *and still to go on working,* is itself reason for celebration.

Because Bresson is a director famous for what he leaves out, for his avoidance of melodrama, sensationalism, and even—as we shall see later—of "acting," the first adjective commentators are tempted to use in describing his work has been "austere." This is not completely inappropriate if we also understand how much beauty may be found in austerity. Roger Greenspun, for example, refers to "an austerity that is, in André Bazin's words, almost unbearable, and yet ravishing in its concentration upon the outward signs of some inward grace."[6] The term provides an occasion for misleading oversimplification, however, when it becomes an excuse to label Bresson "jansenist," especially if this is taken to mean an extreme view of the corruption of human nature along with a negative attitude to pleasure.[7] Those like myself who are not theologians would be well advised to avoid the term completely. Nevertheless, before attending a Bresson retrospective, it might be useful to read Pascal, a seventeenth-century mathematician-philosopher who offers an existential sense of what is meant by "the hiddenness of God," and whose *Provincial Letters* contains a polemic against Jesuit casuistry and a defense of jansenist ideas on grace. But although Pascal's aphorism "All things conceal a mystery" should be kept in mind when attending the director's films, it is pointless to try to pigeonhole Bresson. While his sympathy is with Pascal in the latter's criticism of the Jesuits, at one point he actually started work on a movie—which was never made—about St. Ignatius Loyola, whose career, he believed, embodied the influence of both providence and individual determination. Further insight into Bresson's approach is found in the comments of novelist Julien Green, who prepared a scenario for the Loyola project: "He seems immune to picturesque effects, wants neither crucifix nor miracles. . . . In the scene in which the Virgin appears to St. Ignatius, he doesn't want the Virgin to be seen."[8]

Green's recollections are a good indication of how respect for the audience determined Bresson's refusal to exploit the avenues of cheap emotion. The viewer is not manipulated by the way scenes are staged, and a certain distance is maintained even from characters like Joan of Arc, with whom there is clearly a presumption of sympathy. To convey this sympathetic yet disinterested view of his characters Bresson searched relentlessly for greater precision in relating image and sound, narrative and form, drawing on all the elements that could be brought together to make film an independent art form. The tribute of Jean-Luc Godard—"Bresson is to French film what Dostoevsky is to the Russian novel, what Mozart is to German music"—may be too expansive to account for his achievement. Martin Scorsese's comment, however, is more precise: "Elvis Costello said that whenever he's writing a song he asks himself, is it as tough as Hank Williams? Meaning—is it as ruthlessly pared down, as direct, as unflinching in its gaze at aspects of life I might feel more comfortable ignoring? Young film-makers might well ask themselves: is it as tough as Bresson?"

At the same time, one should keep in mind Bresson's repeated insistence that human existence has meaning; even though there are ominous signs on the horizon, each person is of inestimable value. He never stoops to cheap cynicism, but celebrates the heroism of the unending, never completely successful struggle for freedom. Michel Estève is right, therefore, when he insists:

> Bresson gives his characters the essential qualities of childhood: stubbornness, a healthy pride, a sense of absolute hope. Especially in his first six films, Bresson's heroes save themselves by accepting their existential responsibilities: in fidelity to their own vocation they conquer themselves through a combination of will, freedom, and grace. That is why saying that Bresson is jansenist is a gross misinterpretation.[9]

In *A Man Escaped,* for example, Lieutenant Fontaine, imprisoned by the Nazis as a member of the Resistance during World War II, is a personification of alert intelligence as he knocks on the wall of his cell hoping for a response from the prisoner on the other side. He listens for the jangle of the guard's keys as the latter proceeds down the corridor, then concentrates patiently on using the spoon he has bent into a chisel, scraping away tirelessly in his effort to weaken the panels of his prison door.

Because he was a painter before he began making films, Bresson might have been expected to specialize in the creation of beautiful compositions, but he deliberately avoided shots that would call too much attention to themselves. "He regularly used a 50mm lens, which is not considered very cinematic, framing as little as possible, and respecting as much as possible the vision of the eye. For this reason, he did not like labored dolly or panoramic shots, which do not correspond to our way of seeing because they separate the eye from the body."[10]

For Bresson, all the elements of the movie have to work together; its beauty is to be found in its relationships. Léonce-Henri Burel's photography in *Diary of a Country Priest* is an outstanding example of such an approach. The memorable shots of the curé d'Ambricourt walking past a huge tree as he approaches the chateau of the local aristocrats, or another of him ordering the count's rebellious daughter into the confessional if she wishes to speak to him, do not stop the action but deepen our understanding of what is at stake. The later, color photography of Pasqualo De Sanctis in *Lancelot of the Lake,* with its tournament scene introduced by shots of the horses' legs and continuing with close-ups of lances and armor and the constant hoisting of banners, is an equally striking example of the way in which Bresson marries form to content.

A further reason that Bresson is largely unknown in the United States is that he was an intensely private person. An internationally admired director, he talked freely to critics about his films as they appeared but avoided the publicity-generating celebrity circuit and refused to provide copy for gossip columnists. His biography consists principally of the dates of his movies. His first wife died; his second, Mylène Van der Mersch, worked as his assistant after 1967—that is, on the last six films, beginning with *Mouchette.* He had no children.

All that is known otherwise is that Bresson was born in 1901 in Bromont-Lamothe (Puy de Drôme). He attended secondary school at the lycée Lakanal in Sceaux, where he passed his *baccalauréat* after studying Latin, Greek, and philosophy. He first became a painter but did not exhibit his work, and was quoted as saying "After Cézanne, there is nothing more to do."

In the 1930s he became involved in movies and even directed a short film, *Les Affaires publiques*, in 1934. Bresson described it as a "crazy comedy," largely a vehicle for the well-known circus clown Béby. For a long time it was presumed destroyed during World War II, but a copy was found by the Cinémathèque française in 1986. A satiric work, considered avant-garde at the time, it presents three days in the life of an imaginary dictator, Béby, filmed by a photographer of fantasy newsreels. Firemen try to save a burning house, which flies away, but the chief is decorated. A princess falls from an airplane. As the dictator dedicates his statue, it yawns, putting everyone to sleep; when Béby tries to christen a boat with champagne, it sinks.

Les Affaires publiques gives no hint of the thematic concerns of Bresson's later films. Roger Leenhardt's review sees parallels with the Marx brothers' *Duck Soup* and W. C. Fields's *Million Dollar Legs* but concedes that it doesn't measure up to those farcical successes. He points to an awkwardness understandable in apprentice work and criticizes "a search for visual effects conceived of independently of the dialogue."[11]

Bresson acquired further professional experience in the movies by writing the dialogue for *C'était un musicien* (1933), by working on the adaptation of *Courier Sud*, a novel by Antoine de Saint-Exupéry (1936), by being a partner on the scenario of *Jumeaux de Brighton* (1936), and by acting as director's assistant on *La vierge folle* (1938). He also participated in the preparation of *L'air pur* of René Claire (1939), a movie that was never made. Early in World War II he was taken prisoner by the Germans and held for more than a year, an experience he undoubtedly drew on in making *A Man Escaped* (1956).

Back in Paris, he was able to make his first full-length movie, *Angels of Sin*, in 1943. His last, *L'Argent* (*Money*) appeared forty years later. He continued to develop ideas for other films, notably, *La Genèse* (*Genesis*), a project he nurtured for thirty-five years. As René Prédal wrote in 1992, "Even if this reflection on the origins of humanity is perhaps not really destined to materialize, it suggests the dimensions of the artist's work and makes clear its profound nature: Bresson does not offer an entertainment but a vision of the world that the majority of critics recognize as Christian."[12] A few years later, after an extended illness, Bresson died on December 18, 1999.

Bresson's inner convictions never tempt him to preach; his concern is less with subject matter than with the perfection of a pared-down style. In addition to *Diary of a Country Priest* and *A Man Escaped*, to which reference has already been made, he directed eleven other movies that deal with a great variety of topics and draw on an intriguing range of sources. *Angels of*

Sin tells the story of the efforts of an order of Dominican sisters to rehabilitate women prisoners; *Pickpocket* observes the apprenticeship in crime of a young robber in Paris; *The Trial of Joan of Arc* draws almost exclusively on the transcript of the saint's fifteenth-century trial; *Au hasard Balthasar* presents the stages in the life of a donkey whose career intersects with the destinies of a number of villagers; *The Devil Probably* is a contemporary study of disillusioned young people in Paris; *Lancelot of the Lake* retells the Lancelot-Guinevere story in the context of the collapse of the knightly ideal after the failure to find the Holy Grail.

In addition, Bresson translated four more literary texts into film: *The Ladies of the Bois de Boulogne*, based on a story from Diderot's *Jacques le fataliste*, dealing with the revenge of an eighteenth-century upper-class woman on a lover whose ardor has grown cold; *A Gentle Woman*, from Dostoevsky's novella of that name, which probes the reasons behind a young wife's suicide; *Four Nights of a Dreamer*, which relocates Dostoevsky's "White Nights" from St. Petersburg to contemporary Paris; and *L'Argent*, an adaptation of Tolstoy's short novel *The False Coupon*.

AS IMPORTANT FOR BRESSON AS HIS VARIOUS SUBJECTS AND SOURCES is his vision of the possibilities of cinematography, an art he considered still in its infancy because of the dominance of what he called "photographed theater." *Notes of a Cinematographer*, a collection of highly aphoristic reminders to himself on the priorities of filmmaking, is an indispensable reference for anyone interested in Bresson, but it would be foolish to get terribly involved in theories before looking at his films. His ideas are best appreciated in relation to the specifics of his actual work. Bresson's position on cinematography was refined over a considerable period of time, since it grew out of his experience as a director; he did not start with theory and always left room for improvisation in the actual shooting of a film.

One clear mark of Bresson's art is his sure sense of pacing; he asked for innumerable takes on the set but the finished film moves with speed. His longest movie, *Diary of a Country Priest*, runs an hour and fifty minutes; *The Trial of Joan of Arc*, only sixty-five minutes. The cuts from one scene to another may sometimes seem abrupt; careful examination, however, will reveal a seamless continuity, as when a sound from the following scene intrudes on the ending of the one before it.

The viewer's real difficulty comes from expectations carried over from conventional moviegoing—the assumption that everything will be explained. In contrast, Bresson does not always bother to make clear to the audience that there has been a jump in time. It may take a while to get your bearings, therefore, when one shot is followed without transition by another that indicates a change in place. Spectators may never completely understand why a character does what he or she does and are often forced to reflect on underlying motives long after they have left the theater.

By and large, Bresson's work represents a break with the pre–World War II emphasis on psychology, which had lent considerable prestige to French filmmaking. He presents almost nothing about the past of the characters in his movies, and one sometimes remains unsure what will happen to them at the conclusion. This means that contradictory readings of Bresson's films can legitimately be defended and that he was not speaking theoretically when he said he expected to learn something new from observing the work of his interpreters while a film was being shot.

Above all, Bresson earned widespread praise for his attention to the soundtracks of his moves, for his recording of natural sounds that can affect audiences deeply, even though viewers are usually only partially aware of the sounds. At the same time his career shows a decreasing use of background music; whereas his first movie, *Angels of Sin,* gave a large place to the chanting of the nuns in order to create an emotional atmosphere that would reinforce its central theme, by the time he made *The Trial of Joan of Arc* (1962) we hear only an insistent roll of drums at the beginning and the end.

Bresson's first two movies, which were made within the accepted framework of French studio productions, led him to reject the star system and to raise fundamental questions about the nature of acting for the screen. The first section of his *Notes of a Cinematographer* is dated 1950, but it is obvious that his resistance to overacting and his general unwillingness to overwhelm the audience emotionally came naturally to him. This probably explains his battles with Maria Casarès, a distinguished actress in the French theater, during the making of *The Ladies of the Bois de Boulogne.*

Bresson's approach creates two problems. Understandably enough, even serious students of film often go to the movies primarily to see a particular star. In addition, the kind of performance he tried to elicit from his cast—whose members he would soon call "models" rather than actors—is hardly of a kind that would win them rave reviews and Academy Awards. Instead, it is apt at first to make some people reject Bresson's movies as "cold." It would be more accurate to say that Bresson's films tend to foster a contemplative attitude in audiences, and the emotional experience they help to induce is frequently deeper and longer-lasting than that of even the best conventional productions.

One important result of his rejection of professional actors was that those who attended his films were watching performers whom they had never before seen on the screen. This experience, "as if for the first time," constitutes an important part of Bresson's aesthetic. It was also the reason why there is rarely an identification of the places used as backgrounds in the scenes of his movies. Not only did he not want to duplicate picture postcards of well-known locales; he hoped to ensure the freshness of the spectator's response.

Abandoning what he called "photographed theater," Bresson even rejected the standard French term for director, *metteur en scène*, and pre-ferred to think of himself as one who "puts things in order." "Why hide the fact that everything ends up on a rectangle of white cloth suspended on a wall?" he asked. "(Look on your film as a surface to cover.)"[13]

Bresson's films rarely have any explicit political content, though *The Devil Probably* contains some impassioned ecological footage, a protest against the way in which the modern world is destroying its own home. Sev-eral of his later films include provocative insights regarding the youth cul-ture of contemporary Paris, but in general few clues are provided by which one could clearly date them. Even when he draws on historically grounded subjects in *The Trial of Joan of Arc, Lancelot of the Lake,* and *The Ladies of the Bois de Boulogne,* he makes no effort at total authenticity in costume or background detail. In fact, *Bois de Boulogne* was sharply criticized by some when it first appeared because people used telephones and drove modern automobiles in a story premised on older cultural and ethical values.

All his movies, however, are governed by what he understood as "the real." "There are two sorts of real," he wrote in *Notes:* "1. The crude real recorded as it is by the camera; 2. what we call real and see deformed by our memory and some wrong reckonings."[14] It is obvious that his admiration for such classic documentaries as *Man of Aran* and *Louisiana Story* is not based on the naive assumption that director Robert Flaherty found himself in interesting locations and simply used his camera to make a mechanically cor-rect recording. Bresson had great respect for reality—material objects might almost be considered to play roles in his films—and chose *Bicycle Thieves* (1947) for his list of all-time favorite movies, but he was doing something quite different from what the neo-realist Vittorio de Sica accomplished. Dis-cussing his 1957 movie *A Man Escaped,* Bresson said explicitly, "I wanted all the facts to be exact, but at the same time I tried to get beyond basic real-ism. . . . I was hoping to make a film about objects which would at the same time have a soul."[15]

As Amédée Ayfre points out, Bresson's world "makes no attempt to pass for the everyday universe."

> [Instead, he] wants to show by various devices the essence or soul of concrete
> reality rather than its more or less chaotic workings. . . . How does Bresson

manage to give us only the essence of people without any feeling of thinness? Largely through a very precise choice of details, objects, and accessories, through gestures charged with an extremely solid reality.[16]

In his 1972 study *Transcendental Style in Film,* Paul Schrader, who later achieved distinction both as a screenwriter and as a director, made a pioneering English-language attempt to understand Bresson's approach as a way to go beyond surface realism:

> The realistic surface is just that—a surface—and the raw material taken from real life is the raw material of the Transcendent.
>   Bresson's use of the everyday is not derived from a concern for "real life," but from an opposition to the contrived, dramatic events which pass for real life in movies. These emotional constructs—plot, acting, camerawork, editing, music—are "screens." . . . Screens prevent the viewer from seeing through the surface reality to the supernatural; they suppose that the external reality is self-sufficient.[17]

Sartre criticized the characters of François Mauriac because he believed the latter pretended to be God observing the action of his novels. Bresson is not open to such criticism; he does not assume that he understands his characters fully. "There is always something fundamental and mysterious in them that escapes us," Ayfre comments. "In other words, they are more than characters, more than souls, they are people: 'the most perfect thing in nature' (St. Thomas)."[18]

Although the word "soul" is frequently employed by his critics, one should avoid any airy discussion of "spirituality" in Bresson's work. Indeed, Schmuel Ben-Gad refers astutely to Bresson's "materialist art":

> his precise ordered presentation of carefully chosen and composed non-significant images invites the viewer to what Andrew Sarris called "contemplation," though not a contemplation of vague, spiritual notions. It is rather, at least at first, of physical realities like faces and hands, doorways, and axes. If anything—"spiritual" or otherwise—exists beneath or behind material reality, if physical reality is in fact a surface, then the only possibility of knowing this other reality will be through a profound gaze at this surface.[19]

Whatever his convictions about the nature of the universe, Bresson's primary concentration is on those bits and pieces of the material world he will rearrange during the editing process. No doubt he felt that the common tendency to make the material and the spiritual completely contradictory categories obscures the truth of things.

The donkey who is the title character of *Au hasard Balthasar,* for example, is a very real donkey, yet at the same time a witness to the human blindness and wickedness around him, a living metaphor of our common vulnerability. The fact that the donkey, shortly after birth, was given the salt of baptism by Marie, a young village girl, and that later he carries relics in a village procession, does not prevent his being used in a smuggling operation during which he is shot, abandoned, and left to die a painful death the following day. The quality of the compassion suggested by Bresson's careful selection of details should elicit a deep resonance in the audience, especially if they simultaneously bear in mind his challenging aphorism: "The supernatural in film is only the real rendered more precise. Real things seen close up."[20]

Because his narrative technique is very different from that of most directors, any attempt to present summaries of Bresson's movies has special difficulties. He does not build methodically to a clear climax, and there is a deliberate absence of histrionics. The whole emerges from a collection of fragments; instead of a series of artificial emphases, the various objects, backgrounds, and characters receive an evenly distributed attention. Everything is pared down; there are many ellipses and a relative absence of psychology.

Such an approach requires the viewer to be constantly alert to what is heard on the soundtrack as well as seen on the screen. Meaning emerges from a complex series of relationships, and questions of interpretation inevitably depend on the assumptions and cultural references the audience brings to the theater. In film after film, Bresson leaves interpretation open. Close attention to each of them in turn is the only path that can lead to genuine understanding.

NOTES

1. Jean Cocteau, preface to René Briot, *Robert Bresson* (Paris: Éditions du Cerf, 1957).

2. Robert Bresson, *Notes of a Cinematographer* (Los Angeles: Sun and Moon Press, 1988), 33.

3. Jean Collet, *Télé-ciné*, no. 88 (March–April 1960).

4. Susan Sontag, "Spiritual Style in the Films of Robert Bresson," in *Against Interpretation* (New York: Farrar, Straus and Giroux, 1966), 181.

5. Interview about *Mouchette* in *L'Avant-scène Cinéma* no. 80 (July 1967).

6. Roger Greenspun, *New York Times*, November 26, 1972, section 2.

7. The Jansenist movement, named for Bishop Cornelius Jansen (d. 1638) developed in France in the seventeenth century. Its heavily Augustinian outlook tended to emphasize "a sharp contrast between human corruption . . . and redemption." See *Encyclopedia of Theology*, ed. Karl Rahner (New York: Seabury Press, 1975), 728.

8. Julien Green, "En travaillant avec Robert Bresson," *Cahiers du cinéma* no. 50 (August–September 1955), 19–21.

9. Michel Estève, *Robert Bresson* (Paris: Editions Albatros, 1983), 132.

10. René Prédal, "Robert Bresson: L'aventure intérieure," *L'Avant-scène cinéma* (January-February 1992): 14–15.

11. Roger Leenhardt, in *Roger Bresson: Éloge* (Paris: Cinémathèque française, 1997), 11 (originally in *Esprit* [December 1934]).

12. Prédal, "Robert Bresson," 3.

13. Jean Sémolué, *Bresson ou l'acte pur des Métamorphoses* (Paris: Flammarion, 1993), 268.

14. Bresson, *Notes of a Cinematographer*, 78–79.

15. Quoted in Amédée Ayfre, "The Universe of Robert Bresson," in *The Films of Robert Bresson*, ed. Ian Cameron (New York: Praeger, 1969). 8.

16. Ibid., 7–8.

17. Paul Schrader, *Transcendental Style in Film: Ozu, Bresson, Dreyer* (Berkeley: University of California Press, 1972), 63–64.

18. Ayfre, "Universe of Robert Bresson," 6.

19. Schmuel Ben-Gad, "To See the World Profoundly: The Films of Robert Bresson," *Cross Currents* 47 (summer 1997): 234.

20. James Blue, Excerpts from an Interview with Robert Bresson, June 1965, by the author, 1969, 2.

2

Bresson before Bresson

Angels of Sin and
The Ladies of the Bois de Boulogne

BRESSON CERTAINLY NEVER DISAVOWED HIS FIRST TWO movies and they have always had distinguished admirers, but they are primarily of interest in suggesting ways in which they prepare for substantive changes in what was to become his signature style. *Angels of Sin* (*Les Anges du péché*, 1943) and *The Ladies of the Bois de Boulogne* (*Les Dames du bois de Boulogne*, 1945) are studio productions, essentially conventional black-and-white films made in accordance with pre–World War II French standards. Still worth viewing, they also offer significant clues as to why he was later to call for cinematography rather than cinema.

The first feature Bresson directed grew out of the desire of Père R. L. Brückberger, O.P., a well-known figure in the French Resistance movement, to bring to public attention the work of the Dominican Congregation of Marie-Madeleine. This religious community, the Sisters of Bethany, was dedicated to helping women after they were released from prison. In fact, "Bethany" was the original name of the movie, but the producer decided it wasn't commercial enough.

Angels of Sin avoids the sensationalism of its title; the emphasis is on strong plotting, a somewhat literary dialogue, and the skill of established actors. Its Catholic motifs are much too explicit for Bresson's later taste, though the Christian idea that the sacrifices of one character can work toward the spiritual good of another will recur in later films, especially *Diary of a Country Priest.* In fact, the dramatization of the work of the Sisters of Bethany was also an implicit criticism of bourgeois French Catholicism. The constitution of the Bethany sisters challenged conventional piety by stating that former prisoners who believe they have a religious vocation are eligible for reception into the community.

Angels of Sin has far greater depth than Hollywood "religious" films of that time, which tended to reduce the demands of the supernatural to the simplistic dimensions of individual morality. From the start Bresson shows an instinctive sympathy for rebels: the central plot line of the movie contrasts a conventional following of convent rules with the headstrong spirit of one of the sisters who understands her vocation in extremist terms.

The credits attribute the scenario to Brückberger, Bresson, and Jean Giraudoux, with the dialogue by Giraudoux, the distinguished dramatist whose reputation was then at its height. Brückberger encouraged Bresson to read a book on the subject by Père Lelong, *Les Dominicaines des prisons*, and the fledgling director gathered more background material from the nuns themselves.[1] Although Giraudoux's contribution guaranteed the high quality of the dramatic exchanges, the experience made Bresson reflect on the contradictions between a literary script and the nature of film. He was also unhappy with some of the actresses who played the key roles of the Dominican sisters, even though they were professionally qualified; he was especially disturbed by what he considered the artificial quality of their voices. Michel Estève says that Bresson's first two films, *Angels of Sin* and *The Ladies of the Bois de Boulogne*, are marked by several characteristics that would disappear in his later work: "a lighting that is sometimes overdone, a little artificial, its lack of sobriety giving the photography a somewhat syrupy quality; overly literary dialogue, the use of professional actors, and a classic linear intrigue."[2]

From the beginning Bresson practiced an economy of means. *Angels of Sin* includes a murder, but it is presented in the briefest terms and the spectacular and criminal aspects of the story are minimized. The central action turns on the mysterious relationship between an intense young novice, Anne-Marie, and Thérèse, a former prisoner who murders her ex-lover immediately after release and takes refuge in the convent. If the supernatural dimension of the story was to be meaningful to a contemporary audience, the director believed, it needed to be grounded in a realistic presentation of everyday life in the convent. In this, he largely succeeded: Roland Barthes, no admirer of pious confections, considered *Angels of Sin* a successful movie largely because he believed the actresses were credible as nuns; he was impressed by the way they moved. After calling attention to the images of long, bare corridors and a linear cloister, the discreet use of bells and music, and the fact that the prioress "really looks like a nun for once, not a madam in disguise," Barthes praised the "dialogue for taking us into a higher universe where the convent's intimacy is as warm as sackcloth and as restful."[3]

MUCH OF THE FILM WAS SHOT AT NIGHT, AS IT WAS MADE DURING the German occupation of paris, much of the film was shot at night; though its content is apolitical, its dark background shots create something of the atmosphere of underground struggle that was going on in France at that time. The credits are followed by a text that summarizes the movie's intentions:

> This film is inspired by the life of a French Dominican congregation that was founded in 1867 by Père Lataste.
>
> The authors are responsible for the plot that they have imagined but in the choice of images and the details that have been taken from reality they have tried to respect the atmosphere that reigns in these convents and the spirit which animates their mission.

After an opening shot of the convent garden and the tomb of Père Lataste, a nun emerges from the convent to ring the bell, a group of sisters are seen moving purposefully through a corridor, and another nun goes from room to room to summon the community to chapel. Once the film's background is thus economically established, the prioress (Sylvie) is seen answering the phone before reviewing plans with her chief assistants regarding their upcoming visit to a nearby prison. Conveying a sense of professionalism as she displays a map of the prison area, she asks them to recognize the need for caution but offers reassurance: "After all, our driver is an ex-boxer."

In the chapel the prioress tells the community to continue to pray until she and her assistants return. The scene shifts to a dark street, and the nuns walk with determination to the prison gate, where they receive Agnès, a young woman who has just been discharged. When Agnès tells them she has received threats, the nuns hide in a doorway as a few men go by. There is a sense of relief when they get to the cab that is waiting for them.

This dramatic presentation of the central purpose of the congregation gives greater impact to the following scene, in which Anne-Marie (Renée Faure), a pretty young woman from a bourgeois family, seeks admission to the community. The prioress tests Anne-Marie by telling her she risks being taken for a criminal if she becomes part of a group that makes no distinction between ex-prisoners and other sisters. "That is one reason why I'm here," the young woman responds.

After Agnès and Anne-Marie, the two newcomers, prostrate themselves as a sign of obedience to the rule of the order, they are warmly invited by the prioress to "become part of our family." In conformity with the vow of poverty, Anne-Marie rids herself of most of the possessions she brought with her to the convent, but is understandably upset when she discovers that a chain, a gold pencil, and a small mirror have disappeared. Bresson cuts quickly to a scene between a contrite Agnès and the understanding prioress. "I need your severity," Agnès insists. "Your own will be enough," the latter responds. When Anne-Marie tells Agnès to keep her chain and pencil, the ex-prisoner marvels at the young sister's fervor: "One needs courage to kiss a leper." "Or much pride," responds Anne-Marie.

Despite this suggestion of self-awareness, Anne-Marie insists on going with the prioress on the next prison visit. Sylvie's low-key interpretation of the prioress shows her to be a woman of prudence and humor who can appreciate Anne-Marie's independence. The latter's eagerness to visit the jail was sharpened by Agnès's mention of another prisoner, Thérèse (Jany Holt), described as both beautiful and dangerous. "Someone is calling me," Anne-Marie confides to the prioress.

This sequence is brilliantly counterpointed by the arrival at the convent of Anne-Marie's mother, whose elegant appearance reinforces our awareness that the new postulant comes from a background of luxury. The mother is appalled by the special vocation of the Dominicans of Bethany and tells her daughter, "Devote your life to God, not to crime." Although Anne-Marie tries to be kind, she is immovable: "I'm your little girl, but I'm made of iron." The scene is followed by one in which Anne-Marie symbolically makes a final break with her past, burning letters and photographs in a small fireplace in her room. As a large photograph of her mother dissolves in flames, the musical background reinforces the emotion of the moment, a conventional movie practice which Bresson would later criticize sharply.

The action moves to the prison to observe the prioress's level-headed empathy as she deals with Clotilde, who must serve a twenty-year sentence, and Jenny, to whom she promises real face powder instead of the plaster the young woman has had to use as a substitute. A sullen prisoner named Thérèse pushes the soup wagon from cell to cell; whether through anger or carelessness, she manages to spill some on Anne-Marie's habit. Anne-Marie nevertheless tries to establish a bond with the prisoner but is completely rebuffed. The prioress gently explains to the young novice that Thérèse will inevitably resist any words spoken to her in jail because she will hear them as commands.

The prison attendant tries to hurry Thérèse along, which only increases her anger. As the emotion of the moment is again heightened by music, Thérèse pushes the soup wagon down the stairs, leaving the pots in a heap. She runs desperately through the prison as if hoping to escape; soon she is in solitary confinement, screaming with frustration. Anne-Marie visits her, telling her that she and the prioress are the sisters of all those in prison. "Not mine," Thérèse answers defiantly, "I'm innocent."

Back at the convent, the sisters assemble to receive an individual spiritual maxim, a phrase or sentence intended to offer them special guidance. One receives Pascal's "Everything happens through mystery," a motto that could be applied to Bresson's entire career as a director. The sentences seem appropriate for those who receive them: Mother Saint-Jean (the somewhat legalistic assistant prioress) gets Teresa of Avila's "Don't obey my orders; obey my silences," and Anne-Marie receives advice from Catherine of Siena: "If you hear the word that ties you to another human being, do not listen to any others that follow—they are merely its echo."

Understanding her maxim as confirming her link with Thérèse, Anne-Marie asks the prioress if she may accompany her when the prisoner is released. Mother Saint-Jean is alienated by Anne-Marie's boldness, but the prioress consents, asking her assistant, "Shall we listen to the mischievous or only to the good ones?"

At the prison, however, Thérèse seems unreachable after she is discharged. The prioress gets no response when she tells her she will be welcome at the convent if she has no place to go. Anne-Marie chases after her in the rain but the angry young woman merely cries out, "Let me go!" The camera then follows a determined Thérèse into a gun store where she quickly obtains a revolver. She fires point blank at the man answering the doorbell in a nearby apartment building, believing him responsible for her unjust imprisonment. Back at the convent, Anne-Marie prays for the ex-prisoner, who, she senses, is undergoing a special test.

Thérèse's eventual arrival at the convent comes within another scene documenting the everyday life of the sisters. Anne-Marie is reading the story of the wolf of Gubbio, one of the legends associated with Francis of Assisi, while the community is eating. Twice she interrupts herself to ask if the others have heard the bell ring. She is told no, but when she asks the third time, Thérèse, looking for a safe hiding place, is found knocking at the door.

From here on Bresson offers occasional brief glimpses of police activity as they pursue clues to the murder. Meanwhile Anne-Marie, who has been given the job of introducing Thérèse to community life, decides to relax the discipline by taking the newcomer into the convent garden. As she begins to explain the language of flowers to Thérèse, she is interrupted by Mother Saint-Jean, who tells her she has no right to be in the garden at that time and orders her back to her cell. Although Anne-Marie angrily declares there is only one rule, that of the heart, she prostrates herself, accepting the authority of her superior.

At the convent laundry, where several of the sisters work and gossip, Thérèse complains that Anne-Marie treats her almost as a personal possession. Out of resentment, Thérèse lays a trap for Anne-Marie, telling her that some of the sisters are plotting against her. The latter, however, follows her impulse, expressing her love of beauty by placing flowers in the sisters' cells. When Mother Saint-Jean tells her the rules forbid such a worldly attachment, Anne-Marie makes clear she considers such a position hypocritical.

The following scene makes the convent practice of "fraternal correction" a useful window into religious life and illuminates a stage of Anne-Marie's development. As she goes from sister to sister, she receives both praise and stiff criticism. Understandably, she finds these brief exchanges a difficult experience. The process is a lesson in self-knowledge: the majority consider her gifted but self-centered, clever but hot-headed.

Bresson has already placed Mother Saint-Jean's cat Duffie in the background of convent life, often visible while the sisters are sewing or listening to a reading. Anne-Marie accuses them of currying favor with the assistant prioress by caressing the cat and pretending affection for the animal. Challenged, she even calls the cat an agent of Beelzebub, since Duffie has eaten both the toad in the garden and the blackbird that had given them so much pleasure. This time the prioress feels the young postulant has gone too far and calls on her to do public penance, but Anne-Marie feels unable to comply with her vow of obedience.

The pace of the action quickens: Anne-Marie is dismissed from the order. Alone with the prioress and again wearing street clothes, she is close to despair. Torn between her instinctive admiration for Anne-Marie and "the community's interest," the prioress is convinced that her decision is necessary. Anne-Marie's lonely departure is visually contrasted to a group shot of the nuns chanting as they file into the convent garden.

Suddenly there is a telephone call from Anne-Marie's mother, in which the prioress learns that the young woman has not returned home; she hopes Anne-Marie's absence is simply another manifestation of independence. From here to the end of the film the narrative shifts back and forth from the convent to police headquarters, where they are actively looking for Thérèse, whom they now suspect of murder.

Anne-Marie has spent the evening in the thick shrubbery of the convent garden, sleeping in the bushes. The following night there is a heavy, cold rain, and Anne-Marie prays fervently at the tomb of Fr. Lataste, the founder of the order, to which she still feels loyal. The nuns discover her in the morning, desperately sick, and quickly put her to bed; Thérèse is assigned to nurse her.

The prioress anxiously hovers over Anne-Marie, her smile making clear that she has forgiven the willful postulant. A special light emanates from the young woman's face as she tells the prioress she wants to perform the penance she had previously rejected. Having come to greater self-knowledge, she tells the superior, "I assigned myself a high mission, but could only bully a cat."

Equally significant are the gradual changes in the relationship between Anne-Marie and Thérèse. Anne-Marie tries to apologize for her earlier approach: "I was ridiculous," she confesses, "but I loved you: that was my only excuse. . . . I forced you to lie. I kept showing off." At first Thérèse considers this confession simply a new way to dominate her, and says that there is no cure for a "dead" heart. But when Anne-Marie says that the hope of accomplishing such a cure would keep her alive a hundred years, Thérèse begins to relent.

At this point the police chief calls the prioress, telling her that his men are coming to the convent. By now it is evident that Anne-Marie is dying, and the prioress is summoned. The camera catches the nuns rushing along the corridor to assemble near Anne-Marie's bedside. When the police enter the downstairs area of the convent, the prioress declares with quiet authority, "Let them wait."

Anne-Marie begs permission to profess her formal vows as a member of Bethany but is too weak to pronounce them. It is Thérèse who says the words for her, only seconds before Anne-Marie expires. The prioress asks the community to sing the "Salve Regina," and as their voices rise in the traditional hymn of praise to Mary, the camera returns to the police downstairs. A minute later, after she has composed herself, Thérèse slowly descends the stairs to the waiting police and calmly offers herself to be handcuffed.

—ALTHOUGH THE RELIGIOUS MOTIVATIONS OF THE MAIN CHARACTERS earn respect, and audiences could still be moved by the film's central scenes, it is difficult not to consider the ending of *Angels of Sin* somewhat contrived. In addition, during its first hour, many might mistakenly believe that they are being asked to identify uncritically with Anne-Marie. Cinematographer

Philippe Agostini's lighting seems almost like a halo, underlining Renée Faure's impassioned acting style as she speaks of her special vocation. Bresson was later careful to prevent such excesses. Jany Holt is more successful as Thérèse, in part because she has far fewer lines. Except for her outburst in prison when she deliberately upsets the soup wagon, she must construct her character out of indirect suggestions, ambiguous glances, and a pattern of consistent resistance. When she had to pronounce the words of the vows in place of Anne-Marie, however, Holt tried Bresson's patience by weeping during one take after another. Nevertheless, at the end, she shows both firmness and restraint in walking to her captors, hands outstretched.

Critic Tony Pipolo is perceptive in emphasizing the cut after Anne-Marie asks for permission to accompany the prioress when Thérèse is released from prison and the subsequent shot in which we see the two women waiting for the prisoner. It is clear that, in the interval, the enthusiasm of the new sister has led the prioress to overrule the objections of Mother Saint-Jean.

> Elliptic strategies of this kind can be found in many films, but their significance in Bresson, even at this early stage, is that they bear directly on the moral and thematic foundations of his work. Here, they appear to respond, as if by injunction, to the maxim which Anne-Marie is given—the "word that ties [her] to another human being"—and to make inevitable the effectuation of its directive. The narrative structure itself, in other words, is now committed to fulfilling the truth of the maxim. It is the moral conviction that underpins this connection between narrative trajectory and form that, I believe, gives Bresson's work such undeniable force.[4]

Bresson, of course, is drawing on the theme of the communion of saints, a favorite of such French Catholic writers as Charles Péguy and Georges Bernanos, and later popularized in Graham Greene's *The End of the Affair*. Even if Anne-Marie's death seems too convenient a plot "solution," the sense that her life and that of Thérèse are mysteriously joined becomes almost palpable. The image of Anne-Marie kissing Thérèse at their first meeting in prison is repeated at the end when Thérèse kisses the naked feet of the now-dead sister. The trials and sufferings of one person are shown to be of assistance to another: Thérèse and Anne-Marie are necessary to each other's spiritual flowering.

Before Thérèse's arrival at the convent, Anne-Marie prays aloud: "Tell me that the burden with which you have charged me in allowing me to hear the secret of a poor soul in despair is only a trial that will give birth to my greatest joy." Her excessive confidence seems justified when she "hears" Thérèse ringing the bell at the convent door, but this apparent fulfillment of her prayer makes her forget the prioress's warning in prison on dealing with souls that have been victimized and humiliated. Later, she prays to the founder of Bethany at his tomb: "You are not yet a saint. . . . That is why, before praying, I dare to offer you my sad complaint. Help me; my suffering has been too strong." She had been proud to think she had been chosen to convert the most hardened and guilty sinner; now she can no longer find the strength to go on. The later Bresson will not formulate his themes in such explicit language and would probably consider it melodramatic to have a heavy rain fall on Anne-Marie's face while she is praying, but he will return again and again to the idea of strong spiritual links between characters.

The subtlety of Anne-Marie's interior development is seen in the change she undergoes as she abandons her earlier confidence in order to find genuine humility. When she is reading to the other sisters, she is convinced that she hears the outside bell announcing Thérèse's arrival at the convent. At the end of the fraternal correction she says resolutely, "There is another voice that tells me the path I am to take, and I will follow it to the end. No one will stop me." Later, however, after she has been expelled from the convent, when she prays desperately at the tomb of Fr. Lataste, she employs a more explicit language than we will meet with in Bresson's later films. As Jean Sémolué comments, "She who believed she would lead back the lost sheep finds herself abandoned; she who bragged of her confidence is in despair. But it is this process that puts her on the path to her 'greatest joy.'"[5]

Bresson has already learned how to knit together a seamless narrative; we neither know nor care about the intervals of time between scenes that are linked to each other without interruption. At the outset the prioress announces the visit to the prison; the reception of Agnès follows almost immediately. When Thérèse, still seething with revenge, finally leaves prison, we watch her immediately go to a store to buy a gun, and in the next instant use it. Such an economy of means helps Bresson avoid melodrama. Whatever the limitations of this first directorial effort, *Angels of Sin* reveals an emphasis that becomes characteristic: what is important are not actions but the results of the actions, not so much what is explicit as what remains hidden, less the characters than their destinies.

Ultimately, *Angels of Sin* succeeds because its semi-documentary material is successfully integrated with strands of ongoing action. "The welcome at the prison door, the distribution of maxims, fraternal correction, public penance, and the pronunciation of the vows, all mark a decisive stage in the intrigue while adding a supplementary touch to the psychological portrait that makes Anne-Marie climb each time to a new rung on the ladder of the spirit."[6] The everyday practices of the Sisters of Bethany shed their exotic flavor and become meaningful ways to reveal individual character and shifts in personal relations. Bresson's preoccupation with the theme of imprisonment will repeat itself in later films; his paradoxical expression of the interior search for liberation is already evident as Thérèse finally surrenders to the police.

━━ SHOOTING FOR BRESSON'S NEXT MOVIE, *THE LADIES OF THE BOIS DE Boulogne* (*Les Dames du bois de Boulogne*) began in May 1944, during the last months of the German occupation, and was frequently interrupted when actors had to run into the studio at Epinay in search of an air-raid shelter. After the liberation of Paris in August, there were further delays because of the shortage of electricity, but work was completed in February 1945 and the opening was in September.[7] As Élena Labourdette, who played Agnès, recalled,

> Bresson aimed at perfection even in the smallest detail. He was the first to make use of grays and blacks. He imposed a style, "a climate," and a rhythm on the images and insisted on a sobriety which startled the cinema of that time. People criticized his rigor, his slow pace, and even spoke of a kind of coldness. At the outset, *Les Dames du bois de Boulogne* was not well received, as can be seen by its newspaper reviews. But paradoxically, it later became an immense success, a "cult film" that is still presented in art houses today and is often seen on television. In its scenery, adaptation, dialogue, acting, even costumes, Bresson was looking for a purity that surprised the press and the spectators of the time, but eventually gained widespread acceptance and inspired talented younger directors like Jacques Démy, who cast me in his movie *Lola*, partly as a tribute to Bresson.[8]

Like *Angels of Sin*, Bresson's second film was made within the production framework of its time, with its dependence on established actors, but one can observe Bresson's increasing control of the finished product, and he is responsible above all for *Boulogne*'s emotional tone.

The movie's source is an interpolated narrative in *Jacques le fataliste et son maître*, by Denis Diderot, the eighteenth-century encyclopedist. Bresson, who admired Diderot, was probably attracted by the way in which the story illustrated the fatalistic conviction that "everything has already been written above." The central action is revenge on an unfaithful lover: Madame de La Pommeraye (Hélène), abandoned by the Marquis des Arcis (Jean), succeeds in maneuvering him into a scandalous marriage with Mademoiselle d'Aisnon (Agnès), a dancer with a notorious past. Bresson makes Agnès a more sympathetic and high-minded character than she is in his source. The story fits into Diderot's sardonic assumptions because Hélène believes she can control destiny. Although she is successful in arranging the misalliance, her plot backfires: Jean's impulsive desire grows into genuine love.

In Diderot the framework is that of a story told to Jacques and his teacher, who initially find Mademoiselle d'Aisnon as hypocritical as her mother and Madame de la Pommeraye; she becomes a figure of pathos only at the end. Bresson deliberately softens the portrait of Agnès: her dancing seems more acrobatic than lascivious; she is revolted by the men crowding around her after her performances and keeps reminding her mother that she is not interested in luxury. When Hélène tells Jean that Agnès is an unspoiled country girl who is unattainable by an aristocratic *roué,* she is telling him something closer to the truth than she knows.

Bresson is faithful to the main outline of Diderot's story; "His construction was so tight that I could never reknit it in my own fashion."[9] Although the director was responsible for the framework of the screenplay, he was delighted to have Jean Cocteau compose the dialogue. The basic problem was to maintain the precision and sophistication of the eighteenth-century original in a version with a generalized modern framework. Bresson called for cuts in the exchanges between Hélène and Jean, while the conversations between Agnès and her mother were expanded. Asked if the collaboration had posed problems, Cocteau said, "Hardly any. Bresson gave me the scenes, told me the number of lines that were needed. . . . The difficulty was in keeping the tone of the Encyclopedia, in the written language of today. A tone more artificial, more organized, than the language we are accustomed to."[10] In fact, Cocteau found some elegant abbreviations of Diderot: when Hélène gives Jean a cigarette case in their first scene together, Jean looks at it with admiration: "I love gold. It resembles you. Warm, cold, clear, somber, incorruptible."[11]

The production makes discreet use of tasteful displays of wealth; the jewels, gowns, and furnishings of Hélène's apartment—which represented a significant part of the film's budget—convincingly establish the social world of its central intrigue. But the walls remain bare, there is an absence of décor, and the milieu is never specifically identified. Contemporary U.S. filmgoers might not fully appreciate the class distinctions that are assumed in the story, however, since Bresson chose not to draw explicit attention to their importance.

There are several likely reasons for the public's initial dissatisfaction with the film: some may have considered the story dated; others were probably disappointed that Bresson had not made a historical drama, highlighting the clothes and furniture of the eighteenth century. One critic complained that, since the film was not securely rooted in the society of any particular period, the possibility of a scandalous marriage would not present a clear-cut threat. Finally, it was hard for Paul Bernard, an actor who was neither tall nor particularly dashing, to make Jean a sufficiently commanding figure to arouse such deep passion in Hélène and sweep a romantic young woman like Agnès into his arms.

⬛—THE LADIES OF THE BOIS DE BOULOGNE OPENS ON A PARIS STREET: a well-dressed couple, who have just left the theater, pick up a cab. The man notices that the woman (Hélène) is sunk in melancholy retrospection. "I haven't been able to distract you," he concedes. "You've sacrificed everything for a man who no longer loves you."

She denies it but her eyes betray her. After the couple say goodbye, she enters her apartment to find Jean sitting in front of the fireplace. When he apologizes for forgetting their appointment, she calmly reminds him that it was the anniversary of their relationship and hands him a present: a gold cigarette case. As Jean fumbles for a response, Hélène makes her grand gesture. "There is nothing to reproach ourselves with," she declares. "We promised never to withhold anything from each other. It is I who have changed. . . . My heart has been growing away from you." Jean is surprised but also relieved. "You spoke first but I was guilty first," he says admiringly. "You're remarkable; we've had a narrow escape." As the couple leave the living room of Hélène's apartment, the camera rests on her face, a dark mask emerging from the shadows.

A new sequence opens with Hélène in bed, playing with her pet dog, Katsou. When the phone rings, she tells her servant, "I'm not in." Alone, she is full of defiance. "I'll have my revenge," she says ominously, condensing a much longer declaration in Diderot.

There is a quick cut to a nightclub act featuring an attractive tap-dancer; Hélène is in attendance. The dancer, Agnès, ends her performance with an energetic split, and takes her hat off to wild applause. Back in her dressing room with Madame D, her mother (Lucienne Bogaert), however, she declares she is fed up with her life.

At the stage door several men are waiting in attendance. Hélène, observing the scene, tells her chauffeur to follow the car that takes Agnès and her mother to their home. Hélène arrives, follows them upstairs, and watches what is taking place from behind full-length glass windows. Several of Agnès's admirers are present at this gathering, and one overly confident bon vivant blows smoke at Agnès, who pushes him roughly and rushes off to her room.

Upset at this contretemps, Madame D suddenly recognizes Hélène, whom she has not seen in three years. The two women had known each other in the country at a time when Madame D was well off. She gives Hélène a quick summary of what has happened: Agnès has given up her classes in ballet and now dances in nightclubs to support them. Madame D goes into the next room to comfort her distraught daughter, calling her "My little girl."

"I'm not your little girl," Agnès responds, "I'm a tramp."

But Hélène is ready with a proposal for the anguished mother. She will take care of their debts and install the two women in an apartment, where they will live in seclusion and resume using their old name. Hélène is so self-confident that Madame D hardly stops to ask why she is prepared to do all this. "I simply want to help," Hélène insists. "But Agnès must stop exhibiting herself in public."

The next scene shows the arrival of Agnès and her mother at their new apartment in Port Royal square. Agnès instinctively thinks of the place as a prison, but her mother points out that there is a piano and a wonderful view. "Will I have the right to look outside?" Agnès asks.

Hélène's plan begins to take shape when she tells Madame D to be at the cascade in the Bois de Boulogne with her daughter at three o'clock. When Jean calls, she maneuvers him into taking a walk in the Bois. At the meeting she has arranged, Hélène introduces Madame D and her daughter as old friends from the country. After they part company, Jean admits that he is attracted by Agnès and had even been tempted to drive the two ladies home.

From here on the action shifts back and forth from Port Royal square to Hélène's apartment. Madame D gets a phone call from Hélène, reporting that she was satisfied with the meeting in the park. When her mother repeats this to Agnès, however, the latter is suspicious: "Satisfied with what?"

When Jean expresses interest in "the ladies of the Bois de Boulogne," Hélène explains that they live in simplicity, having lost their fortune. She insists that Agnès is quite inaccessible but "accidentally" reveals her address. When Jean leaves, he forgets his gloves; the maid suggests that they can be returned to him tomorrow. Hélène, aware that relations with Jean have fundamentally changed, announces ominously, "The gentleman will not come tomorrow."

Jean comes to Port Royal square on a rainy night without an umbrella, on the lookout for Agnès. "Since our meeting," he says when she appears, "I have been attached to you by a thread. I had only to follow it." "What do you call your thread," she asks, "indiscretion?" Agnès gets her mother's umbrella and gives it to Jean. "Make it a gift," she says, "for the friend with whom we met you in the Bois" (i.e., for Hélène). "Follow your thread carefully—and don't get lost on the way."

Jean begins to send flowers, a development that delights Madame D, but Agnès insists that it "spoils everything." She rushes to complain to Hélène: "Jean was waiting for me in front of our home; now we are being flooded with flowers." Reassured when Hélène praises her for sending Jean away and advises her to avoid him in the future, she is ready to accept Hélène as an ally, and at her suggestion writes a letter which she hopes will discourage Jean.

When Jean drops in on Hélène to complain that the ladies of Port Royal square refuse to see him, Hélène goes on playing the piano, then hands him the letter Agnès wrote at her direction, in which the young woman asks to be left alone. He promises not to disturb Agnès at her home, but begs Hélène to help him see her again. When Hélène pretends to be shocked at the idea of being a go-between, Jean protests that he is deeply in love. Hélène, continuing to play the piano, insists there is no remedy for his infatuation. Jean leaves in exasperation—"because I don't like the piano"—and there is a beautifully executed scene in which he descends in the elevator while Hélène rushes down the stairs to catch up with him, ultimately agreeing to arrange a meeting.

Agnès dances at home to a record that includes both classical and folk music. Wearing a flowing dress and an embroidered apron, she is the embodiment of spontaneity and happiness, very different from the earlier image of her as a nightclub performer. Suddenly, after declaring that she is through with dancing and its pretenses, she collapses, frightening her mother. "It's nothing," Agnès says. "I won't dance again; it's my heart." At this moment the phone rings: Hélène is inviting them to dinner that evening. At first, Agnès says she is delighted; then she asks her mother, "Will we be alone?"

At Hélène's all is well until Jean arrives, as if by accident. Hélène pretends she is annoyed but allows him to stay, and Madame D is profuse in her appreciation of the flowers he has sent. Agnès becomes so upset, however, that a glass slips out of her hand and falls to the floor, and she and her mother leave hastily. Alone with Hélène, Jean exclaims, "That young woman must belong to me," convincing Hélène that her plot is approaching its desired outcome. Back at her apartment, Agnès says that she does not fully understand what is going on, but she and her mother should not see Hélène any more. Madame D protests that without Hélène they would be on the street. "I know it," Agnès concedes, but "I prefer a destiny of our own to one that is imposed on us."

The next day Jean appears at Port Royal while Agnès is out. At first Madame D says she cannot receive him, then allows him to come in, insisting that Agnès should not find him there. Jean is entranced to see Agnès's room, touch her things, and see pictures of her as a child, while Madame D hastily conceals a photo of Agnès in her nightclub costume. Although the mother warns him that it would be extremely imprudent to leave a letter, he manages to drop one on Agnès's bed before leaving.

Agnès returns in high spirits; they are "saved" from Hélène: she has found a job in an office. She becomes suspicious, however, when she notices that someone has been in her room. Discovering Jean's letter, she reads it quickly before tearing it up. A shot of the wastepaper basket reveals a legible fragment: "Even if you should not come, I will wait for you every day at the cascade."

After her fellow employees have left at the end of Agnès's first day at work, the watchman tells her that there are men outside who have been waiting for her since morning; they know she is the well-known dancer. Agnès is still upset even when she gets home; it seems that she cannot escape her past. Her mother urges calm, and hands her a jewelry box containing pearl earrings. Though suspicious about where they came from, Agnès puts them on while reminding her mother. "It is not the absence of luxury that makes me unhappy. . . . If these pearls were real, I would throw them out the window."

When Hélène arrives, she immediately notices the pearl earrings and tells Madame D they must be returned; Agnès is being treated like a slut. Hélène warns Madame D to prevent her daughter from doing something stupid.

Agnès writes a letter, puts on her raincoat, and quietly leaves the apartment. At the cascade in the Bois de Boulogne, where she finds Jean waiting, she asks him to read the letter, but he refuses. After they take shelter in the grotto behind the cascade, he asks her to go away with him. Driving Agnès back to her house, he tells her to meet him at the Gare de Lyon at seven o'clock.

Agnès begins to pack her bag, apparently intending to run away with Jean. Madame D asks, "Have you told him everything?" When Agnès says no, her mother declares, "You love him," and the two women embrace. The audience only learns that Agnès ultimately decided against leaving with Jean when the latter arrives at Hélène's in despair: he had waited in vain at the railroad station for a long time. The point, of course, is that since Agnès genuinely cares about him, she feels he must know the truth about her past. Yet in making herself "unavailable" to Jean, she is unintentionally following Hélène's strategy.

When Jean visits his former mistress once more, he tells her he has decided to marry Agnès. He asks Hélène, who is delighted at the idea of a large public wedding, to get the consent of Madame D and make the necessary arrangements.

Bresson makes much more of the wedding ceremony than Diderot. At the church, Agnès, in a white dress and veil, walks slowly down the aisle to the accompaniment of organ music. In the large crowd the camera discovers Hélène, wearing a black fur hat; there is a hint of a tear in her eye. After the ceremony, however, Hélène rushes to the sacristy; as Jean kisses her on the cheek, she whispers enigmatically, hoping to arouse doubts about his new bride: "I am afraid I was wrong about the little one."

At Jean's house, Agnès avoids the formal reception and escapes to a room next to the library. When Jean urges her to come and greet the guests, the repentant bride—who now understands Hélène's intentions—collapses on the floor. Jean tells a servant to take care of her and rushes through the noisy reception room to his car outside. Seeing Hélène, he calls her over and begs her to explain the situation. "Nothing simpler," she says, "you have married a slut. She was a dancer, my dear. . . . You played a trick on me; I played another on you."

Jean drives off in near despair, but when he returns that night, he sits down on a chair next to the canopied bed where his wife is lying. Reminding him of the letter he refused to read, Agnès begs for forgiveness: "I loved you; that was my only excuse."

Jean responds in kind. "You are my wife, Agnès. I love you. Stay with me."

◂━━━ THE LADIES OF THE BOIS DE BOULOGNE IS A GOOD DEMONSTRATION of how Bresson could be faithful to his literary source while putting his own distinctive stamp on the finished film. He eliminates everything that does not advance its central action: one scene fades out into black, another begins without interruption. Cocteau worked in complete harmony with Bresson, who admired the dialogue precisely because it did not try to provide psychological explanations for the actions of its main characters. The entire script, even the camera movements in individual scenes, remains focused on its central plot line: the revenge of Hélène on a lover who had become indifferent. The revenge, of course, backfires, as Jean is not only led on by the young woman's apparent unavailability, but comes to genuinely care for her.

The film's emotional complexity is underlined by the fact that Hélène, its active agent as the one setting the trap, always remains "faithful" to Jean. When Jean finally recognizes that his desire to possess Agnès requires him to marry her, he admits to Hélène, "God knows that neither you nor I are the kind who marry."

His ex-mistress answers that in her case he is mistaken. "But only to one man . . . you."

There is a moment of silence as Jean absorbs this confession. "Then you disapprove of my marriage?" he asks.

"No," Hélène replies, "she is a girl who is just right for you."

One needs to see the movie more than once to appreciate fully the way in which the scenes are perfectly knotted together: the manner may seem dry, but the pithy, near-aphoristic exchanges are as sharply timed as the thrusts of a duel. Bresson's primary concern is for the rigor of the narration, and he already demonstrates a knowing use of moments of silence. It is hard not to admire the shrewdness with which Hélène manipulates the other characters, although we have a right to wonder why Madame D doesn't raise more questions about the new life that is being offered her and her daughter. To her credit, Agnès is instinctively resistant and only drops her suspicions when Hélène has her write a letter (to be shown to Jean) demanding that she be allowed to live in peace. Bresson softens the reality of Agnès's past, making it easier to sympathize with her emotional triumph at the end. Although her mother remains venal, the daughter seems never to have been seduced by the lure of luxury.

Boulogne shows a growing mastery of technique and was a revelation to the young François Truffaut, yet Bresson himself was far from satisfied. Though there was critical praise for Maria Casarès as Hélène and Élena Labourdette as Agnès, the experience convinced him to break free from the reliance on "stars," and his departure from the standard production pattern will become increasingly evident in his next films. In a television interview in 1958 Casarès sharply criticized Bresson for wanting to be in control of every detail of the production:

> On the set he was a genuine tyrant. . . . He murdered us so sweetly, so politely. . . . When we entered the studio we abandoned everything that could resemble a life of our own, a personal will, in order to drag before our sweet tyrant—for he was extremely sweet—a body, hands, and a voice that he had chosen.[12]

Casarès, of course, was a renowned stage actress, and the implications of Bresson's rejection of what he called "photographed theater" will emerge more clearly in his next project, *Diary of a Country Priest.* In fairness to the actress, however, the conditions under which she worked in *Boulogne* were particularly difficult. During a good part of the time it was being filmed—under the 1944–1945 restrictions already mentioned—she was also appearing on the stage. In practice, this meant going to bed after midnight and getting up at five to rush to the movie set.

The emotional intensity that is conveyed in *The Ladies of the Bois de Boulogne* is in great part the result of the fact that every detail—the costumes, the white walls of the apartments, the occasional moments of silence, the acuteness of the dialogue—has been chosen with deliberation. At the same time, there is no heavy-handed symbolism: as Jean Sémolué comments, "Whether it is a matter of elevator or stairway, grand piano or upright piano, expensive cloaks or a simple raincoat, a rich toque or a simple hat, long robes or short skirts, many servants or the cook's apron, everything naturally establishes a contrast between Hélène and Agnès."[13]

André Bazin's oft-quoted remark, "The sound of a windshield-wiper against a page of Diderot is all it took to turn it [the text] into a dialogue of Racine," is mystifying without his prior statement: "Bresson has taken the risk of transferring one realistic story" (that of Diderot) "into the context of another" (that of the film). "The result is that these two examples of realism cancel one another out, the passions displayed emerge out of the characters as if from a chrysalis, the actions from the twists and turns of the plot, and the tragedy from the trappings of the drama."[14] Using elevators and modern cars, Bresson deliberately combines a timeless present and an eighteenth-century atmosphere.

The power of *The Ladies of the Bois de Boulogne* resides in the way Hélène controls the other characters like puppets, only to seal her own fate. Sémolué asserts that the result is a "cinematographic equivalent of the rigor desired by Racine in his tragedies, as stated in the preface to *Brittanicus*: 'a simple action, burdened with little matter . . . which, advancing by degrees to its conclusion, is held together merely by the concerns, the feelings, and the passions of the characters.'"[15] Even before he developed his more radical approach to filmmaking, Bresson had realized that one of the most important secrets of art lies in knowing what can be omitted.

NOTES

1. Jean Sémolué, *Bresson ou l'acte pur des Métamorphoses* (Paris: Flammarion, 1993), 31. Sémolué says that Fr. Lelong's book, first published in 1937, was crowned by the French Academy.

2. Michel Estève, *Robert Bresson* (Paris: Editions Albatros, 1983), 16.

3. Roland Barthes, in *Robert Bresson: Éloge* (Paris: Cinémathèque français, 1997), 16.

4. Tony Pipolo, "Rules of the Game: On Bresson's *Les Anges du péché*," in *Robert Bresson*, ed. James Quandt (Toronto: Cinematheque Ontario, 1998), 198.

5. Sémolué, *Bresson ou l'acte pur des Métamorphoses*, 38.

6. René Prédal, "Robert Bresson: L'aventure intérieure," *L'Avant-scène cinéma* (January-February 1992): 41.

7. Paul Guth, *Autour des "Dames du bois de Boulogne": journal d'un film* (Paris: Julliard/Sequana, 1945).

8. Élena Labourdette, in *Le Cinématographie de Robert Bresson* (Tokyo: Tokyo International Foundation for Promotion of Screen Image Culture, 1999), 38.

9. Guth, *Autour des "Dames du bois de Boulogne."*

10. Ibid.

11. *L'Avant-scène cinéma*, no. 196 (November 15, 1977): 10.

12. Maria Casarès, interview in *Radio-Télévision-Cinéma*, no. 426 (March 16, 1958).

13. Sémolué, *Bresson ou l'acte pur des Métamorphoses*, 52.

14. André Bazin, *What Is Cinema?* (Berkeley: University of California Press, 1967), 1:168.

15. Sémolué, *Bresson ou l'acte pur des Métamorphoses*, 51.

3

"All Is Grace"

Diary of a Country Priest

BRESSON'S NEXT PROJECT, THE ADAPTATION OF BERNANOS'S great novel *Journal d'un curé de campagne* (*Diary of a Country Priest*), was a major step in the discovery of his own approach to cinema. Instead of being a studio production, it was shot on location in a small village in the Pas de Calais, and almost all the roles were filled by untrained actors. Bresson made a strenuous effort to put into practice what he calls cinematography: "a writing with images in movement and with sounds."[1]

He not only exercised personal control over the movie—like other directors whose work revealed a personal style and who were beginning to be described as *auteurs*—but consciously rejected what he criticized as "photographed theater." Bresson distinguished between two types of film: "those that employ the resources of the theater (actors, direction, etc.) and use the camera in order to *reproduce*; those that employ the resources of cinematography and use the camera to *create*."[2]

Acclaimed by critics as one of the most successful adaptations of a novel for the screen ever made, *Diary of a Country Priest* is a dazzling achievement, immensely faithful to Bernanos and yet one in which Bresson placed his own signature on almost every detail. *Diary* reached a wide audience in France as well as other countries (including the United States, where it was chosen by the National Board of Review as one of the best foreign films of 1954), although based on a book that seemed impossible to film. Its framework appeared completely anti-cinematic: the daily thoughts and recollections of a village priest in northern France during the 1920s. The novel's minimal plot reflected the processes of the priest's inner life, and there were many interruptions and digressions for reflection on pastoral concerns, poverty, and spirituality. It was out of such seemingly slight material that Bresson fashioned a movie that earned a special accolade from André Bazin: "Probably for the first time, the cinema gives us a film in which the only genuine incidents, the only perceptible movements, are those of the life of the spirit. It also offers us a new dramatic form that is specifically religious—or better still, specifically theological; a phenomenology of salvation and grace."[3]

Two attempts at adaptation had been rejected in 1947. The first, by the successful screenwriting team of Jean Aurenche and Pierre Bost, made a radical change in the novel's tone. A delicate encounter between the country priest and Chantal, the rebellious daughter of the count, was gratuitously distorted by having the young girl spit out the consecrated host she had received at mass. Even worse, the script ended with the despairing comment of a minor character, "When you're dead, you're dead." In contrast, the last line of the novel—and of Bresson's film—is that of the dying curé: "What does it matter? All is grace."[4]

Reviewing this scenario, Bernanos understandably commented that he was afraid "to see his book cruelly falsified." A second scenario, by Père Brückberger, transposed the story to the days of the German occupation, radically displacing the center of interest to the political realm. After Bernanos died in 1948, producer Pierre Gérin asked Bresson to attempt yet another film treatment, but finally decided that the scenario was not sufficiently dramatic. Bernanos's literary executor, Albert Béguin, approved of it, however, and another producer was found, Union Général Cinématographique. Shooting of the film began in February 1950.

Bresson deliberately makes the diary form of the novel, a key factor in concentrating audience attention on the central subject of the film, the life of the spirit. "In my eyes, what was striking was the notebook of the diary, in which, through the curé's pen, an external world becomes an interior world and takes on a spiritual coloration. My scenario concentrated on that, rather than on events that are usually considered more cinematographic."[5] The movie opens simply with a shot of the notebook. The curé of Ambricourt, the priest of the title, reads the entry he has just made: "I don't think I am doing wrong in jotting down, day after day, with absolute frankness the very simple trivial secrets of a very ordinary kind of life." Throughout the film, the same voice either echoes Bernanos's text as the diary entries are written out or prolongs it while subsequent images project the incident that is described. In theory such a presentation ought to be dull. It is redundant, after all, to repeat what the images already reveal. In practice, the largely uninflected reading of the diary reinforces the sense of inner strug-gle, and the doubling of voice and image intensifies the significance of the curé's words and of the experience he is going through.

Sometimes the voice pronouncing the words of the journal covers over those spoken by the curé describing an incident, which are heard again only when the journal's voice has become silent. This happens in the movie's cen-tral scene, in which the curé challenges the countess, who has been deeply embittered ever since the death of her infant son. "Have you heard me?" she suddenly demands. He says no, and we haven't either, because for a moment the voice of the journal is the only one that is audible. Leaving ordinary duration, for a brief time we enter the realm of inner consciousness.

The supreme instance of this technique is an exchange between the curé of Ambricourt and his mentor, the curé of Torcy, in which the older man insists that we all have to find the place in the Gospel where we personally encounter Jesus. Suddenly Torcy exclaims, "What on earth's the matter? What are you blubbering about?" There is a close-up of the young priest's face as Torcy's words are covered by the voice of the journal: "I hadn't real-ized that I was weeping." A tear rolls down the young man's cheek while the voice continues: "The truth is that my place for all time has been the Gar-den of Olives." After a medium shot of the two priests, Torcy continues, "What's up now? You're not even listening to me; are you dreaming?" Again the interior voice: "Suddenly our Lord had granted me the grace of letting me know, through the words of my old teacher . . . that I was the prisoner of the Holy Passion." Bresson makes these words more poignant by refus-ing to overdramatize the situation; we hear the barking of a dog as the cam-era's gradual withdrawal returns us to the world of appearances.[6]

This refusal to exploit situations for sheer emotionalism, marks Bresson's whole work. Although he is concerned with feelings and not abstract ideas, he is unwilling to manipulate his audience. Such an approach complements Bresson's increasing use of nonprofessional actors who have had little or no experience in front of a camera before working in one of his films. Asked to try out for the part of the country priest, Claude Laydu told the director he was just a beginner in acting school, not realizing that this would prejudice Bresson in his favor. During the shooting, Laydu reports, the veteran actors—a small minority in the movie—often felt frustrated because they were not allowed to use the techniques of "expressiveness" they had learned on the stage. Submitting himself completely to Bresson's demands, Laydu says he did not realize he had been portraying a saint until he saw the com-pleted film.

Bresson closely follows Bernanos's structure at the same time that he tightens it. As he said,

> I long ago acquired the conviction that in certain works—those in which the writer wanted to put all of himself, and Bernanos's work is in that category— what shows the author best, and in depth, more than his thoughts or inti- mate experiences, is his particular manner . . . of reuniting and coordinating them. . . . Hence, for me to adapt means fidelity to the spirit of the work by respecting its construction.[7]

Bernanos's novel is composed of glancing insights—short paragraphs of dif- ferent lengths, marked off from each other, that reflect the phases of the curé's development without any obvious logical links. Dialogues, examina- tions of conscience, and personal confidences somehow preserve the unity of the story while reflecting the inner experience of the priest.[8]

──AFTER THE MOVIE'S FIRST WORDS, WHICH ARE HEARD AT THE SAME time as a hand is opening the student notebook, we see a sign "Ambricourt." A slightly built young priest, his luggage tied to his bicycle, arrives at the vil- lage, which is his first parish. As he approaches the chateau, a couple can be detected a little distance from the iron grills of a park. The count and his daughter's tutor, Mlle. Louise, are embracing; they quickly turn away.

No welcome has been prepared for the young priest at the presbytery. He acknowledges his bad health; stomach pains have led him to adopt a diet that is making them worse—he has given up meat and vegetables and takes only some hard bread, soaked in wine and well sugared. His first experi- ences in the parish are discouraging. An elderly widower complains bitterly about what the church is charging to have his wife buried. When the priest goes for counsel to the gruff but fatherly pastor of nearby Torcy (played by another non-actor, Armand Guibert, in real life a Parisian psychiatrist), he is told that a priest's job is to keep order; he shouldn't dream of being loved. After he gets back to the parish, a representative of the village council informs him that they will install electricity in the presbytery, and the curé blames himself for not mentioning the "family dances" the man runs at the café, where young men get the village girls tipsy. In the evening he hears the music from the dance, which only deepens his sense of uselessness.

These encounters make him look forward to teaching catechism to the children, and he is encouraged by one student, Seraphita, who seems to have studied her lesson seriously. When he calls her up to his desk after class to reward her with a holy card, however, she tells him she pays attention in class because "he has beautiful eyes." Her schoolmates titter just out-side the door.

His contacts with the chateau are equally frustrating. Mlle. Louise com-plains that Chantal, the count's daughter, tries to humiliate her. At first he believes the count himself will prove an ally and eventually let the parish use one of his fields for a sports club. The count drops in after hunting and brings him a rabbit—which the curé knows he cannot stomach. When he timidly suggests that Mlle. Louise might show more understanding of Chan-tal, he is told not to be a fool.

Taken ill during a return visit to the chateau, the curé decides to consult a friend of Torcy, Dr. Delbende, a local doctor who tells him that his poor health is the result of generations of poverty and alcoholism. The doctor shows sympathy and insight. He feels that the curé is someone like himself, a person who faces up to adversity and never surrenders.

The atmosphere of the parish, however, appears hostile. On the road, Seraphita suddenly throws her schoolbag down at his feet, and when he returns it to her home, her mother too is unfriendly. When he visits Torcy, the older priest tells the curé he has no practical sense, but possesses the spirit of prayer. He even receives an anonymous letter, advising him to ask for a transfer; the handwriting—which he recognizes from a card in her missal—is that of Mlle. Louise. That night he is in agony because he cannot pray, though prayer is as necessary to him as air. "Before me, there is only a black wall . . . God has withdrawn from me."

The next morning he hears the sound of a shot; the sacristan informs him of Dr. Delbende's death, presumably in a hunting accident. After the funeral, the curé talks to Torcy; his anguished face manifests the fear that their friend might have committed suicide. Torcy says that although the doc-tor did not believe in God, he was a just man, and God is the judge of the just.

The curé has another painful night. No longer feeling joy in prayer, he continues to struggle with himself, murmuring, "I have not lost my faith." He has the impression someone is calling; he opens the window, although he is sure that he will not find anybody. In the next shot Chantal has come into the presbytery, furious about Mlle. Louise's affair with her father. The curé realizes she is asking him to confront her mother, the countess. "Young lady," he says, "what I have promised to do for you, I will do."

All too aware that his pastoral efforts have been a series of failures, the curé rushes off in the hope of receiving counsel from Torcy, but the latter is away. When he returns, Chantal is waiting for him in the church. He insists he can only speak to her in the confessional, but she refuses to kneel. She wants justice; they are sending her away in a few days. She hates her mother and no longer respects her father; she heard him with Mlle. Louise the previous night. With a sudden premonition, the curé orders Chantal to give him a letter she is carrying on her person. "Are you the devil?" the girl cries out, amazed, but she complies. She runs out, leaving the letter behind, and the words "to my father" appear on the screen as the curé burns the letter, unread. He had seen the temptation to suicide in the young woman's eyes but blames himself for having listened to her.

The curé rushes to the chateau, in accordance with his promise to Chantal to plead her case. His ensuing duel with the countess, famous as "the medallion scene," is the center of both the film and the novel. He tells the countess he is afraid her daughter might hurt herself. The mother counters by asking him if he fears death; he lowers his eyes and says, "Yes." The curé insists, however, that driving her daughter out of the house is wrong: "God will break you." "He has broken me already, he has taken my son from me," the countess replies, turning to pictures of the dead infant that lie on the mantel.

The curé finds a sudden strength: "God has removed him for a time, but your hard heart may part you forever." When the countess continues to justify herself, saying she goes to mass regularly, he bursts out, "How dare you treat God like that?" At this point she confesses to a long-felt resentment of God. "I too, Madame, sometimes," he confesses, and his inner voice repeats words from his diary: "the image of Dr. Delbende was before my eyes." He urges her to ask for resignation, and is finally able to get her to repeat "Thy kingdom come, thy will be done." During this conversation the camera reveals Chantal listening outside the window, and sounds can be heard of the gardener raking leaves nearby.

"I might have died with that hate in my heart," the countess confesses gratefully, but remains aware of the pride she still retains. "Surrender your pride along with the rest," the curé insists, and she pulls the locket containing her dead son's picture from her neck and throws it into the fire. The curé rushes to the fireplace and rescues it: "God is no torturer," he reminds her. "He desires that we should be merciful to ourselves." Before leaving, the priest gives the countess his blessing, touching her hair as his hand passes over her.

Later, when he arrives at the presbytery, the gardener hands him a small package and a letter from the countess. The package contains the empty locket and the letter is one of gratitude. The countess refers to the curé as a child who has drawn her out of a terrifying solitude. "I am not resigned; I am happy." Suddenly it is morning: his alarm clock shows half past six and footsteps can be heard. Then come words from the diary: "The countess died during the night."

The curé rushes to the chateau and blesses the corpse, his arm feeling like lead. When he returns in the evening after catechism class, the house is filled with visitors, and he can hear them murmuring about him as he climbs the stairs to the countess's room. He recalls blessing her and saying, "Go in peace." "O marvel," the voice of the diary declares, "that one should be able to give another that which one does not possess."

Since the countess's sudden death had given rise to gossip about the curé's visit the day before, the Canon La Motte-Beuvon, an uncle of the count, comes to see him, hoping to help smooth things over. The canon asks him to write a summary of his conversation with the countess, merely for the eyes of the bishop, but the curé refuses: "Only the countess could have given authority for such a report." Meanwhile, Chantal seems to be taking charge at the chateau. When she tells the curé the governess is leaving immediately, he reminds her of a more implacable enemy: "It's yourself you hate." The count, believing that the priest was a contributing cause of his wife's death, dismisses him rudely: "No priest shall mix in the affairs of my family."

The next scene, a visit from Torcy, becomes the occasion in which the curé comes to realize his place in the Gospels is with Jesus in the Garden of Olives. Torcy criticizes his dress, his diet, and his pastoral judgment in dealing with the countess. Chantal had observed the curé's duel with her mother and has led people to believe that he had forced the mother to throw the locket with her son's picture into the fire. When Torcy leaves, however, he asks for his young colleague's blessing.

The next evening, while making his parish rounds, the curé realizes he is dizzy and leans against the trunk of a large crooked tree. As he falls in the mud, the image of the Blessed Virgin—to whom Torcy had encouraged him to pray—comes into his mind. He has vomited, and when he opens his eyes, he is holding the hand of the child Seraphita. She dips a corner of a towel in a bowl of water, washes his face tenderly, and guides him to the road. Back in his room, the curé realizes he has lost a great deal of blood and decides to go to Lille to consult a specialist.

Dawn, however, comes as a deliverance. As he is putting away some of his things, Chantal comes in. Although intrigued by this priest who seems to have a secret strength, she remains defiant: "I'll damn myself if I want," she tells him. "I will answer for you, soul for soul," he replies calmly. As he leaves the house, her cousin, Oliver, an officer in the foreign legion, offers him a ride to the train on his motorcycle. The curé is deeply moved by the experience, which is the occasion of a few moments of joy and deep inner liberation. By the time they arrive at the station, the two men are speaking to each other like old comrades.

After the train ride, the curé proceeds to the doctor's office; as he leaves, he looks faint and drained. He enters a church, where the voice of the diary comments: "Never had I felt so violently the revolt of the body against prayer." At a table in a café-bar, he repeats the doctor's verdict: "Cancer of the stomach." The woman serving him leaves him alone, believing he is composing his sermon; the curé dozes off, recalling the blessedness of recent mornings, "the cock crowing at my peaceful window. How fresh and pure it all was."

Leaving, he walks through darkened streets until he finds a door with a sign reading: Louis Dufrety, drug salesman—a friend from his seminary days whom he believes has left the ministry. His reception by Dufrety is awkward; the ex-priest rattles on pretentiously while the curé is close to nausea. Referring to the woman "who has sacrificed her life for me," Dufrety comments, "She counts for nothing in my intellectual life." "If I'd broken my ordination promises," the curé replies, "I'd rather it had been for love of a woman than for what you call your intellectual life." When the curé suffers another attack, Dufrety rushes to the druggist. A woman, worn out from her work as a cleaning lady, looks in and apologizes for the condition of the house. In response to a question, she says it was she who rejected marriage: "If ever he wanted to make a fresh start [i.e., if Dufrety wanted to return to the priesthood], I'd not be a trouble."

When Dufrety comes back, the curé insists on talking to him; there is little time left. The curé writes awkwardly in his notebook: "He agrees to meet the curé of Torcy, my old master," and continues with great effort until the diary slips from his hand. He moves toward the window, then sits in a chair in the middle of the room. The camera moves in on a face that seems to be trying to understand what is going on within him. There is a stillness to the curé's stare, punctuated by the sound of a steam whistle, and the screen goes dark.

Then a typed letter appears on the screen, addressed to Torcy. As the latter reads Dufrety's description of the curé's last moments, the screen becomes white, with just a black cross in the center. The dying man had signaled for his rosary and held it against his breast. "Then, in an almost unintelligible voice, he asked me for absolution. . . . While I performed this duty, I tried to express the scruples I felt about doing so. . . . His eyes signaled me to put my ear close to his mouth. He then pronounced, very slowly, these words which I know I am reporting accurately: 'What does it matter? All is grace.'"

━━THIS SUMMARY MAKES CLEAR THAT *THE DIARY OF A COUNTRY PRIEST* has no conventional plot, and it may at first seem hard to account for the strong presence of the supernatural it suggests. Dudley Andrews believes that the film's impact is produced

> by an accumulative method. . . . Through repetitions of scenes, gestures, sounds, lighting and decor, a musical rhythm invades the images, producing a meditation, with themes and variations, on the supernatural. The themes are constant and well known; the variations include dialogues, monologues, landscapes, gestures, scenes of action, scenes of writing, natural sounds, and recorded music.[9]

Many have noted the paradox that although Bresson's fidelity to Bernanos emphasized the literary quality of the film, it was accompanied by ruthless elimination of incidents and characters present in the original. Several moving digressions by Bernanos were sacrificed, and little effort was made to capture the lyricism of the novel. In addition, Bresson suppressed the social and political dimensions of the book to such an extent that some early Catholic critics complained that one was left with almost no sense of the curé's involvement with his parish as a whole. There are also significant omissions in the curé's conversations with Torcy and Dr. Delbende, and even relatively important scenes with the governess and Seraphita were eliminated. When the producer told Bresson that the film was too long, the director was unperturbed. As André Bazin said, "Forced to throw out a third of his final cut for the exhibitor's copy, he ended by declaring with a delicate touch of cynicism that he was delighted to have to do so. Actually, the only 'visual' he really cared about was the blank screen at the finale."[10] For Bresson, fidelity to the spirit of Bernanos's novel meant centering everything on the evolution of the priest's inner life.

The aesthetic form of *Diary of a Country Priest* depends on the duplication of sound and image, emphasizing the interiority of all action. Andrews summarizes a particularly striking example of this near the end of the film, when the curé sits in the café at Lille, after receiving his death sentence from the doctor:

> We watch him write, we hear him say, "I must have dozed off for a while," as we see him lean back and close his eyes. A dissolve to a minutely different camera angle embodies the startled displacement he experiences in voice-over: "I must have dozed off for a while . . . [dissolve]. When I awoke, oh God, I must write this down. . . ." And as he bends forward again, we realize he is writing the very episode we have just seen. It is a daring layering of all three modes of reflection in a single moment, concentrating our imagination with

his as he conjures up the past and tries to give it a place in the story of his spiritual life.[11]

True to his aesthetic principles, Bresson did not encourage his photographer, Léonce-Henri Burel, to look for visuals that would be memorable in isolation. Nevertheless, Jean Sémolué is able to describe interior scenes as having a lighting comparable to that of George de la Tour.[12] When the curé writes in his journal at night the oil light throws a shadow on his face; at the same time the cross on the wall is outlined in black on gray. There is an especially dramatic shot of the curé holding on to a huge tree for support while he is out walking at night; more typically, there is a subtle use of grays that reflect the bad weather of northern France. Burel is masterful in creating "a diffused lighting and precise combinations of shade and light; the crucifix in the curé's room is always in shade because the priest is undergoing the 'dark night' evoked by John of the Cross. . . . Shots are framed to underline the solitude of the hero and suggest the reality of the supernatural, beginning with the depth of his glance and the immobility of his features."[13]

Paradoxically, some of Bernanos's dialogue that would have easily lent itself to film is either eliminated or delivered in monotone, and the only novelistic scene with obvious movie appeal that Bresson retains is the curé's motorcycle ride with Chantal's cousin Oliver. There is a virtual absence of psychology, which serious French films had always prided themselves on, and practically nothing that could be called character development; each scene is complete in itself, as if controlled by some law of necessity. Bresson's rigorous cutting is accompanied by a sure instinct for the telling concrete detail—the wine spilling on the floor, the curé's collapse and loss of blood the night when Seraphita bathes his face, and visuals of doors and grills that underline the barriers between people and things.

Even in his earlier movies, Bresson was teaching his audiences to be attentive to the natural sounds that provide an overall counterpoint to the action. In *Diary of a Country Priest* the previously mentioned raking by the gardener during the curé's confrontation with the countess is a famous example of using sound as both background and counterpoint to the action. In addition, wagons are constantly passing through the village, doors and windows are closed, dogs bark in the background, and we hear footsteps on gravel, dance music from the cabaret, Delbende's gun being fired, and wine barrels being delivered to the presbytery. At this point in his career, Bresson also makes use of discreet, occasional bits of music to support the emotion at the end of a scene, a conventional studio practice he would later abandon.

Much has been written about the astounding success of Claude Laydu as the curé, how he allowed himself to be molded in accordance with the director's intentions, spent some time in a monastery to accustom himself to the rhythms of a life of prayer, and met with Bresson on Sundays for months to discuss the meaning of his role. All this was done with intentions very different from those, say, of the Actors' Studio, since Bresson ultimately did not want him to act at all, but to reveal himself spontaneously. What is remarkable is not only how the recitation of lines in a near-monotone turns out to be so moving but that images of the curé that overwhelm us with the sense of his physical and psychological exhaustion are sometimes followed— as in the encounters with Chantal and the countess—by sudden manifestations of inner strength. Indeed, after the countess comes to a peaceful acceptance of God's will, there is even a sudden smile of joy.

Priest-novelist Jean Sulivan refers to the previously noted paradox that Bresson has created a style of his own in this film even while agreeing to be the slave of a celebrated text:

> After accustoming us to read over and over a text which the curé d'Ambricourt is in the process of writing—a novelty in the cinema—he forces us to look at a man, alone on the screen, and to read on his face all the interior movements of his soul, without deigning to show us his interlocutors, who soon are reduced to delivering monologues, whether it is the curé de Torcy, the defrocked priest, or his friend Oliver, to whom he does not even say goodbye. Often at the end of the shot an imperceptible travelling movement brings the face of the curé d'Ambricourt closer to us.[14]

John E. Keegan helps us understand the basis of Bresson's film style by emphasizing his concentration. "He does not multiply details in order to give us the 'reality' of the person. He intensifies in order to probe to the 'essence' of the *particular* human."[15] The point is reaffirmed by Raymond Durgnat:

> in Bresson the monotone and the dead-pan represent not a mask, but a revelation of the essential man. His personages seem aloof because they are naked. . . . The physical is spiritualized. . . . This intense "physicality" and "materialism" explain how the film feels so intense even though, dramatically, there is so little emphasis and so many omissions.[16]

Keegan maintains that the authenticity of Bresson's characters lies precisely in their immersion in what is at hand, where many would fear that their "self" would get lost:

> The big moments of the curé's existence in *Diary of a Country Priest* are not moments that arise from "marvelous and extraordinary" feats. They arise, rather, out of the "humdrum" of peeling his potatoes and doggedly going

about his tasks . . . the Vicar of Torcy reinforces this with the advice he gives the moribund curé, "Do the simple things . . . faithfully."[17]

Vincent Amiel, lamenting the fact that the physical density of bodies in contemporary film is increasingly excluded because characters "are no longer anything but wills, consciousness, and well-understood interests," says, "The cinema of Bresson is the infinite quest of that first astonishment, that daily and forgotten experience of immediate bursts of perception, which the body is first to receive."[18] Amiel quotes a long letter written by Rilke after seeing Rodin's workshop in Paris; the poet was so overwhelmed by seeing yards and yards of fragments that he began to suspect that viewing the body as a whole is more the job of the scholar, while that of the artist is to create new unities out of smaller, disparate elements. This fits in well with Bresson's declared intention in *Notes of a Cinematographer:* "See beings and things in their separate parts. Render them independent in order to give them a new dependence."[19]

Diary of a Country Priest, Amiel says,

> is the first film in which Bresson makes the experience of this primacy of the body over consciousness, which will become the material of his entire work. . . . Before our contact with the world is named, it is experienced, like each cart that passes and repasses in front of the camera during the film. Those heavy horses and creaking axles are neither signs of agricultural activity, indications of the season, nor geographical emblems of a particular society: they are shrill creakings, spurts of mud, repetition.[20]

He supports his argument by calling attention to the fact that Bresson keeps the journal in the order of the present, while in the novel it is part of the past. "Because we see the curé write and place his hand on the notebook, at the moment when the words form it is not just their significance that remains but the very gesture of the body that traces them."[21] In Bernanos, the countess's death is announced in two lines; there is a graphic division on the page, but immediately afterwards the story of the day reestablishes the narrative order in which these events were included. "On the screen, it is as if the dryness of the words was not enough; there is also the rush of the moment, the panic of gesture. While we see the written word on the screen . . . we hear the breath of a character who extinguishes a candle, then hasty steps moving away. . . . We are in the time of the body, not that of remembrance."[22]

Dudley Andrews emphasizes that "the non-sectarian success of the film testifies to the consistent and radical interiority attained by Bresson. From first to last (from the image of the diary to that of the cross), we are locked within a particular sensibility, a state of being, a soul."[23] Although he draws on an explicitly Catholic spirituality, Bresson makes it possible for agnostics to explain away the actions of the curé as the result of heredity and morbidity, and some of the pious may even feel cheated by his refusal to edify.

"In no sense," Bazin concludes his essay, "is the film 'comparable' to the novel or 'worthy' of it. It is a new aesthetic creation, the novel so to speak multiplied by the cinema."[24] Jean Sémolué points out that at the end of the first chapter of the novel, the curé speaks of the journal as conveying "a sense of inviolable presence which is certainly not God . . . [but] a friend made in my image." Although Bresson omits the line, "when the film is projected, the spectator becomes this friendly presence, a real auditor."[25] *Diary of a Country Priest* was a brilliant success, but it only strengthened Bresson's determination to make an even more total break with standard moviemaking in his next film.

NOTES

1. Robert Bresson, *Notes of a Cinematographer* (Los Angeles: Sun and Moon Press, 1988), 16.

2. Ibid., 15.

3. André Bazin, *What Is Cinema?* (Berkeley: University of California Press, 1967), 1:136.

4. René Prédal, "Robert Bresson: L'aventure intérieure," *L'Avant-scène cinéma* (January-February 1992): 5.

5. Robert Bresson, interview in *Le Figaro littéraire*, March 16, 1967.

6. Jean Sémolué, *Bresson ou l'acte pur des Métamorphoses* (Paris: Flammarion, 1993), 65–66.

7. Robert Bresson, *Recherches et débats*, March 1951.

8. Michel Estève, *Robert Bresson* (Paris: Editions Albatros, 1983), 30.

9. Dudley Andrews, "Desperation and Meditation: Bresson's *Diary of a Country Priest*," in *Modern European Filmmakers and the Art of Adaptation*, ed. Andrew S. Horton and Joan Magretta (New York: Ungar, 1981), 28.

10. Bazin, *What Is Cinema?* 128.

11. Andrews, "Desperation," 29.

12. Sémolué, *Bresson ou l'acte pur des Métamorphoses*, 69.

13. Estève, *Robert Bresson*, 34.

14. Jean Sulivan, "Réflexions sur un style cinématographique," *Dialogues-Ouest* (March 1951).

15. John E. Keegan, "Film Style and Theological Vision in Robert Bresson," *Horizons* 8, no. 1 (1981): 89.

16. Raymond Durgnat, "Le Journal d'un curé de campagne," in *The Films of Robert Bresson*, ed. Ian Cameron (New York: Praeger, 1969), 46.

17. Keegan, "Film Style and Theological Vision," 93.

18. Vincent Amiel, *Le corps au cinéma: Bresson, Keaton, Cassavetes* (Paris: Presses univérsitaires de France, 1997), 7, 40.

19. Bresson, *Notes of a Cinematographer*, 93.

20. Amiel, *Le corps au cinéma*, 40.

21. Ibid., 39.

22. Ibid., 43.

23. Andrews, "Desperation," 30.

24. Bazin, *What Is Cinema?* 142.

25. Sémolué, *Bresson ou l'acte pur des Métamorphoses*, 62.

4

The Spirit Blows through Prison

A Man Escaped

A MAN ESCAPED (1956), BRESSON'S NEXT MOVIE, DEMONSTRATES that the "spiritual" aspect of his work is due more to style than subject matter. (Its more precise French title, *Un condamné à mort s'est échappé*, would translate as *A Man Condemned to Death Has Escaped*.) In *Diary*, the interior struggle of Bernanos's country priest made the employment of Christian symbols unavoidable; here, in making what Jonathan Rosenbaum calls "the greatest of all prison-escape movies,"[1] Bresson manages to make use of that overworked genre in a way that induces reflection on all the complex issues of grace and predestination.

When I took my then-fifteen-year-old son to see *A Man Escaped* years ago, he was hardly interested in the religious subtext but found the film far more "real" than the Hollywood thrillers to which he was accustomed. This is because Bresson brings viewers to appreciate the patience and attention to detail involved in the prisoner's planning. Instead of gunplay or emphasis on violent action, we observe extended moments of silence and seem to experience the prison routine through the watchful eyes of an individual under a death sentence. His fellow prisoners are desperate in their need to communicate with each other, and his struggle for liberation helps develop a deeper sense of community among them. Ultimately, the audience even gets a sense of mysterious forces that seem to favor the efforts of one prisoner rather than another.

The story is based on the actual escape of André Devigny (renamed Fontaine in the movie) from the Nazi prison of Montluc in Lyons in 1943. But unlike the neo-realism of such fashionable Italian directors of that time as Rossellini and de Sica, who wanted their films to directly reflect the society around them, Bresson's realism had a different goal, to convey the reality of the transcendent.[2] A *Man Escaped* has always been one of the most popular of Bresson's films, and it was chosen as one of the best foreign films by the National Board of Review for 1957.

The film provides no background information about the prisoner's activities in the French Resistance, but shots of his face immediately convey intelligence, determination, and self-control. The camera observes Fontaine's hands intently as they patiently scrape away the joints of his cell door, using an iron spoon he has bent into a chisel. The movie's title would seem to eliminate the possibility of suspense, but by concentrating on the everyday details of prison life and avoiding melodramatic effects, Bresson brings us close to Devigny's actual experience and encourages reflection on the meaning of imprisonment and liberation.

As Eric Rohmer observes, after Fontaine's first attempt to escape while being driven to prison he is met by and the brutality of the guards after he is captured, Bresson avoids any direct presentation of violence. His subject, unlike that of *Diary of a Country Priest,* is not the inner life of the soul, but the methodical preparation and hour-by-hour execution of a dangerous attempt to escape:

> It is a question of employing the most humble technique in order to convert everyday objects into instruments for escape. This is a more prosaic combat than that of the curé of Ambricourt. But matter is modeled with as many considerations, if not more difficulties, than the soul. What counts is the respectful prevision of the gesture, the beauty of a man at work. Bresson introduces into his film a tension which is that of the ordinary rhythm of life and owes nothing to the dramatic schemas used by most directors. A period of time that they would insist on embellishing he meticulously fills with nothing but expectation. Each instant is full, and if the idea of boredom is strange to anyone, it is especially to our prisoner, who does not know the day of his execution or that of his escape, whose hour grows further away to the degree that he finishes his preparations. Should we talk about suspense? No, not if what one means by that word is a skillfully measured choice of good or bad signals. Yes, if it is true that nothing is able to distract us from the one thought—escape.[3]

The effect of Bresson's daring aesthetic choice is summarized aptly by J. L. Tallenay:

> Bresson has chosen to tell the story of an adventure but has succeeded in the tour de force of making us forget the actual events. He has forced the public to pay attention only to the reactions of one man. Suspense remains, but its object has changed: it is no longer a matter of what is going to happen, but the passionate desire to know how a man is going to conduct himself.[4]

With Fontaine's running commentary as the backbone of its construction, most of the film is presented in the first person. The voice-overs are not super-imposed on the dialogue, as in *Diary*; in general, we hear the voice after we see the image. Our awareness that Fontaine will ultimately escape is reinforced by the fact that the commentary is in the past tense.

> This final *result* of the narrative cause-effect chain is known. As a result, our suspense is centered on the *causes*—not *whether* Fontaine will escape, but *how* he will escape. The film guides our expectations towards the minute details of Fontaine's work to break out of prison. The commentary and the sound effects draw our attention to tiny gestures and ordinary objects that become crucial to the escape.[5]

Paradoxically, by presenting events with cool detachment, even during moments of great danger, audience involvement becomes even more intense.

A Man Escaped represents a further break with standard moviemaking. As he was finishing work on it, Bresson told François Truffaut, "I wanted to achieve a great purity, a greater asceticism than in *Diary of a Country Priest*. This time I don't have a single professional actor."[6] Bresson's rejection of actors is central to his conception of cinematography. He has great admiration for live actors in the theater who can create with their bodies, but cinematography calls for the use of what he terms "models," whom he does not want to "act" at all. "On the boards," Bresson writes, "acting adds to real presence, intensifies it. In films, acting does away with even the semblance of real presence, and kills the illusion created by the photography."[7] His frequent insistence on many "takes" and his effort to control not only the gestures his models are to employ but even the diction with which they speak their lines are a training in a kind of automatism, undertaken in a belief that we reveal who we truly are when our gestures are automatic.

Regular moviegoers, accustomed to performances based on a very different set of assumptions, may find this approach upsetting at first, or simply complain about "bad acting." Since his rejection of actors made it difficult to acquire financing for his projects, the use of "models" was clearly more than a theoretical quirk for Bresson:

> What I am very pretentiously trying to capture is this essential soul. . . . What I tell them [the models] to do or say must bring to light something they had not realized they contained. The camera catches it; neither they nor I really know it before it happens. The unknown is what I wish to conquer.[8]

Bresson even says, "It would not be ridiculous to say to your models: 'I am inventing you as you are.'"[9]

It is apparent that in *A Man Escaped* Bresson offers a more complete embodiment of his understanding of cinematography than before. There is not only a nearly total control of his non-actors, but of the flow as well. We never have a clear sense of the overall layout of the jail; space itself is deliberately fragmented. This approach forces the spectator to an extra alertness; it is almost as if we have to work out the specifics of the escape ourselves, facing the same difficulties as Fontaine.

In the overall effort to ensure authenticity, the exterior shooting of *A Man Escaped* took place at Lyon and Fort Montluc in the presence of André Devigny himself, and the prison cell was reconstructed with real materials at studio Saint Maurice. In his earlier movies Bresson used the music of Jean-Jacques Grünewald to heighten the emotion of individual scenes. Here he practices greater restraint: music is restricted to a leitmotif of chords from Mozart's Mass in C minor, which are heard at several points during the action. At the same time, natural sounds, whose importance has already been noted in *Diary* (and even in Bresson's earlier work), become a major factor in the film's composition. He was deeply convinced that sounds were more expressive than images: "When a sound can replace an image, cut the image or neutralize it. The ear goes more toward the interior, the eye to the exterior."[10]

Devigny had published the story of his escape in *Figaro littéraire* (November 20–27, 1954). In a press conference at the 1956 Cannes festival Bresson spoke of his reaction to the narrative: "It was a very precise, even technical, account of the escape. The effect was of great beauty; written in a very precise, cold tone, even its construction was beautiful. . . . It had both the coldness and simplicity that make one feel this is the work of a man who writes with his heart."[11]

The film deliberately concentrates on the escape itself; nothing is said of Fontaine's resistance activities, nor do we learn about what happened to him after leaving prison. (In reality he was captured and escaped again.) As the credits roll, Bresson projects a brief signed statement: "This story is true. I present it as it is, without ornaments." At the same time, neither in *Escaped* nor in later films is he aiming at a complete historical reconstruction of events; "even if historical circumstances play a determining role in regard to external events and interior reactions, these circumstances nevertheless remain secondary in regard to them."[12]

Bresson retains all the exact material details that made the escape possible; as François Leterrier, the model for Fontaine, said, "the objects against which the prisoner struggles should have been listed in the credits." In addition to the bent spoon, there is the hatpin that initially enabled him to open his handcuffs, the latticework of the bed, a lantern, fabricated hooks, and the shirts and sheets that Fontaine transformed into ropes. Note how all these objects had to be forced into a new shape in order to see the prisoner's needs. In the process, the attempt to dominate matter becomes a kind of spiritual transformation.

Bresson's first title for the film was *Help Yourself*; when this was discarded, he chose a subtitle, "the spirit blows where it wills," from St. John's Gospel (3:8). Fontaine is acting out a complex dialectic between faith and free will: God is with him, but at the same time he has an obligation to employ all human resources to achieve his own liberation. Bresson explained his underlying intention: "I want to show this miracle: an invisible hand over the prison directing events and making something succeed for one person and not for another."[13] As Amédée Ayfre comments, however, this is "an invisible hand which never acts except by the hand of Fontaine, by that obstinate hand that makes tools and forces doors."[14]

▬▬ A *MAN ESCAPED* BEGINS WITH A SHOT OF A PLAQUE AT FORT MONTLUC, announcing that seven thousand of the ten thousand prisoners sent there died during the German occupation; during the credits we hear the "Kyrie" from Mozart's Mass in C minor. The film itself is made up of innumerable quick-moving, chronologically ordered fragments. Although there are six hundred separate shots, the escape itself, which has several stages, is its only extended sequence. "It was a matter," Bresson said, "of making a rapid film out of slow-moving things, suggesting the ponderous life of prison." No summary can do justice to the small encounters between prisoners who are forbidden by their German guards to talk to each other. Details that seem unimportant during a first viewing can ultimately be seen as preparing a significant change in attitude that will later affect the central action. For example, less than a third of the way through the film Fontaine is moved to a cell on an upper floor of the prison, where Blanchet, the elderly prisoner in the adjoining cell, is close to despair and at first rejects all communication. When Blanchet falls in the courtyard, Fontaine helps him up, but the old man, afraid that the scraping Fontaine makes as he tries to weaken a panel of his door will bring reprisals, remains resistant. Gradually, however, Fontaine's struggle for freedom becomes infectious and Blanchet gives him a blanket which he converts into material useful in the escape.

The first shot of the film itself is of Fontaine's hands. He is riding in the back seat of a Gestapo car with two other men, all of whom are handcuffed together; there is an exchange of tense glances with one of the men after

Fontaine's left hand seems to seek the door handle. With such an orientation, we naturally watch the road in expectation of a propitious moment to jump out. The car's progress is temporarily blocked by a wagon, but the opportunity passes too quickly. Then a trolley seems to be blocking the road and Fontaine disappears. We hear German voices shouting, then the sound of a club striking something, and Fontaine is back in the car, manacled. When the car gets to the prison, he is dragged roughly into a room where guards are obviously about to beat him. Bresson does not show the violence; the next thing seen, however, is a bloody Fontaine brought to his cell on a stretcher. The cell door closes heavily.

"I wasn't a pretty sight," Fontaine says in an exhausted voice, and after further reflection, "I got used to the idea of dying." When his solitude is interrupted by a knock on the wall from a prisoner in the adjoining cell, he cannot restrain his tears. Bresson never presents an overall view of the cell; we see only what Fontaine observes. Soon he notices a shelf, which enables him to look out the window. Two prisoners are walking in the yard beneath him. A possibility dawns: one of them, a man named Terry, says he knows a way to send a message. Fontaine is anxious to let his Resistance unit know that the transmitter they were using was actually helping the Germans. Terry manages to send paper and a pencil up to him via a rope with a sling, and promises to pick up Fontaine's letter the next day. When Fontaine sees Terry again, he asks for a pin; Terry picks one up in the women's barracks and passes it up, wishing Fontaine "Courage!" A little later Fontaine learns from the prisoner in the next cell how to use the pin to remove his handcuffs, and this first success gives him such a heady sense of victory that he raps on the wall, imitating the rhythm of a song. He still has no idea of the layout of the prison, much less what lies beyond it. His overall sense of location is based on the sound of a tram that passes close to the prison, but he is forcibly reminded of the constant danger around him by a burst of gunfire announcing another execution.

Fontaine is taken to German headquarters and asked to promise that he will not try to escape, a request he regards as simply a formality. When he is returned to prison, he is tranferred to a cell on the top floor, next door to Blanchet, the older prisoner who is close to despair. The daily lineup and procession for the emptying of the prisoners' slop buckets becomes a treasured moment of communication among prisoners, which Bresson highlights by a repetition of the brief passage from Mozart's Mass that was heard at the beginning.

Back in his cell, Fontaine experiences a bleak solitude yet retains an interior confidence that escape is his destiny. As he stares at his door he is struck by the way it has been constructed, which convinces him that it could be taken apart with a simple tool. He begins work with an iron spoon that he has bent into a kind of chisel, and the camera concentrates on Fontaine's hand working patiently at its task. A voice-over declares that five days elapse before he is able to make a gap in the wood. He has to work very slowly because of the fear of making so much noise that the guards would notice. Despite growing excitement, Fontaine remains cautious, and sweeps shavings under the door. He falls back into deep discouragement on hearing that Terry is leaving prison but remains determined: "I had to open that door."

During the daily washing of the slop buckets, Fontaine gives a pencil to one of the prisoners, a Protestant pastor, who wants to write out a few key passages from the Bible. Back in his cell, he uses paper to plug up the holes in the door panels that he has loosened. When the elderly Blanchet has a dizzy spell during the daily routine of emptying their slop buckets, Fontaine gives him a hand, insisting that everyone in their situation has to help one another.

After working on the door for three weeks and managing to separate a few panels from the frame, Fontaine realizes that he needs another spoon to pry the boards apart. Chance—or grace—is at work in the prison: at the daily wash-up, the pastor has obtained a Bible, and Fontaine picks up a discarded spoon. There is also a beginning of communication through the wall with Blanchet, even though the older man is still afraid the guards will hear the scraping.

Another prisoner is singled out by the camera during the emptying of the buckets—Orsini, whose wife had informed on him but who has managed to overcome his initial bitterness. Orsini, occupying the cell opposite Fontaine's, becomes his accomplice, acting as lookout while he is working on his door. After a month's slow labor, using great caution, Fontaine is finally able to open it. Late at night when there are no guards making the rounds, he has a sense of exultation as he roams the prison corridor.

During an encounter in the washroom, the Protestant pastor gives Fontaine a slip of paper with the text of John 3:8. In it Jesus speaks to Nicodemus of the need to be born again, and the line also contains the words of the movie's subtitle, "The spirit blows where it wills." The pastor counsels prayer and reliance on divine help, but Fontaine responds realistically that the individual must do his part: "it would be too easy if God took care of everything."

Fontaine's plan is developing. He will need twelve meters of rope; netting from the bed provides him with needed wire, and he can make rope from the bolster on his bed. Blanchet, emerging from his despair, begins to review escape plans with him.

Orsini, who was to be a partner in Fontaine's escape attempt, is taken in for questioning. Out of a sense of desperation, he tries to get away by himself, but is captured and brought back to his cell. He manages, however, to pass on some important information to Fontaine. Orsini explains that his effort failed because his rope broke; Fontaine will need hooks to ensure that it will hold. They can be obtained from the lantern frame in the cell.

As Orsini is taken away, Fontaine reflects on Jesus' words to Nicodemus. Suddenly the prison is shaken by the sounds of Orsini's execution. In order to understand more clearly what will be needed for his escape, Fontaine diagrams the roof and the outside walls. Using wire and loops, he makes the three hooks which he hopes to use to support his rope.

The prisoners receive a new order: turn in all pencils. Despite the threat of death if he is caught, Fontaine refuses to give in. Next day guards come through the prison searching each cell. Fortunately, a package arrives as they enter Fontaine's cell; although they inspect the package carefully, they forget to search his bed and the rest of the room. Using the clothes that have been sent him, as well as a blanket that Blanchet donates, Fontaine constructs the additional feet of rope that are needed.

The prison is filling up, and friends who know Fontaine's intentions warn him that he cannot wait any longer. This is confirmed when he is summoned to Nazi headquarters (the infamous Hotel Terminus), where he is told his case has been decided: he has received a death sentence.

Though shaken, he is relieved that he has been placed back in his old cell. Suddenly, he hears steps approaching and a guard enters with a young man who is wearing parts of a German uniform. His name is Jost. Worrying that he may be a spy, Fontaine gradually draws out the boy's story, which leave the latter's loyalties ambiguous. Again we hear a fragment of Mozart, while Fontaine reflects on the situation: he must either kill Jost or make him a partner in his escape. He decides to take the risk. After showing Jost the pencil he has retained, he tells him the Germans will lose the war.

Fontaine knows he must act quickly. The following night should be dark, and he resolves to take advantage of the darkness for his escape attempt. Exerting his moral authority over Jost, he gets the boy to agree to come with him. He says his goodbyes to the other prisoners during the washing of the buckets and asks a priest-prisoner and the Protestant pastor to pray for him.

Confident about his equipment, Fontaine reviews final preparations, making sure that the rope is ready and the cell is swept. Then he knocks on the wall to say goodbye to Blanchet. Once in the corridor, he cautions Jost to walk as softly as possible. On the roof, Fontaine goes over the side first, then Jost. They observe steam from a train that is going by and have to stop for a minute because the crunching of gravel under their feet is making too much noise. When they reach the edge overlooking the courtyard, a quick shot reveals the upper part of their faces in the light. They see a guard below them, armed with a machine gun, bayonet, and grenade. A pause indicates a wait from midnight till one in the morning.

When the guard is changed, Fontaine observes his movements closely: "This man had to die." A whistle blows, Fontaine shimmies down the rope and hides in a corner ledge. His heart is pounding so much he can't act. He hears the footsteps of the German sentry. Is he lighting a cigarette? He's only a meter away, now he's turning around. Fontaine grabs the German from behind, but Bresson doesn't show the actual violence with which he is dispatched; we simply hear Fontaine looking up and signaling to Jost, "Come."

Fontaine passes over another hurdle, climbing on Jost's shoulders. They have left their jackets and shoes behind. Fontaine reflects that if he were alone, he might have remained there all night. When they go over the side again, they note that the sentry box is not occupied and the sentry is patrolling by bike. Fontaine tells Jost to cut the electricity. With the help of a hook, the rope catches, but Fontaine still hesitates. Time is running out before they go over the last wall at four o'clock in the morning.

The ending is brief and restrained. After the two men embrace, Jost says, "If my mother could see me now!" As they hustle off into the darkness, their figures disappearing into the steam from a train, there is a final triumphant burst of the Mozart Mass.

IN BRESSON'S HANDLING, FONTAINE'S ESCAPE IS CLEARLY FAR MORE than a carefully observed adventure story. As Allen Thiher maintains, "The manifest struggle for freedom in the world is doubled by a spiritual determinism, for it is grace that allows him to overcome his captors."[15] It is important to recall Fontaine's insistence that leaving everything to God would make things too easy; he must make every effort to work for his own liberty. As Ayfre said, "In Bresson's universe, 'all is grace,' but simultaneously 'all is freedom.'"[16] This fits in well with Thiher's insistence that the influence of Christian existentialism in French intellectual life during the fifties is a more important element in the background of *A Man Escaped* than the World War II Resistance movement. For Virgilio Fantuzzi the film's theme is that "Life is a relentless struggle whose aim is the soul's liberation from the individualism of prison. Limits and obstacles exist in order to be over-come. Without these limits and obstacles there would be no struggle, and without struggle there would be no liberation."[17] At the same time, Bresson never had any intention of turning his film into religious preaching: when during the shooting he was offered a tiny (four-millimeter) cross for the pastor to wear, he told his prop director, "I'm afraid that might be a little big."

Janick Arbois sees *A Man Escaped* as a unique film which "makes us see death, not Fontaine's, but the only one which truly represents death—our own. . . . This movie, which does not show us any executions or scenes of violence, which even avoids those its subject includes, is the first movie in which death is the star, invisible but present in each image and each glance of its principal interpreter."[18]

At the same time Fontaine's story dramatizes the movement from soli-tude to communication, repeating the theme of the communion of saints already present in *Angels of Sin* and *Diary of a Country Priest.* Terry, a fellow prisoner, shows him how he can communicate with those outside the walls, and another prisoner explains how to unlock his handcuffs. Even more sig-nificantly, after a reckless, unsuccessful attempt to escape, Orsini informs him of the importance of additional hooks in descending the prison walls. The exchanges with the Protestant pastor help confirm Fontaine's sense that he will have God's help in this adventure. It is especially appropriate that Blanchet, the old prisoner who had been close to despair, is the one who points out: "It was necessary for Orsini to fail so you could succeed." Nor is it by chance that Fontaine's final test is the necessity of showing trust—to Jost, a confused, "unworthy" adolescent—who will turn out to be necessary in the escape.

As Thiher insists,

> The prison actually allows these prisoners to overcome isolation and to enter into true communion. To give another pointed opposition, one might con-sider the relation between the natural presence of evil and the despair to which it might lead, on one hand, and on the other hand, the seemingly gra-tuitous faith that never abandons the hero, a paradox that is expressed exis-tentially as a constant leap of faith.[19]

The Japanese novelist Shûsaku Endo comments, "The film speaks of things that we have lost sight of since the end of the war: hope in trust and mutual assistance. . . . Fontaine has to rely on strangers, the man in the opposite cell, or the one next to him. Perhaps they will betray him, but the lieutenant puts his confidence in them. To wager on the everyday, to have confidence, that is what we least know how to do."[20]

Many commentators have called special attention to the moment in *A Man Escaped* in which Fontaine hides behind a ledge, calming himself before rushing into the darkness to overpower the German guard. What is instructive, of course, is that Bresson does not show the violence; he even says that the surrounding objects in the episode are more important than the hands that strangle:

> The subject is not in those hands; it is elsewhere, in the currents that are passing through. At that particular moment the objects are—and this is very curious—a great deal more important than the characters. The terrace above, that wall, this blackness, the sound of the train—these are more important than what takes place. The objects and the noises, therefore, are in intimate communion with man (perhaps in a mystical sense), and that is a good deal more serious and more important than the hands that strangle a guard.[21]

François Truffaut describes Bresson's treatment of actors as "holding them back from acting 'dramatically,' from adding emphasis, forcing them to abstract from their 'art.' He achieves this by killing their will, exhausting them with an endless number of repetitions and takes, by almost hypnotizing them."[22] At least in *A Man Escaped* the result is nearly miraculous: "With amateur interpreters who know nothing about theater, he creates the ultimately real character, whose every gesture, look, attitude, reaction, and word—not one of which is louder than the other—is essential. The whole takes on a form that *makes* the film."[23] François Leterrier (Fontaine) understood very well what Bresson wanted of him: "He did not want us to ever express ourselves. He made us become part of the composition of an image. We had to locate ourselves, as precisely as possible, in relation to the background, the lighting, and the camera."[24] Reviewers who complained about the awkwardness of some of the acting in *Diary of a Country Priest* were won over by the homogeneity of the performances, all by amateurs.

Truffaut also calls attention to the way Bresson revolutionized standard film cutting. Normally, "a shot of someone looking at something is valid only in relation to the next shot showing what he is looking at—a form of cutting that made cinema a dramatic art, a kind of photographed theater. Bresson's approach is quite different; if in *A Man Escaped* closeups of hands and objects lead to closeups of the faces, the succession is . . . in the service of a preestablished harmony of subtle relations among visual and aural elements. Each shot of hands or of a look is autonomous."[25]

Earlier films had demonstrated Bresson's subtle use of natural sounds; *A Man Escaped* is an even more brilliant example of his practice than *Diary of a Country Priest*. The slamming of a cell door, noises made by the handcuffs, keys grating against the bars, the loud scraping as Fontaine sharpens a spoon handle into a chisel, the gunfire when one of the prisoners is executed, the motor of a streetcar, the whistle of a train passing close by the prison—all are experienced by the audience as if they too were prisoners. We see very little direct violence on the part of the Nazi guards, but their voices are harsh and ominous; even when an officer speaks with formal politeness, he conveys a sinister sense of entrapment. In contrast, Fontaine's own voice, though it expresses determination and confidence, never betrays inner violence or an inflated sense of self.

Through a detailed analysis of the brief scene in which Jost is put into Fontaine's cell, David Bordwell and Kristin Thompson demonstrate "how silence and shifts between sounds that are internal and external, simultaneous and non-simultaneous, guide our expectations."[26] The importance of Bresson's use of natural sounds is especially evident during the final escape, a night sequence. "Often sound is our main guide to what is happening. This has the effect of intensifying the spectators' attention greatly. We must strain to understand the action from what we can glimpse and hear. We judge the pair's progress from the church bells tolling the hour. The train outside the walls helps cover the noise the fugitives make. Each strange noise suggests an unseen threat."[27]

Another brilliant use of sound has already been noted: Bresson's subtle and restrained use of Mozart's Mass in C Minor, heard first over the credits.[28] During the film proper it does not occur until the first time Fontaine goes with the other prisoners to empty their slop buckets. It returns seven more times, primarily when he makes contact with someone who will affect his escape. It reappears when Orsini tries to escape, when Blanchet donates his blanket for the needed rope-making, and when Fontaine is debating as to whether he should trust Jost. At the end, when Fontaine jumps to safety from the outer wall, the "Kyrie" reverberates in thanksgiving, while continuing to intercede for all who remain within the walls, whether prisoners or jailers.

NOTES

1. Jonathan Rosenbaum, "The Last Filmmaker: A Local Interim Report," in *Robert Bresson*, ed. James Quandt (Toronto: Cinematheque Ontario, 1998), 20.

2. Quoted in Amédée Ayfre, "The Universe of Robert Bresson," in *The Films of Robert Bresson*, ed. Ian Cameron (New York: Praeger, 1969), 8.

3. Eric Rohmer, *Cahiers du Cinéma* no. 64 (December 1956).

4. J. L. Tallenay, *Radio-Cinéma* no. 58 (1956).

5. David Bordwell and Kristin Thompson, *Film Art: An Introduction,* 6th ed. (New York: McGraw Hill, 2001), 316.

6. *Arts* no. 574 (June 27–July 3, 1956).

7. Robert Bresson, *Notes of a Cinematographer* (Los Angeles: Sun and Moon Press, 1988), 37–38.

8. Charles T. Samuels, *Encountering Directors* (New York: G. P. Putnam & Sons, 1972), 61.

9. Bresson, *Notes of a Cinematographer,* 37.

10. Ibid.

11. Jean Sémolué, *Bresson ou l'acte pur des Métamorphoses* (Paris: Flammarion, 1993), 74.

12. Michel Estève, *Robert Bresson* (Paris: Editions Albatros, 1983), 40.

13. See Robert Monod, "En travaillant avec Robert Bresson," *Cahiers du cinéma* no. 64 (November 1956).

14. Ayfre, "Universe of Robert Bresson," 22.

15. Allen Thiher, "Bresson's *Un condamné à mort:* The Semiotics of Grace," in *Robert Bresson,* ed. James Quandt (Toronto: Cinematheque Ontario, 1998), 225.

16. Ayfre, "Universe of Robert Bresson," 22. Ayfre goes on to say, "No formula could be more orthodox if the Doctor of Grace, St. Augustine, is to be believed: 'as the law is not made void but established through faith, since faith procures the grace whereby the law is fulfilled, so the freedom of the will is not made void through grace, but rather is thereby established'" (*De spiritu et littera,* 30.52).

17. "Robert Bresson," special issue of *Rivista del Cinematografo* no. 9 (December 2000).

18. Janick Arbois, fiche *Télé-ciné* no. 295 (1956): 6.

19. Thiher, "Bresson's *Un condamné à mort,*" 225.

20. Shûsaku Endo, in *Le Cinématographie de Robert Bresson* (Tokyo: Tokyo International Foundation for the Promotion of Screen Image Culture, 1999), 109.

21. Robert Bresson, *Cahiers du cinéma* no. 75 (October 1957).

22. François Truffaut, *The Films in My Life* (New York: Simon & Schuster, 1978), 192–93.

23. François Leterrier, *Express,* Sept. 21, 1956.

24. Truffaut, *Films in My Life,* 195.

25. Ibid.

26. Bordwell and Thompson, *Film Art,* 319.

27. Ibid., 318.

28. Ibid., 319.

5

A Ballet of Hands

Pickpocket

"*PICKPOCKET* IS ROBERT BRESSON'S FIRST FILM," SAYS FRENCH director Louis Malle. "Those that he made before were only rough sketches. . . . Its release is one of the four or five great dates in the history of cinema." Even Bresson's admirers had assumed he could go no further in the refinement of his style; Malle suggests that, for the new generation of directors who were given the collective title "*la nouvelle vague*," the movie seemed like a trumpet call for the liberation of cinema: "*Pickpocket* is a work of profound inspiration, instinctive, burning, imperfect, and overwhelming. It resolves all misunderstandings: if you reject this film, it is as if you are doubting the possibility of cinema as an autonomous art."[1]

After *A Man Escaped*, Bresson had begun working on *Lancelot of the Lake*, but the project was put off for lack of funding. Disappointed, Bresson threw his energies into *Pickpocket* (1959), and only ten months after he conceived the idea, the movie had its Paris opening. The speed with which he worked is reflected in the rhythm of the film, which reveals the hand of a master working with the same confidence and excitement that pickpockets themselves exhibit as they practice their art at the Gare de Lyon, a masterfully composed scene that was filmed in the midst of a crowd. Here Bresson mixes close-ups and medium shots, employing a variety of camera movements, including panoramic shots and brief lateral traveling shots.

It is worth keeping in mind that *Pickpocket* is Bresson's first completely personal film—that is, one for which he composed the screenplay himself instead of adapting it from an existing text. "*Pickpocket* is a break with a cinema inspired by literature," Michel Estève comments. "More and more, the subject is only a pretext; theme and symbols are reflected through portraits. The story itself is placed in question."[2] By "reducing" its actors to models,

Philippe Arnaud asserts, "*Pickpocket* annexes for the cinema the new domain of unconscious automatism, guided by the hand and its quasi-autonomous will."[3] Convinced that "[i]t is anti-nature to subordinate [our movements] to will and thought," Bresson argues that

> models who have become automatic (everything weighed, measured, timed, repeated ten, twenty times) and are then dropped in the medium of the events of your film—their relations with the objects and persons around them will be *right*, because they will not be *thought*.[4]

Pierre Étaix, who was one of the pickpockets in the film, confirmed this in a personal interview. Étaix, who is now a film director in his own right, said that Bresson kept correcting his actor-models, insisting on many takes—sometimes more than forty. He didn't want them to think or interpret, but to achieve a natural rendering of the lines. Étaix admits being both confused and terrified at times but maintains that it was an enriching experience.

Despite the enthusiasm of the avant-garde, responses to the film were divided. Some, thinking confusedly of the director as someone who dealt only with the sublime, thought the subject rather sordid. Certainly its hero, Michel, a somewhat pretentious and self-conscious young thief, is a sharp contrast to Fontaine and the curé d'Ambricourt. Those who were not already familiar with Bresson's work read the title as a promise of a crime movie and did not understand the absence of melodrama and exaggeratedly emotional acting they were accustomed to finding in a thriller. The surprising brevity of *Pickpocket*—seventy minutes—makes it clear that Bresson is deliberately leaving out the links between different stages of the action and is indifferent to standard movie realism.

Estève celebrates the film as opening the way to the modern conception of cinema. He calls attention to its "rejection of classical linear intrigue, the traditional 'play' of the actor, outdoor shooting, the subjective perception of space and time, and the primacy of image over word—or their strict union."[5] As in *Diary of a Country Priest* and *A Man Escaped*, Bresson employs a narrator; but in contrast to the earlier films, in *Pickpocket*, when Michel reads extracts from the spiral notebook in which he keeps his journal, he speaks in the past tense, except at the very end. The device serves to interiorize the images of the film; "the strange paths of pickpocketing and the strange paths of love become ways of discovery and self-knowledge in the account that Michel draws up."[6]

There are occasional hints of Dostoevsky's *Crime and Punishment*, especially in Michel's justification of crimes carried out by "superior people" and the cat-and-mouse game he plays with the police inspector, but *Pickpocket* is by no means an adaptation of the novel. Malle gives us an accurate idea of what to expect:

> There is no longer any *anecdote,* that is, any pretext foreign to the real subject of the film (which more often hides it)—what producers call "a good subject," "a good story," with psychology and dramatic development as its keys. We find only symbols of a luminous simplicity which together make up an allegory, or more precisely what the Gospel calls a *parable.*[7]

But if it is legitimate to speak of parable, it is one presented by an extremely painstaking artist who believes that "the role of cinema ought to consist less in showing than in *suggesting,* by means of rhythms, relationships, a crossroad of relationships." As Jean Pelegri comments,

> It is curious to recognize that Bresson, in defining cinema, speaks of rhythms rather than images. For him cinema is not an art of the director or photographer, but the art of placing things in order. It is a matter of orchestrating and composing them in a musical manner. "The eye listens," Claudel insisted. Bresson's films prove it.[8]

Pelegri, who played the part of the police inspector in the movie, says, "People have the impression that everything is completely organized, but with Bresson, working on the set gives him ideas. He used a lot of improvisation in *Pickpocket.*"[9] The endless retakes led to predictable, but sometimes amusing responses. Some boxers, for example, who had been hired as extras for a scene in a working-class café in the suburbs, were given tomato salad to eat during a particular shot. After the twelfth repetition, one of them became impatient. "Can't you change things a little, and give us a bit of sausage now?" he asked.[10]

The scenario for *Pickpocket* shows Bresson's increasing resistance to psychological analysis. Because he has "reduced" his actors to "models," it is hardly surprising that Bresson's characters are sometimes accused of unreality. For the director, however, there is a strong link between automatism and chance, or even a sense of fate.

Since the use of "models" is so central to Bresson's practice, Pelegri's reflections on his experience are especially pertinent:

> If one had to classify him, Bresson would be placed among the portraitists. What interests him are gestures, glances, and attitudes: the implicit and latent personality of his models. The often held idea is that he considers them as objects—objects of which he would be both master and creator. But for Cézanne, was an apple simply an apple? Was it not a model? For a painter there are different ways of sketching an apple. Bresson's response is precise: "Model. Between you and him, not just to reduce but to suppress the distance."[11]

Drawing on an analogy between what Bresson asked of his interpreters and what St. John of the Cross insisted on with his novices, Pelegri reminds us that portrait painters like to surround their models with silence. The avoidance of all theatrical acting, the practice of speaking mechanically, can be a kind of "dark night" for Bresson's models, but "if they submit, there is a strange feeling of absence, of interior liberty. Ready to live the instant, we are tractable, separated from ourselves. This is a little like Bresson can be on the set, where, in contrast to the general assumption, he always seemed to be in the process of waiting, spying on his models, on the look-out for signs. Beginning with them, he is ready to improvise, to find connections."[12]

■— LIKE A MAN ESCAPED, PICKPOCKET BEGINS WITH AN INTRODUCTORY text, white letters against a black background: "This is not a crime film. The author is trying to express, through images and sounds, the nightmare of a young man pushed by weakness into an adventure in pickpocketing for which he was not made. This adventure, however, following strange paths, will unite two souls who otherwise would never have known each other."

Next a spiral notebook appears; under several lines already written, a hand traces phrases that a voice speaks at the same time: "I know that ordinarily people who have done such things keep quiet, and those who speak about them have not done them. And nevertheless I have done them." The film will frequently return to this notebook, which presumably contains the written account of its central character, Michel, usually for brief voice-offs.

Bresson then shows us a crocodile handbag, from which the right hand of an elegantly dressed woman pulls bank notes. She passes them on to a man, who presents them at the betting booth of a racetrack. Michel, the young man who had previously spoken, observes them: "My decision had been taken some time ago; would I have the necessary boldness?" He places himself behind the couple, succeeds in opening the woman's bag, and takes out some notes. We return to the voice of the narrator: "I no longer had my feet on the ground; I was in control of the world." He turns around, and two policemen follow him: "But a minute later I was grabbed." After his moment of elation, he had been arrested. He is soon released, however; the police inspector acknowledges that they have no proof. Michel leaves the police station, walks up to the top floor of the building in which he has rented a room, and falls asleep with his clothes on.

The next day he stops before the door of his mother, whom he hasn't seen in a month. Jeanne, a young woman neighbor, offers to let him in, but he hesitates, gives her some money for his mother, and rushes off.

At a café with his friend Jacques that night, he asks for help in finding some kind of a job. Jacques says, "You are very good with your hands. Obviously, you deserve something better. One must know how to wait and be satisfied with what is offered, thanks to which you will soon own a new suit and a tie." The inspector who had released Michel happens to come by, and the three men sit at a table together. Urged on by Jacques, as well as by his own pride and the desire to play with fire, Michel presents his theory that society should allow a few superior people who are down on their luck to break the law in certain cases. When the police officer criticizes this idea of giving a kind of license to criminals, Michel says it would only be for a few times; afterwards, they would stop. No, the inspector insists, such men never stop.

Riding the metro gives Michel a chance to observe a man who turns out to be a skillful pickpocket. The thief holds a newspaper that is spread out; by the time he folds it, he has succeeded in pilfering a passenger's wallet. Back in his room, Michel practices this by himself. There is a dissolve from the newspaper he used in the room for practice to the metro where he holds a newspaper in the manner he had seen employed by the pickpocket. His hands tremble—"my heart beat rapidly"— but he is successful. Michel continues with this activity, deliberately taking different train routes each time. He is somewhat successful, but profits are minimal, and once he has a close call: he is stopped by a man who realizes he has been robbed, and orders Michel to return his wallet.

One evening Michel sees a stranger waiting outside the door of his house and wonders if he is being watched by the police. Going up the stairs to his room, he bumps into Jacques, who passes on a message from Jeanne that his mother is dying. Although Michel tells Jacques that he loves his mother more than himself, he is so curious about the man waiting on the street that instead of rushing to her he hurries out to find the stranger. Soon they are talking like old friends in a café on the boulevard Rochechouart. As the stranger initiates Michel into the secrets of a pickpocket, elegant dance music by Jean-Baptiste Lully, the seventeenth-century composer who was a favorite of Louis XIV, can be heard in the background. Michel's new friend emphasizes the need for stringent training in order to make one's fingers supple.

When he returns home, he steps over a note that had been put under his door: "Come quickly, Jeanne." At his mother's sickbed, he tells the old woman that he wants to make her happy and offers facile reassurance: "Tomorrow you will feel better." In a typical Bresson reversal, the next shot shows Jacques, Jeanne, and Michel sitting beside the mother's coffin during the funeral Mass. As he prepares to kneel, Michel turns to Jeanne, his face bathed in tears.

Back at his place, where Jeanne has helped him bring back his mother's belongings, he says, "And that's all that is left—papers, letters, a few photographs. No way to turn back. Jeanne, do you believe we will be judged?"

"Yes, but don't worry about her—she was perfect."

"Judged how? According to a code? What code? It's absurd."

"Don't you believe in anything?" Jeanne asks.

"I believed in God, Jeanne," he responds, "for about three minutes."

The camera shifts again to show Michel writing his journal. He describes a visit to a bank where a man with a handsome suitcase takes out some bills and puts them in his wallet. During the scene as presented, when the man looks at Michel, he is afraid to act, but his confederate—the one who had initiated him at Rochechouart—strips the victim of his wallet as he is getting a taxi. The two thieves split the proceeds at a café, where a third accomplice joins them.

Once again Jacques and Michel meet the police inspector at a café. The latter notices a book of Michel's that Jacques has borrowed, *The Prince of Pickpockets,* by an Englishman named Barrington. The officer asks Michel if Barrington was one of those superior men whom he had praised during their last conversation. Although he realizes the commissioner suspects him, Michel brings the book to the police station, but soon decides that the interview "was a trap": the authorities had arranged the occasion in order to have a chance to search his room. When he gets home, however, he feels reassured; nothing seems to have been moved.

Jacques, Michel, and Jeanne go to a café on Sunday. The atmosphere around them is that of a carnival and there is a merry-go-round nearby, but Michel remains distant. "You're pathetic," Jeanne say to him sharply. "You're not in real life; you're not interested in what other people are interested in." She and Jacques go for a ride on the merry-go-round, and Michel leaves, driven by his passion for stealing. Abruptly, the camera shows Michel climbing the stairs to his room, his trousers torn and his hands scraped: "I had to run, I fell. . . ." Despite the accident, he is excited by the handsome watch he had managed to steal. Another return to the journal: "I had become extremely daring. My two accomplices and I understood perfectly that it couldn't last."

At the Gare de Lyon the three pickpockets are hard at work: it is a sustained and complex sequence, difficult to summarize. At the ticket window the men grab a woman's handbag, then the money of an older man. One of the accomplices puts his hand on the right shoulder of a man who turns around, while from the other side a confederate takes his wallet. A train is waiting on one of the platforms; in the corridor a man carrying a heavy suitcase passes in front of an accomplice who takes his wallet. The money is removed, but when the same man passes going in the other direction the empty wallet is put back in its place. Michel notices a policeman he has seen before; what he doesn't remember is meeting him at headquarters.

Running into Michel on the stairway of his building, Jacques tells him that Jeanne has been summoned to the police. "I wanted to alert you so that you could be prepared." Back at the Gare de Lyon, two policemen arrest Michel's collaborators but pass in front of him without looking at him.

The police inspector visits Michel, who becomes quite upset and complains that the officer is playing with him. The inspector informs him that Jeanne had made a complaint a year ago about a theft of money from an elderly woman neighbor, but withdrew it a few days later. This was not an unusual situation; people often come to suspect that a theft has been committed by a near relative whom they do not want to implicate. "A little later," the inspector continues, "the son of that old lady was arrested at Longchamps. It was you. I wanted to open your eyes. In the future, you can be arrested simply on the word of one of my agents."

Michel rushes to tell Jeanne he is going to be arrested. She cannot understand how he could have stolen from his mother. "People can know that an act is ugly and still commit it," he reminds her.

"I don't know," Jeanne comments, "perhaps everything has a reason."

Now that she knows he is a thief, Michel says, perhaps she will not want to have anything to do with him. Her response is to throw her arms around his neck, asking, "Are you going to leave?" He says no, but a voice-over reveals his thinking: "The idea immediately seemed possible to me."

Michel rushes to the Gare de Lyon, this time to catch a train headed for Milan. His journal gives a brief summary of the more than two years he is away. He travels to Rome, then to London, where he carries out two successful robberies, but wastes his money on gambling and women. Returning to Paris almost broke, he goes to Jeanne's place, where he discovers she has had a child. Jacques, the father, abandoned the young mother three months ago; Jeanne explains she did not want to marry him because she did not love him enough. Michel says he wants to help support the child, and that from now on he will try to be honest.

There follows a brief shot of Michel receiving his pay in an envelope and handing it over to Jeanne. The voice-over announces confidently, "The police and I had lost sight of each other." In a café, however, he cannot prevent himself from looking over the shoulder of a customer who is studying the racing charts in a newspaper. The stranger asks him if he is a gambler and whether he will be going to the races.

At the racetrack, between races the stranger shows Michel a bundle of bank notes that he has won. The young man fails to see that the horse that had just come in first was not the one the stranger had bet on. The police had set a trap: as soon as Michel extends his hand to steal the bank notes, the stranger (who is a police officer) takes out handcuffs and locks them around his wrist. Michel's career as a pickpocket is shown with perfect symmetry, beginning and ending at the racetrack.

The scene shifts to prison, where Jeanne is visiting Michel. At first he is angry at himself simply for having been caught and asks her if she has come just to tell him he was in the wrong. As she gets up to leave, however, he begs her to stay. Back in his cell, he rehearses a deeper temptation, "Why live? I haven't decided anything yet."

A letter arrives from Jeanne: she hasn't visited him for several months because her little boy was sick. Now that the child is out of danger, she will come again. A voice-over betrays an impulse to tenderness: "When I read that letter, my heart beat violently."

As soon as he sees Jeanne in the visitor's parlor, Michel becomes exultant: "Something lights up her face." Through the bars, he kisses her forehead and hands. The music of Lully, which has been heard several times since its first use over the credits, returns triumphantly as Michel declares: "O Jeanne, in order to get to you, what a strange path I had to take."

BRESSON'S CINEMATIC FASCINATION WITH HANDS, SO CENTRAL TO *A Man Escaped,* is even more evident in *Pickpocket.* In an interview he even describes the film "as the adventure of Michel's hands, which drag their proprietor into the adventure in theft. Later, they drag him beyond theft into an inner adventure, the adventure of the soul. In Michel's case, crime leads to the 'reign of morality.'"[13] In preparation for this film Bresson did research at police headquarters, gathered as much information as possible about pickpockets, and came to understand that their legerdemain fit in perfectly with his ideas about cinematography. The film credits list the magician-illusionist Kassagi as technical counselor; he is also the pickpocket-model who instructs Michel.

Pickpocket also repeats Bresson's convictions regarding the significance of chance: Michel has taken a strange path, but it has been pursued under the influence of a benevolent power. Though he is not as attractive a hero as Fontaine and does not have the spiritual depth of the curé d'Ambricourt, his journal reveals the talent of a potential writer. As with the curé, the journal is a companion in solitude, but Michel's account reveals considerable pride and makes frequent use of irony. Unlike the situation in *Diary of a Country Priest*, however, everything is told in the past tense until the conclusion.

The speed with which the story develops, along with Bresson's lack of interest in psychological explanation, makes it inevitable that *Pickpocket* includes some narrative leaps that do not stand up to realistic scrutiny. Jacques had seemed to be a genuine friend of Michel and was trying to help get him a job; we are completely unprepared for the revelation that he fathered a child with Jeanne and then abandoned her. And although the fear of arrest is enough motivation for Michel to get on a train for Milan, his period away from Paris is summarized far too briefly. Instead of the camera showing anything directly, there is a throwaway line from his journal; in addition, the idea of Michel spending the proceeds from his robberies on women seems at odds with everything we see of him.

Jean Collet's analysis of the scene in which Michel goes to a café on a Sunday with Jeanne and Jacques is especially enlightening. In a sequence that offers a promise of euphoria, with street noises, music from the fairground, and the airplanes of the merry-go-round constantly turning, silence weighs at the table. In such a context Jeanne's harsh criticism of Michel—"You are not in real life"—has extra force, containing a truth that will ultimately permit love to emerge. The camera "translates an isolation, a withdrawal into oneself, while managing to suggest, in a domain that escapes the senses, a far-off communion."[14]

Jean Sémolué makes a pertinent connection between the introduction of Lully's music and the three uses of the notebook in which Michel keeps his journal. Although the music's primary function is to ensure the continuity of the transitions, its purpose the first time we hear it after the credits is to show Michel's initiation into the art of pickpocketing, which takes place in a dingy neighborhood café. Elegant seventeenth-century dances represent an ironic accompaniment to the nimble saraband of hands and quick changes that Michel's mysterious instructor is explaining. In contrast, during the "ballet" at the Gare de Lyon, all we can hear are the noises of reality. Music intervenes again and with greater frequency during the later scenes as events quicken, and in the film's final images another burst of Lully's music brings Michel and Jeanne together despite prison bars.[15]

The entire soundtrack of *Pickpocket* could be analyzed in detail; as in *A Man Escaped*, many small sounds that could go unnoticed on a first viewing would be seen to have considerable value. A valuable insight into Bresson's subtle use of sound is provided by René Prédal's comment on the screech of the train wheel when Michel leaves hurriedly for Milan. Because getting away was such a relief for Michel, the sound had to be amplified to create an awareness of its subjective value. In fact, Bresson recorded the wheels on real rails, but in the middle of the night, in a silent station, and with a train that was going to the depot. "It was, indeed, real sound, but detached from everything else so that it would assert itself, that is, give it an unreal tonality."[16]

A number of critics have called attention to the sexual overtones of the pickpocketing scenes, since the secret touches that are central to this action produce an overwhelming sense of excitement. Louis Malle, for example, says, "*Pickpocket* is also an erotic film, since pickpocketing is only a symbol, scarcely transposed, of the sin of the flesh—note the spasm produced in the hero by his first theft."[17] Philippe Arnaud points out that the first time Michel stole successfully in the subway, the voice-over comments, "My heart beat wildly," and that he uses the same phrase in prison when he receives Jeanne's letter after a long period in which he had no news of her. As Arnaud continues,

> The very gestures of theft, whose entire strategy consists in not having the victim see them—through the use of camouflage (the newspaper), and dexterity (rapidity of execution, that precise area in which the hand that has slid between the cloth of a shirt and that of a jacket ought to avoid touching in order to remain imperceptible) have all the signs of a sexual approach, as the status of the victim suggests. The technical success of the actions of Michel is achieved only when that other is as if absent from himself. . . . But this other, the one who is going to be robbed, is always capable, because of a false move, of pulling himself out of that anesthesia of vigilance which represents the pickpocket's simple strategy. It is this narrow, uncertain, potentially reversible edge of perception, this precise but unknown limit that constitutes the specifically sexual stimulus of the action.[18]

This sexual interpretation should not be exaggerated, however; the combination of danger and tension, followed by the heady sense of success when a wallet or a watch has been taken unobserved, could in itself account for the obvious interior excitement. Some commentators have pushed the evidence to fit their theories to such an extent that Bresson flatly stated, "There is no latent homosexuality in the main character of *Pickpocket*."[19] Perhaps a more useful clue is to be found in Pierre Gabaston's analogy between the pickpocket's occupation and the sleight-of-hand practiced in cinematography itself.[20]

For John Russell Taylor, there is a weakness of the film that is mostly related to the choice of Martin Lassalle as the model for Michel. Since Bresson's method is so dependent on his finding models whose faces will reveal "the spiritual affinities between actor and character," the wrong choice can be disastrous to the whole movie. Though Bresson praised Lassalle's work in *Pickpocket,* he admits that such an affinity may not have come through "because of Lassalle's lack of ease with the French language (his background was Uruguayan)." Taylor accuses Lassalle of putting expression into the commentary, "even to act it, and thereby weaken its effect."[21]

Such a criticism contradicts the testimony of Marika Green, the model for Jeanne in *Pickpocket,* who says that Lassalle corresponded extremely well to what Bresson wanted Michel to be. She also recalls how exhausting Bresson was with Lassalle, making him "repeat the text to expel all the psychology of the character. He was stubborn in eliminating any attempt at personal interpretation in order to recover what he calls the natural." Green's comments seem reliable, especially since she also repeats the typical complaint of those who have been in Bresson movies: "Since I had been a Bresson heroine, [other directors] perceived that it would be almost impossible to make me act. . . . This shows once again that a Bresson model can only represent one character."[22]

Pierre Étaix, one of Michel's pickpocket confederates in the movie, remains convinced that "with his occasional actors, Robert Bresson has always obtained, through surprise, abandon, or simply fatigue, what in painting is called perfection of tone. His concern has never been 'to play true' but to be more true than true." Étaix, who collaborated for a time with Jacques Tati, famous for the deadpan humor of *Monsieur Hulot's Holiday* and other comedies, believes that "paradoxical as it may appear, there is a close kinship between Bresson and the work of Jacques Tati, who for analogous reasons, made little use of professional actors."[23]

Logically enough, because he was dissatisfied with the performance of Lassalle (and also that of Marika Green), the ending of *Pickpocket* did not give John Russell Taylor a "sense of a process completed, but only of an inexplicable change of character." The enthusiasm of most critics, however, suggests that, though they may initially have experienced the ending as abrupt, they quickly came to assent to its appropriateness. Marika Green's recollections regarding the shooting of the last scene are especially useful: "Bresson wanted an immense tenderness to pass between Michel and Jeanne. . . . Something happened that was astonishing with Bresson; he told me, 'Do what you want, do what you feel!' I was stupefied to be able to benefit from this show of favor."[24]

The "redemption" of Michel is perhaps prepared for by a few fleeting shots in which Bresson suggests that everything is to be understood in relation to the death of his mother, especially since this also brings him close to Jeanne.[25] In the last meeting between Michel and his mother, we see Jeanne's reflection in the mirror of the wardrobe, and she is at his side again at the funeral service. Even though his mother's death makes him rebel against any notion of God's justice, as Jeanne later reminds him, "Perhaps everything has a meaning." As Prédal says, "It is possible to see in almost all of Bresson's films a way of the cross, the passion coming to seem the common lot in which men and women find an understanding of the world and the place they occupy in it."[26]

Keith Reader maintains that the status of Michel's final words,

> "Jeanne, what a strange path I had to take," spoken but not transcribed in the journal, is ambiguous. As David Bordwell says, "we cannot tell if it is a line of dialogue he murmurs to her, or the final voice-over commentary."[27] That undecidability, which calls into question the status of the journal and the commentary as metatext, is fundamental to the rhetoric of grace in *Pickpocket*, preventing us from situating Michel's salvation unequivocally either within or outside himself.[28]

It is nevertheless understandable that, on first viewing, many spectators will find the ending of *Pickpocket* sudden. Despite the hints established by the scenes between Jeanne and Michel at the death of his mother, it would be easy to argue that the pickpocket's final declaration is not psychologically justified by visible character development. Even if Jean Collet's comment does not definitvely resolve the issue, it captures a paradox that is central to Bresson: "If this final illumination was caused by some necessity of plot, we would no longer be required to speak of grace. By definition grace is that which is free of any necessity, and hence gratuitous. Isn't that enough to make the conversion of Michel not appear improbable?"[29]

Pickpocket is surely a continuation of the prison theme of *A Man Escaped*, an ongoing meditation on the mystery of grace. Appropriately enough, Louis Malle explains its construction in terms of Pascal:

> The film opens with a blinding experience of Evil ("My heart seemed to burst") and ends with the blinding experience of Good ("My heart beat violently"). Between these two carefully identified extremes, the hero is in the grip of the two pascalian dangers, despair and pride. His grandeur is obvious: in the Christian tradition man is the fragment of God, "the deposed king," at once the protagonist and victim of the great mystery of Grace. That is what gives this film its surprising developments, quick movements, repetitions, contradictions, and surprises, its intuitive and learned rhythms, suggesting the irregular beating of a heart. "The ways of God are impenetrable."[30]

NOTES

1. Louis Malle, *Arts* no. 755 (30 December 1959).

2. Michel Estève, *Robert Bresson* (Paris: Editions Albatros, 1983), 20.

3. Philippe Arnaud, *Robert Bresson* (Paris: Cahiers du Cinéma, 1986), 29.

4. Robert Bresson, *Notes of a Cinematographer* (Los Angeles: Sun and Moon Press, 1988), 32.

5. Estève, *Robert Bresson*, 10.

6. Jean Sémolué, *Bresson ou l'acte pur des Métamorphoses* (Paris: Flammarion, 1993), 94.

7. Malle, *Arts* no. 755 (30 December 1959).

8. Jean Pelegri, *Les Lettres françaises* no. 805 (December 31–January 6, 1960).

9. Quoted in Pierre Gabaston, *Pickpocket* (Editions Yellow Now, 1990), 23.

10. Ibid., 25.

11. Ibid., 13.

12. Ibid., 14–15.

13. Interview with Jacques Domol-Valcroze and Jean-Luc Godard, *Cahiers du cinéma* no. 104 (February 1960): 4–5.

14. Jean Collet, fiche filmographique, *Télé-ciné* no. 88 (March–April 1960): 8.

15. Sémolué, *Bresson ou l'acte pur des Métamorphoses*, 96–97.

16. René Prédal, "Robert Bresson: L'aventure intérieure," in *Robert Bresson*, ed. James Quandt (Toronto: Cinematheque Ontario, 1998), 88, or René Prédal, "L'aventure intérieure," special issue of *L'Avant-scène cinéma* (January–February 1992).

17. Quoted in Philippe Arnaud, *Robert Bresson*, 129.

18. Ibid.

19. See the inside back cover of *L'Avant-scène cinéma* (January–February 1992).

20. Gabaston, *Pickpocket*, 27.

21. John Russell Taylor, *Cinema Eye, Cinema Ear* (New York: Hill and Wang, 1964), 133.

22. Gabaston, *Pickpocket*, 19–20.

23. Pierre Étaix, in *Le Cinématographie de Robert Bresson* (Tokyo: Tokyo International Foundation for Promotion of Screen Image Culture, 1999), 59.

24. Marika Green, in *Le Cinématographie de Robert Bresson* (Tokyo: Tokyo International Foundation for Promotion of Screen Image Culture, 1999), 55.

25. Jean Collet, fiche filmographique, *Télé-ciné* no. 88 (March–April 1960): 8.

26. Prédal, "Robert Bresson," 12.

27. David Bordwell, *Narration in Fiction Film* (London: Methuen, 1985), 309.

28. Keith Reader, *Robert Bresson* (Manchester: Manchester University Press, 2000), 54.

29. Jean Collet, fiche filmographique, *Télé-ciné* no. 88 (March–April 1960): 18.

30. Malle, *Arts* no. 755 (30 December 1959).

6

A Saint Jousts with Her Judges

The Trial of Joan of Arc

PERHAPS MORE CLEARLY THAN ANY OTHER OF BRESSON'S films, *The Trial of Joan of Arc* shows that his art emerges from his sense of what he can eliminate. It is his shortest work, only sixty-five minutes. Almost all movie versions of Joan have emphasized extravagant spectacle, historical costumes, and the exploitation of predigested responses. Mary Gordon rightly castigates the distortions in Hollywood attempts to tell Joan's story and praises Carl Dreyer's great 1928 silent movie *The Passion of Joan of Arc*, with its moving close-ups of Maria Falconetti. She regrets, however, that Dreyer's film has "none of Joan's sprightly, impatient give-and-take with her judges," and that it presents her as a victim "from the first moment we see her on the screen."[1] It's too bad she never saw Bresson's *Joan*, which concentrates on the actual trial text and demonstrates the young woman's spirited independence, while refusing to exploit the obvious possibilities for pathos. Consistent with Bresson's usual caution regarding the exploitation of emotion, *Notes of a Cinematographer* even refers disparagingly to Falconetti's habit, in Dreyer's memorable film, of repeatedly casting her eyes to heaven.[2]

Joan is a perfect heroine for Bresson; as he says, "Joan is the sum of a mysterious operation. She proves that there is a world that is closed to us but that opens itself to her through a naive alchemy of her senses. She places in broad daylight the profound night in which our acts normally take place."[3] Despite his great admiration for Joan, however, and his judgment that the text of her trial represents a great moment in French literature, some viewers, seeing *The Trial of Joan of Arc* for the first time, will find it cold. As René Prédal comments,

This character touches us, but does not move us with the habitual methods for the representation of feelings. Joan does not offer herself in sacrifice in spectacular fashion; she simply says what she feels in herself and which, moreover, in some degree goes beyond her. In this she is like the curé d'Ambricourt, who also often seems to be pronouncing words that did not belong to him. Both are possessed beings, whose modest bodily envelopes shelter an extraordinary force coming from the supernatural.[4]

Although *Trial* has not been one of his most popular films, it won the 1962 Jury Prize at Cannes and was hailed by Otto Preminger: "We all have our Joan but yours is the best."

As with *A Man Escaped,* Bresson is not interested in historical reconstruction, which would only be a distraction from the inner truth he is hoping to convey. "In *The Trial of Joan of Arc*," he says, "I tried, without creating 'theater' or 'masquerade,' to discover a non-historical truth by means of historical words."[5] In an interview on the making of the film, he adds, "In responding to her judges, Joan has done the work of a writer without touching a pen. She has written a pure masterpiece. Her book is a portrait, the only one we have of her."[6] Even before the credits, Bresson highlights the movie's extraordinary source: "I have made use of authentic texts and the precise minutes of the trial of condemnation." The historical authenticity of the film is not lessened because it was shot, not at Rouen, but in the Ile-de-France, making use of the chateau of Meudon. As Michel Estève says, "Historical reconstruction . . . would have dispersed attention, turning the spectator away from the essential. Hence neither decors nor costumes have autonomous existence, and the medieval crowd is heard but not shown. The past becomes hazy through concentration on the picturesque; only the present can produce genuine involvement, inciting the spectator to participate in the tragedy."[7] It is worth recalling that Bresson insists on offering each of his films, but especially this one, in the present.

A distinguished historian and authority on Joan, Régine Pernoud, has put Bresson's work in context:

> His approach meant that all the pictures of Joan as seen by someone else would be avoided—even those that were beautiful when their author was Michelet, Péguy, or Claudel. Bresson wanted to know nothing except "Joan by herself." His work seems like what was done by the researchers at the time of her rehabilitation, when they tried to learn the truth about the earlier trial and obtained all the documents that had remained in the possession of the English while Rouen was under their control. . . . And the historian can also be grateful to Bresson for not having been too faithful to history—that is, to

have avoided everything that smelled like "historical reconstruction," the decorations, the leftovers. Everything that would have fixed Joan in another age, and would thereby have screened the quality of life that emanates from her words and makes her always contemporary, always a presence.[8]

The constraints involved in developing a screenplay for *Joan* were even greater than those Bresson worked with in *Diary of a Country Priest* or *A Man Escaped*. Filming the trial meant including the five formal interrogations in the great hall of the chateau, a further series of hearings in her cell, and the reading of the formal accusation. "There is no opportunity to draw on interior commentary, which enlivened those earlier works," Jean Sémolué comments. "Typically, Bresson relies on these very constraints."[9] Keith Reader repeats and extends this point:

> Bresson's dialogues effectively give us a documentary reconstruction, cutting him off thereby from the interior monologues that have been an important part of his previous three films. Yet that does not mean that he is cutting himself off from the transcendental that is so fundamental to his work. His assertion that in this film he tried "to find with historical words a non-historical truth"[10] suggests a dialectic between the material and the spiritual similar to that we have seen with particular force in *Diary of a Country Priest*.[11]

"The rhythm of the cutting is so rapid," Estève remarks, "the editing so judicious, that objective time seems to be modeled on interior time and to be experienced as a constant harassment."[12] "What I had to fear," Bresson said, "was the slowness, the ponderousness of the trial. Hence I kept the film moving at a very rapid rhythm. A film can be written in eighth and sixteenth notes because it is music."[13]

As in *A Man Escaped*, where the topography of the prison is never available to us as a whole, in *Joan* the courtroom is never shown in its entirety. This strategy is used to emphasize the obvious, that Joan and her judges come from totally different worlds. During the trial, Isambert, a young Dominican who is located in the courtroom in a place close to that of the audience, will on several occasions seem to offer encouragement or discreet counsel to Joan. Keith Reader points out that "[i]t is almost as if Bresson were providing the spectator with a sympathetic representative or surrogate . . . during Joan's public ordeal."[14] Above all, Bresson hoped to get beyond the patriotic and pious clichés about Joan and confront the audience with her ongoing challenge. "It is the privilege of the cinematographer to place the past in the present. . . . Last summer, when I filmed *Joan*, I was not concerned merely to make her sublime words resound; I hoped to make this marvelous young girl present for audiences today."[15]

THE MOVIE OPENS WITH JOAN'S MOTHER, IN MOURNING, ADVANCING to the chair where the archbishop awaits her, along with envoys of the pope. She kneels, and reads her appeal: "I gave birth in marriage to a daughter who had the honor of receiving the sacraments of baptism and confirmation. I raised her in the fear of God and respect and fidelity to the church . . . envious people who wished harm to her, her parents, and the public good of princes and people, dragged her to a trial of faith; they falsely imputed to her a number of crimes, and wickedly condemned and burned her."[16] There is a long roll of drums, then Bresson's statement that Joan died May 30, 1431; "there is no tomb, no portrait, but we have better than her portrait, her words before the judges at Rouen." What follows is the authentic record of the trial, as well as the testimony at her rehabilitation twenty-five years later. "At the outset," he concludes, "Joan has been imprisoned for several months in a room of the chateau at Rouen." Another roll of drums; as it grows silent, we see Joan, her hands manacled. Her face is unclear but her voice is firm: "My name is Joan. I am nineteen."

She is standing in the great hall of the chateau, appearing before Bishop Cauchon, the vicar inquisitor, the promoter, and his substitute, who are all seated at a large table. She swears on the Gospels, then sits down; around her are judges and assessors; far behind her, the crowd. Joan tells them that her mother taught her the Pater, the Ave Maria, and the Credo. When asked to say the Our Father, however, she responds, "Confess me. I will say it in confession."

Joan explains that she worked at home, not in the fields, and learned to sew and to spin. The bishop announces that she is forbidden to leave the prison in the chateau, prompting her to declare that she does not accept this prohibition. There is an outcry, and Cauchon points out that she has already tried several times to escape.

"As every prisoner has a right to," she responds, and leaves the hall, walking behind the bailiff. She descends the stairway from the tower to her cell, where her hands are untied. Alone, she bursts into tears.

After ascending the stairs for the second interrogation, she protests again: "If you ask me to say something I have sworn not to say, I would be a perjurer, which you ought not to want. I have revelations concerning the king that I will not tell you." The vicar inquisitor interrupts to ask if the voice she claims to have heard comes from God. "I believe firmly that it comes from God and by his order. And I am more afraid of deceiving myself by saying what would displease this voice than of responding to you." The bishop then asks, "Do you believe you are in God's grace?" which elicits the well-known reply: "If I am not, may God place me there, and if I am, may God keep me in it."

Cauchon, hoping to implicate Joan in witchcraft, asks about a certain tree at Domrémy. Joan concedes there was a so-called tree of fairies near her village, and a fountain where the sick came to drink: "We sang and danced around that tree, but I never saw fairies there." Has she seen them elsewhere? There is a signal for prudence from Brother Isambert, a Dominican. "Not that I know," Joan says simply.

A brief scene follows in which Joan sleeps in her cell while dogs bark outside. Two guards approach, steps resound in the stairway, and she wakes up. The guards about face, a lantern sweeps down the stairway and disappears before reappearing in a hole in the wall; Joan is being spied on.

Before the third hearing begins, Warwick tells Cauchon that Joan must be burned. The bishop reminds Joan she must tell the truth to her judge, which brings a sharp response. "Take care, you who call yourself my judge. You assume a great responsibility." After several exchanges about her oath, she says, "I will tell the truth, but will not tell everything." Even after further insistence, Joan remains stubborn: "I have nothing to do here, and ask you to send me back to God from whom I have come."

There are cries from the crowd, and a command from Cauchon: "On your knees!" She takes the oath, is seated, and begins her testimony: "I recognized the voice of an angel. It told me I had to leave and that I would raise the siege of Orléans." She has no hesitation in reporting that she was wearing men's clothes, but when she is asked who advised her to do this, she is impatient: "Let's move on."

The bishop tries to pin her down as to the time and place of her voices. She warns him again: "Be careful about what you are doing, for in truth I am sent by God and you put yourself in great danger." When Joan is back in her room at twilight, a faraway trumpet is heard, and she prays in a low voice: "Sweet God, I beseech you, if you love me, tell me clearly what I ought to answer these church people." Warwick, consulting with Cauchon, warns the bishop: "Tell them that anyone who tries to counsel her shall go to the stake with her."

At the fourth hearing the judges try to trap Joan on the details of her apparitions—are they men or women, do they have hair, how do they speak if they do not have a body? Depending on God for an explanation of the voice she has heard, she can only say, "This voice is sweet and speaks the language of France."

Cauchon gets nowhere with questions about magic rings or the use of a mandragora, a poisonous plant with a human-shaped root which had mythical associations with magic. When the bishop asks her if there were mandrake plants in her village, there is again a signal for caution from Brother Isambert. "Yes," she concedes, "they say it helps a person accumulate money, but I don't believe it." The crowd outside is so inflamed that they throw stones at the window of Joan's cell.

Beaupère, one of Cauchon's assistants, continues to question Joan about her voices. He tries to trip her up on details: Do St. Catherine and St. Margaret speak together or one after the other? Another signal from Brother Isambert, and Joan speaks of being comforted by St. Michael, accompanied by angels from heaven: "I have seen them with the eyes of my body, as I see you." Asked what sign the king had before believing in her, she simply answers, "Pass on. I will not tell you." As for her sword, "I carried it to avoid killing anyone; I have never killed." These exchanges leave Warwick even more impatient. "If you don't hurry," he tells Cauchon, "the crowd will be clamoring for your death."

At the fifth hearing Joan is asked about her followers carrying pennants with her image. If some put holy water on such pennants, she answers, it was not by her order. Her judges try to show that she exalted herself by wearing a ring and beautiful clothes, but Joan rejects the implications: "If those of my party prayed for me, it is my opinion that they have not done evil." Reminded that some approached her to kiss her hands and clothes, she simply explains, "The poor come because I don't give them displeasure." Joan makes similar disavowals regarding a horse belonging to the bishop of Senlis (she contends that she paid for it) and a baby that she prayed for (she does not claim to have revived it), and Cauchon orders her to be returned to prison.

The secret interrogation in prison proceeds quickly to the subject of Joan's virginity. St. Catherine and St. Margaret, she insists, help her preserve it. Would her voices continue if she were married? She will leave that up to Our Lord. (At this point Warwick mutters that this is a woman who has lived with soldiers; her claim of virginity is a farce.) D'Estivet, the prosecutor of the trial, explodes angrily, "No more lies; you are not a virgin!"

JOAN: I can surely say that I am. If you don't believe me, that's just too bad.

D'ESTIVET: You don't belong to God, you corrupt girl, but to the devil.

JOAN: I belong and have always belonged only to Our Lord Jesus Christ.

Warwick, the bishop, and D'Estivet leave, determined to expose her, and three women surround Joan, who is stretched out on her bed. After they withdraw, the prosecutor mounts the stairs to the tower: "The women have examined her and say she is intact and a virgin."

Beaupère questions her about the sign the angel gave to show the king she came from God. After an initial refusal, Joan says the sign was a crown brought by an angel: it means that the king will possess all of France.

CAUCHON: Is it because of your merit that God sent his angel?

JOAN: It pleased God to do this through an intermediary, a simple girl.

Joan's chains are reinforced. Asked whether God hates the English, she says, "I don't know about the love or hate that God has for the English, but I know they will be driven out of France, except for those who die here."

CAUCHON: What clothes was Michael wearing when he appeared to you?

JOAN: I know nothing of his clothes.

CAUCHON: Was he naked?

JOAN: Do you think God doesn't have anything with which to clothe him?

CAUCHON: Did he have hair?

JOAN: Why would they have cut it?

CAUCHON: How did you know it was Michael?

JOAN: I soon believed it. *I had the will to believe it* . . . . A good part of what he taught me is in that book (the register of the notary).

The judges turn next to the matter of Joan wearing men's clothes. Beaupère asks if she will agree to put on women's clothes, and Joan agrees: "Yes, to go away. What I have on, it pleases God that I wear it." Lemâitre cites Leviticus to argue that she must wear women's rather than men's clothes but Joan says she makes no distinction between them.

Warwick growls, "We'll make her lose her virginity," and brings a young English gentleman down the stairway to look in on Joan. At the spyhole, the Englishman says, "I'd thrash her with pleasure, but her virginity—no one could strip her of those clothes that protect her."

A woman carries a robe down the stairway from the tower and puts it on Joan's bed. When she notices it, Joan says, "I will not take it, so long as it pleases Our Lord. But if I am condemned and need to be clothed, I ask the favor of having women's dress and something on my head." The bishop insists that she cannot hear mass or receive communion unless she takes off men's clothes. Wiping away a tear, she cries out, "Have those of my party forgotten me?"

A new subject is introduced by Cauchon, coming to her room with his colleagues: "Do you believe you are subject to the church on earth?"

JOAN: Our Lord is to be served first.

The scene shifts to the hearing room, where Jean de Chatillon reads a long statement, charging that Joan claims to belong to God without an intermediary and does not accept the judgment of the church. She is indignant: "I protest with all my strength against these false accusations which do not correspond to the interrogatory and my responses." Joan is taken away as her accuser drones on. But not every member of the court is under Cauchon's control. Nicholas de Houppeville argues: "One does not judge by constraint and under menaces." Challenged by Cauchon, he refuses to submit and leaves, along with Jean Lohier.

In her cell, meanwhile, Joan complains that the food sent by the bishop has made her so ill she believes she is dying. She asks to be buried in holy ground, while her enemies juggle her responses and the words of St. Matthew in order to show that her position has placed her outside the church. A ray of hope is offered when Br. Isambert and a companion visit Joan in her room and advise her to appeal to the pope, who is present at the council of Basel.

At the next hearing, Joan asks to be taken to the pope, but Cauchon continues to insist that she submit to the church. "What is the church?" she responds. "I don't want to submit to you, since you are my chief enemy." Even in the torture chamber, she holds fast: "If I saw the fire lighted and was in the fire, I would not say another thing." Cauchon says the pope is too far away to be bothered with her case and reads the sentence of condemnation. "I believe in the twelve articles of faith and the ten commandments," Joan pleads. "I wish to believe all that the holy church believes."

But when the fire is lighted, she breaks down: "I will do all that you wish." An English prelate is angry that Joan can save herself by signing a statement, but Cauchon says, "I ought to search for her salvation rather than her death." He reads the pardon, but the crowd cries out for her burning. Joan is taken back to the chateau and dressed in women's clothes.

Joan puts men's clothes on again, however, after an English lord tries to rape her. She also reaffirms the truth of her earlier testimony: she has heard the voices. "If I said God had not sent me, I would damn myself. . . . What I did was out of fear of the fire." In response, Cauchon proclaims her a heretic.

Back in her cell, Brothers Isambert and Martin visit a sleeping Joan to prepare her for death. Surprisingly, she is allowed to receive communion. "Yes," she says, "I believe that only Christ can deliver me." Asked if she has hope in God, she replies, "With God's help, I shall be in paradise."

At the marketplace, the crowd cheers the announcement that the church is passing Joan over to the secular arm. After the executioner collects Joan's clothes and belongings in a sack, there is a traveling shot of her small, rapid steps to the spot where the bishop reads the formula of condemnation. She asks for a cross and Isambert goes to get one from the nearby church; meanwhile an English soldier gives her a small cross made of two twigs.

On her knees, Joan commends herself to God, covers her cross with kisses, and calls on Sts. Michael, Catherine, and Margaret. The crowd hurls insults as she proceeds to the stake, but grows quiet when the church clock announces the time. After Isambert gives Joan the large cross, she makes a last affirmation: "Those voices I heard were from God." After the fire is lit, everyone rises; Joan cries out to Jesus, and disappears in the smoke. A dog approaches the stake tentatively before moving off; pigeons on the roof fly away. When the stake has been burned to ashes, the chain that had held Joan is shown to be empty. The rolling of drums echoes the sounds heard during the film's credits.

——ALTHOUGH BRESSON WAS ABLE TO DRAW ON THE ACTUAL WORDS of the trial transcript, he had to do an exhaustive (and extremely complex) job of cutting, rearranging, and eliminating repetitions, even giving the words a certain rhythm.[17] The problem was immense, since the six public hearings lasted from February 21 to March 3, 1431; the sessions in her cell from March 10 to 25; and the reading of the formal accusation took place on March 28. During April there were appeals to accept the decision of church authorities; on May 9 Joan was brought in to look at the instruments of torture, and a final sermon preached to her on May 23. She repudiated her testimony the following day, retracted this disavowal four days later, and was burned May 30. In the film, however, because of quick transitions and ellipses, one has a sense of continuity and inevitability.

Florence Delay, the Joan of *The Trial*, was only twenty at the time; now a highly regarded novelist, she was elected to the Académie Française in 2001. She expresses her admiration as a writer

> for the extraordinary work accomplished by Bresson in his scenario—I was going to say his score. The minutes of The Trial of Condemnation and The Trial of Rehabilitation that he used make up an inextricable tangle of texts. It is from this jumble that he extracted his sequence of questioning. He has

made eliminations and condensations, and tightened up the exchanges with a luminous strength. That is the reason for the extraordinary brevity of the film. Which matches its tension.[18]

Sémolué recalls that Bresson's three previous movies were presented in the first person, establishing a constant counterpoint: the face of the protagonist was seen in opposition to the perception of the world and of others.

> Here the face-to-face confrontation of Joan and the Judges imposes a shot/countershot structure. To accentuate this perspective, the film privileges the medium shot, which is the most neutral and objective. . . . For the passages situated in Joan's cell and the interrogations that take place there, the camera, conjointly effaced and avid, like the eye of the bishop or those of the English looking through the spy-hole, makes us spies and examiners—we become voyeurs.[19]

If the emphasis on the trial would seem to make *The Trial of Joan of Arc* an overly static movie, a close viewing makes it clear that the many small variations that Bresson includes are all the more effective because of such a controlled context. Although the trial is rightly seen as a duel between Joan and Cauchon, underlined by a shot-countershot structure, the subtle glances between Joan and Isambert, the young Dominican, introduce a significant new element, especially since the latter's concerned face contrasts sharply with the closed countenances of the bishop's collaborators.

Bresson deliberately suppressed the use of musical backgrounds in *Joan*, largely because he hoped that a musical sense would be sufficiently suggested by the trial dialogue itself. As Michel Estève points out, "for Bresson, music is born from the very responses of Joan. A background use of religious music would have undermined the nobility of the debate." The formulas of incantation ("I beg you; I beseech you by that piety that you bear to your creator," etc.) and the poetic rhythm of many of Joan's responses help to reinforce the tragic atmosphere.[20]

Bresson was never a propagandist, but by reducing Joan's story to its basic elements, even eliminating the names of all her judges except for Bishop Cauchon, he could not have helped seeing that her trial was all too contemporary—or rather, timeless. Nor did he want us to avoid Joan's challenge by saying, "Oh well, it was easy for her: she was a saint." As René Prédal reminds us,

> The only words [used in the film] that were not drawn from the interrogatories are those in which on the morning of her death Joan says to the Bishop that her voices have misled her. If Bresson insisted on including this scene, drawing on two testimonies from the rehabilitation trial twenty-five years

later, it is obviously in order to insist on the doubt that insinuated itself in a moment of discouragement before the condemned young woman recovered a still livelier faith in the middle of the flames and was then able to affirm, "The voices that I heard were from God."[21]

Léonce-Henri Burel, the great cameraman who had worked successfully with Bresson on *Diary of a Country Priest* and *A Man Escaped*, gave a negative appraisal of *The Trial of Joan of Arc*. He felt that Bresson didn't make good use of the setting and left him no opportunity to convey the feeling that the trial was being held in an enormous room. In addition, he complained, "You never saw Joan and her judges together, not once. There was no interrelation between them." Burel's bitterest disagreement with Bresson was over what he considered the failure to make the most effective use of Florence Delay as Joan. "Here we had this sweet, simple, charming girl with the most marvelous beautiful eyes, and Bresson would never let her look up at the camera. Never. She always had to look down, even when she was answering the judges. I told Bresson that if I believed in God, which I don't, I would look up when I thought of him."[22] Burel implied that this made Joan look "shifty," which Bresson, of course, has denied.[23]

Wisely, Bresson does not pretend to explain the mystery of Joan. As he said in an interview, "People might say that she was a more perfect being than us, more sensitive. She combines her five senses in a new way. She hears Voices. She convinces us of a world at the limit of our faculties. She penetrates into this supernatural world, but she closes the door behind her."[24]

Bresson avoided cliché by not choosing an earthy peasant girl as the "model" for Joan. When I spoke to Florence Delay about her experience in the film, she conceded that her understanding of the saint has grown over the years. At the time she was chosen to be in the film, she thought of Joan primarily as a shepherdess and a captain—and she was more interested in the captain. Today she shares Bresson's view that she was a poet, a thinker, a woman of normal desires. She thinks of Bresson as a rebel like Joan, a provocateur, not a conventional thinker. Rejecting simplistic clichés about his austerity, she believes that Bresson's sensuality led him to make films in which all the senses were involved. In particular she reminded me of the delight with which Marie, the young woman in *Au hasard Balthasar*, licks the jam off her spoon in the scene with the miser.

It is only appropriate that the last word on *The Trial* should go to the model for Joan:

Robert Bresson has filmed the invisible. By limiting—I would say, almost by enclosing—the visible in such a concrete manner that shots of it become timeless. What is there to see in prison, in whatever prison? Corners, walls, a bed, a door, a spy-hole, chains. Our whole attention is fixed on the interior freedom of the captive, on her face, or to say it in another way, her soul. . . . What can someone condemned to death read in the faces of her judges except death? Except that Joan, who sees her own death—and is afraid of it, as we all are—does not look at it all the time. Her face tilted up, she listens to the questions—all the traps—and then listens to what God, her heart, her voices, say about it. It is in that brief time, that tiny interval indicated during the shooting (listening to one's interior being), and created by the rhythm of montage, that Joan, like every hero of Bresson, escapes. Toward invisible life, the other life, that she rejoins, body and soul. Flown away, like a bird filmed from below the tent where it was resting.[25]

NOTES

1. Mary Gordon, *Joan of Arc* (New York: Viking Penguin, 2000), 149–65.

2. Robert Bresson, *Notes of a Cinematographer* (Los Angeles: Sun and Moon Press, 1988), 127.

3. Robert Bresson, *Procès de Jeanne d'Arc (film)* (Paris: Mercure de France, 2002), 8.

4. René Prédal, "Robert Bresson: L'aventure intérieure," in *Robert Bresson*, ed. James Quandt (Toronto: Cinematheque Ontario, 1998), 73.

5. Jean Sémolué, *Bresson ou l'acte pur des Métamorphoses* (Paris: Flammarion, 1993), 120

6. Ibid., 108.

7. Michel Estève, *Robert Bresson* (Paris: Editions Albatros, 1983), 43.

8. Régine Pernoud, *Les nouvelles littéraires*, December 6, 1962.

9. Sémolué, *Bresson ou l'acte pur des Métamorphoses*, 109.

10. Bresson, *Notes of a Cinematographer*, 128.

11. Keith Reader, *Robert Bresson* (Manchester: Manchester University Press, 2000), 61.

12. Estève, *Robert Bresson*, 48.

13. Robert Bresson, *Études cinématographiques*, no. 18–19.

14. Reader, *Robert Bresson*, 68.

15. Bresson, *Procès de Jeanne d'Arc*, 7.

16. Ibid., 11. All quotations from the trial are translated from this book.

17. Robert Bresson, *Cahiers du cinéma* no. 140 (February 1963). Florence Delay speaks of Bresson as "composing the score" for *Trial*.

18. Florence Delay, in *Le Cinématographie de Robert Bresson* (Tokyo: Tokyo International Foundation for Promotion of Screen Image Culture, 1999), 64.

19. Sémolué, *Bresson ou l'acte pur des Métamorphoses*, 118.

20. Estève, *Robert Bresson*, 49.

21. Prédal, "Robert Bresson," 75.

22. Léonce-Henri Burel, "Interview by Rui Nogueira," in *Robert Bresson*, ed. James Quandt (Toronto: Cinematheque Ontario, 1998), 520.

23. See inside back cover of *L'Avant-scène cinéma* (January–February 1992).

24. Robert Bresson, interview in *Études cinématographiques* no. 18 (1962), 95.

25. Delay, in *Le Cinématographie de Robert Bresson*, 66.

1. Béby the clown and Marcel Dalio in *Public Affairs* (*Les affaires oubliques*), 1934.

2. Anne-Marie (Renée Faure) in *Angels of Sin* (*Les anges du péché*), 1943.

3. Hélène (Maria Casarès) in *The Ladies of the Bois de Boulogne* (*Les dames du bois de Boulogne*), 1945.

4. The curé d'Ambricourt (Claude Laydu) in *Diary of a Country Priest* (*Journal d'un curé de campagne*), 1951.

5. Lieutenant Fontaine (François Leterrier) and Orsini (Jacques Ertaud) in *A Man Escaped* (*Un condamné à mort s'est éshappé*), 1956.

6. Michel (Martin Lassalle) and Jeanne (Marika Green) in *Pickpocket*, 1959.

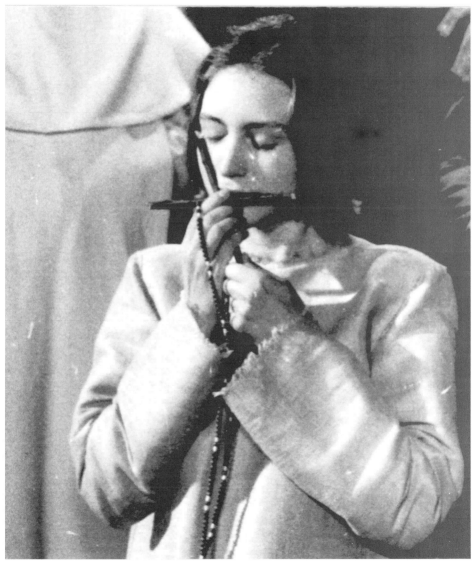

7. Joan of Arc (Florence Delay) in *The Trial of Joan of Arc* (*Procès de Jeanne d'Arc*), 1962.

8. Balthasar training for the circus (*Au hasard Balthasar*, 1966).

9. Mouchette (Nadine Mortier) riding a bumper-car (*Mouchette*, 1967).

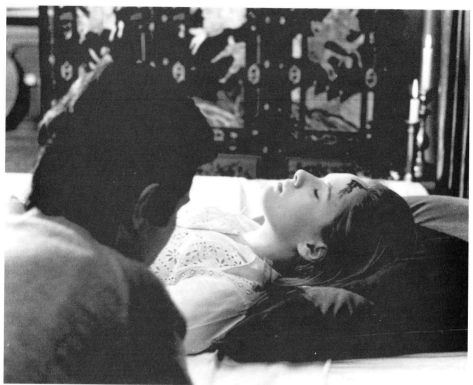

10. He (Guy Frangin) and she (Dominique Sanda) in *A Gentle Woman (Une femme douce)*, 1969.

11. Jacques (Guillaume des Forêts) in *Four Nights of a Dreamer* (*Quatre nuits d'un rêveur*), 1971.

12. Lancelot (Luc Simon) and Queen Guihnevere (Laura Duke Condominas) in *Lancelot of the Lake*, 1974.

13. Alberte (Tina Irssari) in *The Devil Probably (Le diable probablement)*, 1977.

14. Yvon (Christian Patey) being restrained in prison in *Money* (*L'Argent*), 1983.

15. Robert Bresson.

16. Robert and Mylène Bresson, standing behind a knight on horseback, during the shooting of *Lancelot of the Lake*.

7

The Donkey as Witness

Au hasard Balthasar

THE CENTRAL CHARACTER OF BRESSON'S NEXT MOVIE, *Au hasard Balthasar*, is a donkey. Shot in a village in the foothills of the Pyrenees, it is filled with memories of the director's own childhood. Bresson called *Balthasar* "the freest film I have made, the one into which I have put the most of myself."[1] He had been thinking of it since 1950. "If with this film I succeed in touching the public, it is especially, as happens in literature, thanks to that autobiographical element. . . . The beginning of the film bathes in my childhood—the countryside, the fields, the trees, and the animals—these are my vacations as a child and an adolescent."[2]

Someone unfamiliar with his work and seeing the baby donkey and the children in its first shots could be misled into thinking it was going to be a children's movie or perhaps an exercise in nostalgic sentimentality. Instead, Bresson wanted "to show that the stages in the life of a donkey are the same as those in the life of a man: in childhood, caresses; at maturity, work; talent and genius when one is older; and the mystic period before death."[3] Andrew Sarris understood this when he wrote, "If we weep at the fate of Balthasar, it is not through a misplaced sentimentality for the fate of a creature unmindful of its ultimate destiny but through a displaced response to the heightened awareness Balthasar has inspired in us."[4] As Jean-Luc Godard recognized, "This movie is really the world in an hour and a half, the whole world from childhood to death."[5] Perhaps the most powerful and beautiful of Bresson's films, it does not offer the exultant sense of liberation found in the endings of *A Man Escaped* and *Pickpocket* and yet, mixed with its pain, it carries an ineffable sense of consolation.

Bresson, of course, is counting on our recognition of the donkey as an image of humility, and perhaps the animal's association with the ordinary people among whom Jesus chose to live. Remembering a scene from Dostoevsky's *The Idiot,* Bresson was impressed with Prince Myshkin's account of how the cry of a donkey helped restore his lucidity:

> I completely recovered from my depression, I remember, one evening at Basel, on reaching Switzerland, and the thing that roused me was the braying of a donkey in the market-place. I was quite extraordinarily struck with the donkey, and for some reason very pleased with it, and at once everything in my head seemed to clear up.[6]

The director was delighted to think of "an idiot taught by an animal, to have someone who passes for an idiot but is of a rare intelligence see life through an animal." Bresson connected this with the episode in the life of Ignatius Loyola when the saint wanted to kill a Moor who, he believed, had offended the Virgin Mary. While pursuing the "infidel," however, Ignatius had a scruple and let his mule decide on which path to take. "The animal chose the way of clemency, not that of punishment."[7]

Everyone is familiar with the donkey's time-honored place both at the Christmas crib and in Christ's triumphal entry into Jerusalem on Palm Sunday. Bresson even exclaimed in hyperbole, "The donkey is the entire Bible, Old Testament and New Testament,"[8] and recalled seeing donkeys on the tympanum of countless little romanesque churches in France. Art historian Thomas Mathews reminds us that the image of Christ riding a donkey implies a radical reversal both of the meaning of power and the human attitude to animals. In the fourth century the ass was sometimes venerated; there were even ass-headed crucifixes.[9] Marco Bongiovanni comments on a suggestive image in early art: "Conserved by time on the wall of ancient Rome there exists a rough caricature traced by the inexperienced hand of a student: a donkey on the cross, faced by a boy engaged in prayer. Under the cross is written, 'Alexander adores his God.' Bresson's donkey has turned this mockery of the faith of a Christian boy upside down, and after twenty centuries turned it into praise."[10] During the Middle Ages, as is widely known, at the feast of fools at Notre Dame in Paris, the archbishop would ride backwards on a mule.

Bresson pointed out that the title of his movie is the motto of the ancient counts of Baux, the presumptive heirs of the Magi king Balthasar; "hasard," of course, carries all the ambiguous significance which the director customarily gave to "chance" and "destiny." He spoke directly of his intentions in this film:

> *Au hasard Balthasar* is our agitation, our passions, in the face of a living creature that is completely humble, completely holy, but happens to be a donkey.

Depending on whose hands he falls into by chance, he suffers from pride, avarice, the need to inflict suffering, or sensuality, and finally dies. He is a little bit like the Charlot character in the earliest films of Chaplin, but he is nevertheless an animal, a donkey, who brings with him eroticism and at the same time a kind of spirituality or Christian mysticism.[11]

On first viewing, *Balthasar* is hard to follow because there are so many characters and a variety of plot lines. Even an abbreviated summary can seem confusing and long-winded, though the time of the film itself is only one hour and thirty-five minutes. We are so accustomed to the mechanics of conventional dramatic plotting, to a construction that builds to an inevitable climax, that it is easy to be disconcerted by the organization of a film in fragments; we have to trust our feelings to gradually detect the relationships between successive shots and sequences. After one becomes more familiar with the movie, however, it is possible to appreciate the mastery of Bresson's construction: the donkey serves as the connecting thread for the action, and the various plot lines keep crisscrossing in surprising ways. *Balthasar* presents almost a catalogue of the capital sins of humanity, with pride, drunkenness, laziness, and lust competing with greed for the central role. The indictment of the donkey's successive owners is all the more powerful because Balthasar's expression offers no explicit judgment; all he can do when a master treats him too cruelly is to run away.

Perhaps whimsically, Bresson had originally thought of the story as "a donkey's journal," continuing the series of those kept by the curé d'Ambricourt, Lieutenant Fontaine, and Michel the pickpocket; he himself would be the narrator. Though he did not carry out this proposal literally, the point of view in the movie is clearly that of Balthasar; the animal is presented as a sympathetic observer of the evil visited on others and as victim of the same evil.[12] In particular, Bresson stresses his silent presence in scenes showing the humiliation of Marie, whose pet he was when she was a little girl.

Philippe Arnaud, after a minute examination of the scenario of *Au hasard Balthasar* at the Cinémathèque française, emphasizes the way in which Bresson eliminated certain shots and continued to tighten the construction of the movie. The procession of disasters that engulf Marie, the donkey, and many others is an indication of the ongoing circulation of evil. Arnaud believes that

> the great subject of this film is the cause of causes, the impossible cause that is linked with so many others: the mockery of innocence, pride, the christic connotations of Balthasar, avarice, and eroticism. . . . This invisible empire and its structure can be justified only by a belief like that of Jeanne in *Pickpocket:* "Perhaps everything has a reason."[13]

▬▬THE OPENING CREDITS ARE ACCOMPANIED BY THE ANDANTE OF
Schubert's Piano Sonata no. 20, which is interrupted by the braying of a
donkey, after which the music continues undisturbed. Since Schubert's
piece has much of the quality of a lullaby, its occasional recurrence during
the rest of the film brings nostalgic reminders of childhood. The first shot
of the movie itself is of a mountain pasture, with a baby donkey sucking at
his mother. There follows a scene of instant reversal, typical of Bresson.
Two young children, a boy and a girl, appeal to their father, "We have to
have him." "It's impossible, children," the father says, but in the next shot
the three are leading the donkey home to La Prairie, where the family has
been vacationing.

Jacques, the boy, calls Marie, a young neighbor, to come quickly; he bap-
tizes the donkey as Balthasar, and she administers the salt. Jacques and
Marie play with the baby donkey in the straw; he even carves their names
on a wooden bench. Jacques is told to get in the car as the family is about
to leave for home, when the lyrical atmosphere of childhood is shattered. A
nurse signals the father to come into the house: his older invalid daughter
has suddenly died.

A subtitle announces: "The years pass." The realities of growing up are
seen as Balthasar is whipped, fitted with shoes, and hitched up to transport
people and baggage. After the cart Balthasar is pulling overturns, a group
of peasants pursue him, but the donkey escapes and finds his way back to
La Prairie, where he is welcomed by Marie, who is now sixteen, and her
schoolteacher father. The latter, who now manages the property of Jacques's
father, brags about the success of his modern farming methods. It gradually
becomes clear that Jacques's father no longer wants to return to La Prairie,
because of its association with his daughter's death.

The action switches abruptly to a leather-jacket gang, led by the handsome, aggressively confident Gérard. The young men deliberately knock an
oil can into the road and wait around to watch cars skidding on the oil slick.
That night Gérard watches Marie as she pets Balthasar and crowns him
with flowers. "She may really be in love with him and he with her," he comments. She sits down on a bench but runs away when she feels a hand on
hers. Back in her house she can see Gérard and one of his cronies thrashing
the donkey. At mass the next day, however, Marie looks back with curiosity
at the choir loft, where Gérard, in his Sunday best, is singing enthusiastically.

Despite the shifts of the narrative, characters and events constantly criss-
cross within the village, with Balthasar a spectator at key moments. At a
lawyer's office, the notary reads a letter from Jacques's father, brusquely

asking for an accounting on the management of his property. Although the lawyer advises him to comply, Marie's father is indignant and storms out. The effect of his reaction is seen when Jacques returns, hoping to clear up the family disagreement. He tells Marie he still loves her, and though Marie is not sure she feels the same way, she is surprised a minute later to see Jacques get back in his car to leave. Marie's mother criticizes her husband, making clear what transpired: "You only had to say a word and everything would have ended happily. Out of pride you didn't say it." But her husband believes he will be vindicated in a trial and declares there is no reason for them to keep "that ridiculous donkey."

Balthasar is next shown working for a new master, the village baker, where Gérard, who has been taken on as an assistant, takes advantage of opportunities to beat him. After delivering the bread, the young man observes the baker putting cash receipts away in a drawer and goes upstairs to his room, after throwing equivocal glances at the baker's wife.

The narrative thread centering on Gérard then follows his aggressive pursuit of Marie; when she leaves her car to caress Balthasar, he gets in and refuses to leave. He puts his hand around her waist; she wipes away a tear but does not seem altogether unhappy. She gets out of the car and he chases her, with Balthasar between them. That evening he looks in at the door of Marie's house. "I'm looking for what belongs to me," he says brazenly, before Marie's father chases him away.

Meanwhile, the baker's wife has discovered the empty drawer from which Gérard has taken the money. Managing to control her disappointment, she tells the young man, "If you need something, tell me." After she offers him a transistor radio and a motorbike, he kisses her on the cheek. "But you'll have to give everything back," she warns, "if I see you again with Marie."

As if in response, the next sequence shows the growing relationship between Gérard and Marie. When her father calls out for her, there is no answer: she is in a sheepfold nearby with Gérard, who turns off his radio. The father passes by without stopping, continuing to call out to his daughter.

Here Bresson further complicates the plot line: a murder (about which we are given no details) brings a summons for Gérard to come to the police station, where we encounter a new character, Arnold, an alcoholic vagabond. As Arnold leaves the police station, Gérard and his gang accuse him of the murder and of forgetting what he did because he was drunk. Gérard's supporters even knock Arnold down. Marie arrives, calls them cowards, and slaps Gérard; he hits her back. Although she weeps, they soon leave, arm in arm, with Gérard's transistor radio blaring out a pop song, "I'm caught in the trap . . . of your eyes."

The changing seasons are reflected in a brief sequence showing a neglected Balthasar pacing outside in rain and snow while Marie is in the sheepfold with Gérard. The donkey becomes so ill that the veterinarian is about to put him out of his misery when Arnold volunteers to take care of him. The tramp soon comes to believe that "the road has cured Balthasar" and employs him and another donkey to carry tourists traveling in the mountains.

After a bad dream at night, Arnold swears he will give up drinking but in another quick reversal, we see him in a bistro with a full glass. Drunk, he pursues his donkeys with a chair before leaving them in front of the Palais de Justice, facilitating the transition to a scene between a lawyer and Marie's father. The latter, believing he is in the right, refuses to prepare a defense in the impending case with Jacques's father.

Baffled that Arnold had turned cruel after first showing him kindness, Balthasar runs away; in his next appearance he is working in a circus. An extraordinary brief scene follows, in which the donkey exchanges glances with a lion, a white bear, a monkey, and a young elephant. Their countenances remain opaque, but one has the sense that genuine communication is taking place. Drums roll, and Balthasar performs a circus act, solving a few carefully prepared math problems. When Arnold joins the audience and begins drinking, his presence upsets Balthasar and there is general confusion, but at the end the vagabond leads his two donkeys away.

The next scene contains the film's sharpest reversal. Arnold is stretched out in a cabin, when Gérard wakes him up, saying the police are coming. Hoping to make Arnold appear guilty, he hands the worried vagabond a revolver. After a search shows that the gun is unloaded, however, the police make a surprise announcement: Arnold has inherited a fortune from a remote relative.

After signing the bequest papers, the former tramp throws a party for everyone at the local café, with free drinks, music, and fireworks. When Marie's mother sees her daughter with Gérard, she tells her to leave, but the young woman tells her mother that she loves Gérard: "Does one know why one loves? I would kill myself for him."

Tied up in front of the café, Balthasar is again a witness, reacting nervously to the fireworks set off during the festivities. Even when Gérard throws a bottle against the mirror behind the counter, the dancing continues. Marie's mother reminds her that her father is suffering, but the young woman only replies, "He likes his unhappiness more than us." When she is ordered to come home, Marie runs over to Gérard and pleads, "Save me. . . .

Take me far away." But Gérard, slow-dancing with another young woman, ignores her. In response, Marie begins to dance with another boy and is warned by the grain merchant, "Your father will break you." Her partner responds, "If you want her, you'll have to pay."

Outside, the lawyer salutes Arnold, who says he is going on a long journey, and mounts Balthasar. Deeply inebriated, he suddenly stops and salutes a milestone on the side of the road: "Goodbye, my poor dear friend, condemned to pass the rest of your days seeing the same imbeciles go by." But when he leans over to say goodbye to his comrade Balthasar, he falls heavily, hitting his head on the ground.

Back at the police station, we learn that Arnold had died instantly. As soon as the proper papers are filled out, Balthasar is sold to a new owner, the grain merchant. We next see the donkey attached to a waterwheel, trotting around a well beneath the hot sun. Badly wounded, the animal refuses to drink; the merchant says he will get rid of Balthasar as soon as there is a rainstorm.

It is a stormy night; someone is knocking at the merchant's door—it is Marie. He tells her to go back to her father but she refuses. She is just asking for a place on the straw; she is finished with Gérard. Marie takes off her wet cloak as the miser lifts his lamp over her, then gives him her blouse and skirt. "Has anyone seen you come in?" he inquires. She reassures him, and then inquires, "Don't you believe in anything?" "I believe in what I possess." Marie is so hungry she grabs a pot of jam from a cupboard. She eats with delight, stopping only to goad him: "People say you hide pieces of gold and paper money in your slippers; what's the point of that?"

The miser gets up, comes back with money, and puts it on the table. She looks at him a moment, then takes the money. The merchant explains his philosophy of life: "Your papa has given his last penny to his creditors—that's what happens when one puts honesty and honor above everything else. . . . I am a free man, obligated to no one and nothing, except to what is useful to me and from which I can draw profit, preferably a large profit. . . . Life is just a fair, a market where one's word is not needed, a bank note will suffice."

Marie puts the gold pieces back on the table. "Take them back. It's not money I need, but a friend—a friend who will share my pleasures and my pains."

The merchant says, "I will share your pleasures and pains, but I hope that for me there will be more pleasures than pains." He takes her in his arms, and there is a dissolve; in the next shot Marie rebuttons her blouse and rushes away. In the morning her parents arrive and the merchant gives Marie's father the donkey to pay for whatever he owes.

There is another reversal: Balthasar and Marie's parents are back home again when Jacques arrives. Suddenly he and Marie are back on the bench where they were happy as children. Jacques explains that he has been sent to return the money that her father has unjustly lost in the trial. He won't accept it, she sighs; he is buried in the pride of his suffering. "O Jacques," she bursts out, "how many times have I dreamed of a boy like you—honest, a little silly." The camera shows Balthasar nibbling grass during an interval in which Marie makes a confession to Jacques: "Now you know everything; do you still want to marry me?" When he says yes, she insists that marriage has become outdated. Even when Jacques tries to remind her of earlier days, she still holds out: "Our childish promises—it was an imaginary world. Reality is something else." But when she goes to the stable and stands in front of Balthasar, she tells herself, "I will love him, I will love him."

When Marie leaves to have a final explanation with Gérard, Jacques hurries to stop her, but she ignores him. Entering a deserted building, she opens the doors to various rooms. Next we see Gérard and his gang leaving, having scattered Marie's clothes on the ground, beaten the young woman, and locked her in. Her father and Jacques rush to the building; a naked Marie can be dimly seen through the window at the back. The father breaks the pane, and they return in the wagon with Balthasar. But when Jacques comes later to look for Marie, her mother tells him, "She has gone . . . she will never come back."

Marie's mother suffers another blow: a priest arrives to prepare her husband for death. "My God," she prays, "don't take him away from me, too." The following scene shows her in mourning. Later, when Gérard and his cronies come to borrow Balthasar, Marie's mother moans, "He is a saint." The next instant we see Balthasar being incensed and covered with relics, as he takes part in a procession to the local shrine.

At night, however, Gérard's gang takes Balthasar away; they load the poor animal with contraband for a trip across the Spanish border. We hear gunshots; the young men run off; Balthasar is wounded. In the morning, the donkey is seen bleeding and suddenly the sound of bells is heard. Sheep come into the picture, bleating, and surround Balthasar. The Schubert sonata returns, along with the sheep-bells, as the donkey collapses. The sheep go their way; Balthasar dies.

▬—*AU HASARD BALTHASAR* IS A DARING ACHIEVEMENT, A COMPLEX design that embraces a greater variety of characters than Bresson used in earlier films. Left with questions about the motivations of characters, many spectators, Keith Reader suggests, "will probably find themselves oscillating

. . . between filling in the film's gaps and leaving its sense(s) to speak through them, so that *Balthasar*'s challenge—the donkey's and the film's—to our ways of viewing becomes an integral part of its meaning."[14] Lloyd Baugh rightly emphasizes the central role of the donkey, "both because of what happens to him, his story from birth to death . . . and also because of his quiet but intense presence, his witnessing, his participation in the experiences of the other characters." I believe he is straining for a theological reading of the film, however, when he adds: "In the double experience of Balthasar, as sympathetic participant in the evil visited on others and as victim of the same evil . . . he becomes a Christ-figure."[15] Despite his high praise of the film, J. Hoberman avoids such terminology: "The donkey who is the eponymous protagonist of the heartbreakingly sublime and ridiculous *Au hasard Balthasar*—the director's supreme masterpiece and one of the greatest movies ever made—is the ultimate example of a Bressonian subject."[16]

Marie represents Bresson's fullest presentation of a young woman, who shocks us by her almost passive submission to Gérard. Her humiliation and final disappearance is especially hard to bear because of our memories of her as a little girl and her identification with Balthasar. Xavier Tilliette refers to her as "the soiled angel," describing the blanket that covers her naked shoulders in the frightening scene with the miser "a discreet symbol of compassion. . . . What a trembling gleam the film receives from the tears of this young girl, the innocence that persists in her decline. She bears witness without knowing it to infinite mercy."[17]

In his interview with Roger Stéphane, Bresson throws further light on Marie's scene with the merchant:

> There were contradictory movements which basically were dominated by an uprightness, a great honesty. That is, she accepts money at first because she needs it badly and she is thinking of giving it to her father who no longer has a sou, and has been cheated by the miser. Then, after hearing the cynical declaration of the miser. which makes her very unhappy, she sees clearly that money "is not everything," as the miser claims, and she gives him back the money. In this she shows a genuine grandeur. As for what takes place after that, I know no more about it than you do.[18]

In terms of trying to give an "explanation" for everything that takes place, *Balthasar* may be Bresson's most difficult film, but for those who allow themselves to be carried along by its rhythm, it may also be the most powerful: everything holds together. A second viewing will show that its sudden shifts are subtly connected, even the apparent digression when Balthasar and Arnold's other donkey are providing transportation for an artist and his companion. The scene satirizes the artistic pretentiousness of the tourists, but the men's discussion of criminal responsibility for actions committed under the influence of drink reminds us of the probability of Arnold's connection with the murder.

Bresson deliberately leaves a certain opacity in the characters and situations: we don't know what happens to Marie at the end, or why Gérard hates Arnold, or where Arnold came from, yet we are carried along by the feelings that attach to their interactions. As Jean Collet writes,

> The discontinuity of the story masks its profound unity, which exists not at the level of story, or psychology, but in revealing the mystic bonds between all beings—the secret solidarity of innocence and cruelty, good and evil, purity and vice. The whole movement of the film is that of a sensitive balance that never finishes wavering. Balthasar is the yardstick of innocence helping to light up the virtues and vices around him.[19]

Here, as elsewhere in Bresson, the difficulty is due to his determination to offer a stripped-down version of reality, to omit psychological explanations, to present the cause *after* the effect. Such a method follows from his conviction that all art is both abstract and suggestive:

> Everything should not be shown, or there is no art; art lies in suggestion. . . . Things should be presented, therefore, under a single angle, which would evoke all the others. Little by little the spectator should suspect, or hope to suspect, and should always be kept in a kind of expectation which comes from the cause being shown after the effect.
>
> Mystery should be preserved; since we live in mystery; mystery should be on the screen.[20]

Bresson's choice of a donkey as the center of the movie seems a perfect realization of his use of models. Amusingly, in keeping with his shunning of professionals, Bresson chose an untrained donkey instead of a trained "performer"; this resulted in several exasperating delays during which he had to wait for the donkey to follow his directions. Jean Collet is perceptive in suggesting that Bresson's conception of cinema acting leads sooner or later to the exploration of animal mystery:

> In rejecting everything that belongs to dramatic art, Bresson exhausts his models by multiplying the number of takes of the same shot. What is he looking for in this? Automatism, a diction and behavior that is no longer reflected on. It is exciting to discover this automatism, these reflexes, in the animal. The innocence Bresson is looking for in the non-professional actor already exists in the innocence of the animal.
>
> What we can decipher in seeing them is only an overflow of soul, or nothing. But this nothing obliges us to scrutinize with increased attention the

smallest physical trace of interior life. By no longer acting, the people whom Bresson films make us aware of the smallest nuance of voice, of a glance that reveals itself, a hand that shows panic, not knowing that it is observed. Or of nothing, of the opacity of all existence.

The boldness and honesty of Bresson's approach is that he never used montage to violate the mystery of the animal. On the contrary, he wanted us to experience it to the point of agony.[21]

This lengthy quotation will repay reflection before one looks—or looks for a second time—at that remarkable sequence in which Balthasar exchanges glances with several of the animals in the circus. It certainly supports Bresson's earlier statement on preserving mystery. Perhaps it can even help explain why this movie, despite all the pain and cruelty it includes, is not simply depressing. The bright colors, the wide, panoramic shots of the meadow, the sheep's bell continuing to call out even after Balthasar dies, and a final return of the Schubert sonata create what the *New York Times* reviewer Roger Greenspun called "surely one of the most affecting passages in the history of film."[22] A French theologian has even written that "everything happens as if the 'holiness' of Balthasar permitted him to bring to completion the aspirations to the good . . . which exist in the other characters."[23]

For some, this will seem an overly positive reading of this cinematic parable; more measuredly, Jean Sémolué writes,

The ending of *Balthasar* gives the impression that, in spite of incertitudes and so many chaotic appearances, there ultimately exists an order, if only that of silence and repose. In this ending, and its relation with all that precedes it, things appear to be ordered on a cosmic level, if we recall that the word "cosmos" in Greek refers to the world considered as a cosmic whole.[24]

Andrew Sarris's comment may be especially telling since he is sometimes critical of aspects of Bresson's technique: "All in all, no film I have ever seen has come as close to convulsing my entire being as has *Au hasard Balthasar*. . . . it stands by itself as one of the loftiest pinnacles of artistically realized emotional experience."[25]

The ending of *Balthasar* takes on added significance when it is compared to those of *A Man Escaped* and *Pickpocket*, both of which contain hope-filled visitations of grace. Some commentators argue that with *Balthasar* the director falls into an undiluted pessimism, a question that will recur in reviewing his later films. The issue is explicitly raised in Roger Stéphane's interview with Bresson which is worth quoting at length:

STÉPHANE: From *Angels of Sin* until *Au hasard Balthasar* God is present, explicitly present. He is there, redeemer. In *Au hasard Balthasar*

I have the impression of a world without God, a world closed to God.

BRESSON: To begin with, I don't think that speaking of God, pronouncing God's name, indicates his presence. If I succeed, through the means of cinematography, in representing a human being, that is, someone who has a soul, who is not a marionette who wiggles, if there is a human presence, there is a divine presence. It is not because the name of God is pronounced that God is more or less present.

STÉPHANE: No, but it is the first time, to my knowledge, in one of your films, that a character, Marie's father, rejects God.

BRESSON: If he rejects God, it means that God exists, and hence God is present.[26]

The recollections of Anne Wiazemsky, the Marie of *Au hasard Balthasar*, are especially revealing. She was seventeen when she met Bresson after losing her biological father; Bresson, she says, was her artistic father. Her grandfather was François Mauriac, who had to give his assent to her appearance in the movie, since she was a minor. The film was shot in the country, and it was apparently a happy time for her; she found it very reassuring to work with someone who knew what she had to do. "Bresson created a climate of empathy that undoubtedly helped me to understand what he wanted without asking him. . . . Never, in any other cinema, has youth been so present, grasped so subtly at the moment when it is still youth but is beginning to tip over into something else."

Against Bresson's wishes, Ms. Wiazemsky embarked on an acting career after *Balthasar*, making films with directors like Godard and Pasolini. In 1999, while attending a retrospective of Bresson's work in Tokyo, she was asked to offer a few anecdotes on her experience with the director. First came the presentation of *Au hasard Balthasar;* "When I came on stage, I saw in front of me four hundred Japanese in tears. It was very moving, and it was obviously impossible to present little anecdotes in the midst of that emotion. Then I spoke of the urgency of making Bresson's work better known. Every time people want to present any of my films it is always *Au hasard Balthasar* that I most hope that they will use, because it is the one I like best of all that I have made, and I consider it artistically far above the others. I am someone who is usually uncertain about everything, but I am sure that the work of Bresson will not cease to grow. For the moment, it seems as if it has been seen and loved by individuals, but the public is going to come, and Bresson's films will always speak to it."[27]

NOTES

1. Interview with Jean-Luc Godard and Michel Delahaye, *Cahiers du cinéma* no. 176 (March 1966).

2. Interview with Yvonne Baby, *Le Monde*, May 26, 1966.

3. Interview in *Cahiers du Cinéma* no. 180 (July 1966).

4. Andrew Sarris, *The Primal Screen* (New York: Simon & Schuster, 1973), 158.

5. Jean-Luc Godard, in *Les nouvelles littéraires*, May 26, 1966.

6. Fyodor Dostoevsky, *The Idiot* (New York: Penguin Books, 1935), 82.

7. Interview in *Cahiers du cinéma* no. 178 (May 1966).

8. René Maurice, "De Lucifer à Balthasar, en suivant Robert Bresson," *Lumière et vie* no. 78 (1966): 46.

9. Thomas F. Mathews, *The Clash of Gods: A Reinterpretation of Christian Art* (Princeton, N.J.: Princeton University Press, 1993), chapter 2, "The Chariot and the Donkey," 48.

10. Marco Bongiovanni, "Robert Bresson: dalla non-violenza alla grazia," *Revista del Cinematografo* no. 9 (December 2000): 51.

11. Television interview with Roger Stéphane, in *Télé-ciné* no. 173 (March–April 1967): 4.

12. Ibid., 5, for Bresson's sage comment: "The love of adolescents can be addressed to vague, hazy objects. Love needs to find an object. The donkey is already an intermediary."

13. Philippe Arnaud, *Robert Bresson* (Paris: Cahiers du Cinéma, 1986), 59.

14. Keith Reader, *Robert Bresson* (Manchester: Manchester University Press, 2000), 80.

15. Lloyd Baugh, "An Exceptional Christ-Figure, *Au hasard Balthasar*," in *Imaging the Divine* (Kansas City, Mo.: Sheed & Ward, 1997), 191.

16. J. Hoberman, *Village Voice*, January 26, 1989.

17. Xavier Tilliette, "Des ânes et des hommes," *Études* (June 1966): 831–32.

18. Interview with Stéphane, in *Télé-ciné* no. 173 (March–April 1967): 6.

19. Jean Collet, "Le drôle de chemin de Bresson à Balthasar," *Études* (July–August, 1966): 88–89.

20. Interview with Stéphane, in *Télé-ciné* no. 173 (March–April 1967): 6.

21. Collet, "Le drôle de chemin de Bresson à Balthasar," 86–87.

22. Roger Greenspun, *New York Times*, February 20, 1970.

23. Maurice, "De Lucifer à Balthasar," 41.

24. Jean Sémolué, *Bresson ou l'acte pur des Métamorphoses* (Paris: Flammarion, 1993), 150.

25. Andrew Sarris, *The Primal Screen* (New York: Simon & Schuster, 1973), 160.

26. Interview with Stéphane, in *Télé-ciné* no. 173 (March–April 1967): 6.

27. Anne Wiazemsky, "400 Japonais en larmes," remarks recorded by Frédéric Straus, *Cahiers du Cinéma*, special issue on Bresson (February 2000).

8

The Purity of Rebellion

Mouchette

SHOOTING ON BRESSON'S NEXT FILM, MOUCHETTE, BASED ON Georges Bernanos's novella, began only a few months after *Balthasar*; it was released in 1967. Though less ambitious than *Diary of a Country Priest, Nouvelle Histoire de Mouchette* is a work of great purity and depth which closed the writer's novelistic career. Composed in 1936 while he was living in Majorca, its essential source of inspiration was the terror he observed during the Spanish Civil War, which broke out in July. As Bernanos affirmed,

> I began writing *La nouvelle histoire de Mouchette* after watching trucks go by commanded by armed men, holding wretched prisoners with their hands on their knees, their faces covered with dust. They sat up quite straight, their heads raised, with that dignity that the Spanish have even during the most atrocious misery. They were going to be shot the following morning. It was the one thing they were sure of. As regards anything else, they did not understand. If we could imagine their being interrogated, they would have been incapable of defending themselves. Against what? That would have to be explained to them first.
>
> Well, I was struck by how impossible it was for poor people to understand the frightful game in which their lives were involved. I was struck by the horrible injustice of the powerful who, in order to condemn these unhappy men, speak to them in a language that is foreign to them. There is an odious deception in this. And later, I would not know how to express the admiration that the courage and dignity with which I saw these men die inspired in me.
>
> Naturally, I did not deliberately decide to make a novel out of all this. I did not say to myself, I am going to transpose what I have seen into the story of a little girl hunted down by misfortune and injustice. But what is true is, that if I had not seen these things, I would not have written *Nouvelle histoire de Mouchette.*[1]

Bresson wasn't thinking of the Spanish Civil War in making *Mouchette*, but was undoubtedly drawn to the book's fourteen-year-old heroine and challenged by the problem of making the story credible without reducing her to just another example of victimhood. Since *Mouchette* was a far less celebrated text than *Diary of a Country Priest*, Bresson did not have to worry so much about "fidelity" to the original. He could dispense with a narrator, there was no need of voice-offs, and there was no problem about changing the locale from the Artois to a small village in the Vaucluse.

Mouchette was a child of poverty, with an alcoholic father and older brother, and a desperately ill mother who has to call on her daughter's help to take care of a baby boy. The girl is passing through adolescence with few resources beyond her stubbornness and a healthy streak of independence. When she gets lost in the woods one evening, she meets Arsène, the village poacher; he confides that he has killed Mathieu the gamekeeper and she proudly promises to keep his secret. They take shelter in his hut, where he has an epileptic fit. After he recovers, he takes advantage of her sympathy and rapes her. She returns home in the morning, but is unable to seek comfort or guidance from her mother, who is dying. Later, she has a disturbing encounter with an old woman who makes it a practice to visit the homes of the bereaved and watch over the dead.

Bresson's changes from the novel highlight images of the village and the surrounding landscape, which substitute for the novelist's long passages of interior meditation and lyrical commentary. In contrast to his source, Bresson spreads the action over several days, filling in a more detailed picture of village life. He also adds an important scene at the village carnival, which becomes the occasion of Mouchette's childlike joy while riding a bumper-car. Her moment of "escape" is all the more touching because it is quickly punctured by her father's anger when she becomes friendly with a boy who was riding another car. A further important addition that Bresson makes is to complicate his heroine's final action, making it partly a game, in which she rolls three times down an incline to the pond. Bernanos, on the other hand, is more successful in communicating the supernatural element in Mouchette's death. After a dreamlike atmosphere has been established by the girl's encounter with the old woman, the novelist shares her inmost reflections:

And now she was thinking of her own death, with her heart gripped not by fear but by the excitement of a great discovery, the feeling that she was about to learn what she had been unable to learn from her brief experience of love. What she thought about death was childish, but what could never have touched her in the past now filled her with poignant tenderness, as some-

times a familiar face we see suddenly with the eyes of love makes us aware that
it has been dearer to us than life itself for longer than we have ever realized.[2]

The tragic tone and opaqueness of reality already present in *Au hasard
Balthasar* are again evident, though in simpler, more direct form. *Mouchette*
is perhaps the most touching of Bresson's films, and its poetic realism succeeds in giving the girl's "suicide" the overtones of liberation. The film is
emotionally accessible to a broad public, except for those who are unable to
see anything but bleakness in its ending.

Interviewed at the time of its opening, Bresson said that "the domain of
cinematography is the domain of the unsayable."[3] In *Mouchette* this is
achieved largely "by the strangeness of the psychology, especially discernible
during the epileptic sequence, at the instant when the girl is finally able to
sing, the birth of love having, for a short time, finally reconciled her with
herself."[4]

Bresson told Jean-Luc Godard that he wanted to do *Mouchette* as an
"*essai*," an exercise. "Instead of a whole group of lives and different characters . . . I want to concentrate, constantly, absolutely, on one face, the face
of this little girl, to see her reactions. . . . And I will choose, yes, the most
awkward little girl there is, and try to draw from her everything that she will
not suspect I am drawing from her. That is what interests me, and the camera will not leave her."[5] Bresson won his wager: Nadine Nortier was especially affecting as Mouchette and received the prize for best actress at the
Festival of Panama.

━━BEFORE THE CREDITS, THERE IS THE IMAGE OF A WOMAN IN
church—it is Mouchette's mother. "Without me, what will become of them?"
she moans, and leaves the church. The credits are accompanied by Monteverdi's "Magnificat," from his *Vespers for the Blessed Virgin*.

The opening sequence, which takes place in the woods just outside the
village, summarizes the action of the movie and suggests Mouchette's role.
Hands are seen placing traps. Observant eyes detect the captured partridges. At the same time, other eyes are watching the poacher, Arsène.
There is a close-up of his eyes; then another of Mathieu, the guard, watching the poacher's every gesture. Dogs howl in the distance, the camera
returns to Arsène's hands as they move from one snare to the next. Close-
ups follow of a partridge approaching a snare; suddenly its head is caught.
Arsène, aware that he is being watched, gradually withdraws. Another close-
up: Mathieu removes the snare from an injured partridge. For a moment
his two hands hold the game bird, which then flies away. A rustling of wings
leads to a panoramic shot of the partridge flying to the top of the trees.

The camera then follows Mathieu, his gun on his shoulder, walking on the road to the hamlet, passing by the school just as some school girls (from nine to fifteen years old) enter. One of them stops in front of the door and looks across the road. "Mouchette," one of her schoolmates cries.

That night, at the café, Arsène brings two partridges to Louisa, the waitress. She tells him to go away—but also to come back. Mathieu arrives and tries to grab Louisa's hand; although she seems disapproving, she serves him a drink. Outside the café, a man and his son (Mouchette's father and older brother) wait until a police car moves away before unloading boxes from a small truck. The owner pays them, and they have a drink. By the time father and son drive to their ramshackle home they are already drunk. Mouchette applies a poultice to her mother (the woman seen before the credits) and calms her baby brother before sitting down on a straw mattress and closing her eyes.

The next morning the schoolgirls hurry to class while Mouchette, wearing galoshes that are too big for her, sludges along at her own pace. Her face seems hard and closed as she reaches her place in class. The exasperated teacher lines the girls up in two rows to sing a song about Columbus pleading with his sailors to keep up their hopes for three more days. At first Mouchette only pretends to sing, but the teacher grabs her by the neck, brings her up next to the harmonium and forces her to try. The girl's voice is husky and false; she seems close to tears.

When school is over, Mouchette rests her satchel on the grass and begins to throw balls of mud at her classmates. Most of the girls go off in groups toward the village. Two boys call from a shed to get Mouchette's attention: one of them unbuttons his trousers.

At home the next day, Mouchette takes off her galoshes, kisses her mother's hand, and prepares the coffee. It is Sunday, and she helps out at the café. Mathieu arrives in pursuit of Louisa, following her even when she goes down to the cellar to get more wine. He is jealous but she remains evasive; when she becomes too busy with customers, he leaves for church. Mouchette dawdles outside church, getting her shoes and socks wet by stepping in a puddle. Aware of her father's approach, she goes up the steps. He shoves her against the holy water font, where she makes a sign of the cross and moves away.

After church Mouchette works at the café, washing and drying glasses. When the manager pays her, she gives the money to her father who, already tipsy, is sitting at a table outside with his son. To thank her, he hands Mouchette his half-full glass to drink. Hearing the music of an outdoor fair, the girl gets up, passes by the merry-go-round, and leans against the railing of a bumper-car rink as the attendant alerts customers to get into their cars. A young mother with a baby gives Mouchette a ticket for a ride; the girl looks up with surprise, but the woman has disappeared. Mouchette looks delighted as she gets in, spins her vehicle around, shifts into reverse, and avoids a few cars that are trying to hit hers. Jazz fills the air as a young male driver bumps her, and she smiles as she gets into the spirit of the game. At the end of the ride the young man, after looking back at Mouchette, proceeds to a shooting gallery. She follows, eyes lowered, only to have her father grab her by the shoulder, spin her around, and slap her. She does not flinch, but sitting again at her father's table, puts her hand on her cheek.

Arsène and Louisa hurry over to the fair and take their seats side by side in a miniature plane. When Mathieu returns to a table outside the café and sits with his wife, a customer suggests that Arsène is making a fool of him. The game warden puts his glass down and goes inside to confront Louisa, but she ignores his threats, insisting that the poacher isn't afraid of him.

The next morning Mouchette kisses her mother, takes her satchel, and goes to class. After school, when it is almost twilight, she hides in a ditch next to a meadow to spy on her classmates. After watching one girl put perfume on two of her companions, Mouchette throws a ball of mud at them, but the girls ride off with boys on motorized bikes. Mouchette runs to the edge of the meadow and into a small woods where she suddenly stops. A fluttering of wings makes her lift up her eyes: a panoramic shot shows a partridge flying to the top of a tree.

Black clouds appear and the wind rises as Mouchette proceeds deeper into the woods. The rain has become heavy and the sky is dark; her skirt is wet and her galoshes become buried in mud. She rushes to the foot of an old oak tree and sits down. Night has fallen; a pale moon is visible. Through the branches of the tree Mouchette sees Mathieu, who has stopped at a stream, and then Arsène, who is laying a trap. The guard tells the poacher to leave Louisa alone and the enmity between the two men turns to blows: Arsène knocks Mathieu down, and they roll over on each other. When the top of Arsène's canteen falls out, he rushes to take several gulps of whiskey before passing it on to Mathieu.

After a general shot of a dark sky, the camera closes in on Mouchette, squeezing out her wet skirt. Petrified when Arsène turns his flashlight on her, she explains that she got lost. He tells her she can't go home with only one of her galoshes, and directs her to a little cabin, where he throws a log on the fire, fishes out a bottle of alcohol, and tells her to take a gulp to warm up. After questioning Mouchette closely about her movements since school, Arsène instructs her to say that she saw him leave the bar on the route de

Linières. He finds her other galosh, then astonishes her by saying that a cyclone has passed through the area, and finally takes her to a barn where he lights another fire.

Asking her to look him in the face, Arsène tells Mouchette that he thinks he has killed someone. He remembers that he and Mathieu had been drinking, but is unclear how things turned out. Mathieu's nose was in the water, which turned red, he recalls; more recently, however, there were rifle shots which sounded as if they came from the guard's gun. Mouchette isn't clear what Arsène wants her to say as an alibi, but assures him of her willingness: "You can count on me. I hate them. I will stand up to all of them."

Suddenly Arsène has an epileptic attack, and Mouchette cradles his head in her hands. He has difficulty breathing and even slobbers on her; she takes out a handkerchief and wipes his face. As Arsène grows calmer he gradually loses consciousness. Mouchette begins to sing, first hoarsely, then her voice clears and becomes pure. "Keep on hoping for three more days"—it is Columbus's song, the one they tried to teach her in school. When Arsène recovers, he first talks of taking her home to get a drink from her father, but when she tries to leave, he threatens her if she tells a word of what he has told her. "Monsieur Arsène," she pleads, "I'd rather kill myself than injure you." He puts his arms around her and she doesn't move, but when he tightens his grip, she pushes him and hides under a table. Finally, he kicks over the table; in trying to get away, she falls in front of the fireplace, and he gets on top of her. Mouchette groans and raises her arms; then, little by little, her arms encircle his back. . . . Later, she is seen with her satchel, after running away from Arsène.

As soon as Mouchette opens the door of her home, her mother asks her to warm the baby's bottle. Since the boxes of matches are empty, she holds the bottle against her breast. Held tenderly by his big sister, the baby stops crying and drinks from the bottle, and the mother reminds her daughter that she should put away the washing and not leave it damp. The girl struggles with her tears; she is anxious to talk to her mother, but the baby begins to cry again. The mother is in such pain that she asks Mouchette to bring some gin. After wiping her mother's mouth and chin, the girl makes a last appeal—"I have to tell you something"—but it is too late: the mother is dead. The father and older brother come in; there is a panoramic shot of the two of them kneeling at the mother's bed, then we see Mouchette asleep on a straw mattress next to her baby brother who has become quiet.

In the morning a woman neighbor brings a pot of coffee. Mouchette, ready to go out to get milk for the baby, stares at her father. When he insults her, calling her a boor, she simply answers "*Merde*" and leaves quickly.

Mouchette, carrying her milk can, passes the grocer's and is called in to have a cup of coffee. The woman gives her a croissant, but when the girl accidentally breaks the bowl of coffee, she calls her a slut. Mouchette continues walking through the village as peasant women enter the church. At Mathieu's house she is asked to come in, and the game warden informs her that Arsène has been arrested for dynamiting the river, but claims that he met Mouchette at a different spot. Hoping to help the poacher, Mouchette says that she spent the whole night with Arsène in the cabin. When Mme. Mathieu, realizing that the girl is still reeking of gin, asks her to come back and talk to her, Mouchette bursts out, "Monsieur Arsène is my lover," and leaves.

As she returns through the village, the old woman whose practice is to watch over dead people calls her into her house. She tells Mouchette that the dead are no longer being properly cared for and that she has some clothes for her. "I love the dead," she says, "I understand them very well." When Mouchette tells the woman she is disgusting, the latter replies that the girl is evil but nevertheless hands her a package of clothes.

Mouchette jumps a ditch and starts out across the fields, observing hares that are being killed by hunters. She reaches the edge of a pond, pulls a white muslin dress out of the package, and places it against her body. With the robe held around her, she rolls down the slope to the edge of the water. She gets up and makes a sign to someone driving a tractor, who continues on his way. She rolls down a second time. The third time, we hear the sound of Mouchette falling into the water. After a moment the stream seems smooth again. The film ends with a return to the healing music of Monteverdi's "Magnificat."

━━━ IF *MOUCHETTE* HAS A LESS COMPLEX PLOT STRUCTURE AND FEWER missing pieces to puzzle out than the majority of his films, it remains a work of Bresson's maturity, most noticeably in its suggestive use of sound. The extreme sparseness of language leaves the audience free to give full attention to every oral cue. As in his earlier movies, sometimes the sounds announce a scene that is about to begin; at others, one noise blends into another. The locale, an out-of-the-way country area in northern Vaucluse, is constantly filled with the din of trucks passing close to the village; appropriately enough, this sound is far more insistent than that of church bells. The pelting rain the night Mouchette gets lost in the woods, the constant slapping of her galoshes as she walks, the pom-pom of the fairground music, the clinking of the glasses on the counter of the bar, the cries of the baby, the movement of the straw as Mouchette struggles with Arsène—all contribute to the film's overall impact. At the end it is likely that the passing trucks make it impossible for the man driving the tractor to hear Mouchette when she makes what may have been a last appeal for help.

Bresson's choice of another text by Bernanos has a great deal to do with his rejection of the elaborate psychologizing in the previous generation of French films. As he responded in a questionnaire in *L'Avant-scène,*

> The absence of psychology and analysis in his [Bernanos's] books coincides with the absence of psychology and analysis in my films. His perspective in regard to the supernatural is sublime. For my part, I have always considered the supernatural as the natural seen up close. . . . Agony? I am often astonished to see how tranquil people are. . . . It is precisely incommunicability that makes union, and ultimately communion, possible.[6]

Mouchette is also another demonstration of Bresson's preference for images over dialogue. With the exception of the conversation between Arsène and Mouchette in the cabin, the reliance on language is minimal. "If there is painting in a novel in place of analysis and psychology, it is still with words," Bresson insisted. "If there is analysis and psychology in my films, it is with images and rather in the manner of portrait-painters."[7] In his novella, of course, Bernanos could use authorial reflection to indicate interior changes of feeling; in the film, since there is no narrator, and Mouchette is only partly conscious of what she is going through, Bresson has to find other ways to express her loneliness, stubbornness, independence, and deep need of affection.

Mouchette's lack of parental guidance is obvious: her father is an alcoholic who shows no tenderness for her; her mother is ill throughout, and has to pass on a good deal of the responsibility of caring for a baby brother. Just as Mouchette comes back in the morning hoping to be able to tell her mother what had happened during the night, the poor woman expires. The father slaps his daughter just as she is enjoying a moment of escape at the fair; when she hands over the coins she has earned by helping out in the café, he simply hands her what is left of his gin. Her isolation from the other girls at school is extreme, and her "revenge" by throwing mud balls is pathetic. Bresson's use of Columbus's song of hope is brilliant: under compulsion from her teacher Mouchette seems unable to sing and produces nothing but a hoarse creaking; the clear, pure sounds she utters after comforting Arsène during his epileptic attack create the most touching moment in the film.

The movie's opening sequence with Arsène setting traps and Mathieu spying on him is repeated with a difference when, near the conclusion, Mouchette walks across the fields where men are hunting. The fact that at the beginning one partridge is killed while the other flies into the sky is open to varied interpretations; in any case, Mouchette is clearly linked with the imagery of an animal being tracked down. Of course, it is no accident that *Mouchette* follows *Au hasard Balthasar;* both movies, shot in country areas, make an important use of animals.

Jean-Claude Gilbert, who had been Arnold in *Balthasar,* is used here again as Arsène, the only such "return" of a Bresson model. Obviously, there is considerable complexity in both characters; despite his attack on Mouchette and his heavy drinking, the poacher is seen with a degree of sympathy. His poaching is looked on with indulgence, and even though he is making use of Mouchette to create an alibi, she is glad of the chance to help: it is the first time someone has treated her like an adult.

Apart from Bresson's prior interest in Bernanos, the director was probably especially drawn to Mouchette as a character between childhood and adolescence, where a certain toughness is worn as a defense.[8] On several occasions, she gives way to tears; she shows her childishness by splashing her feet in little pools of water and throwing balls of mud; and she enjoys pouring the café au lait in bowls placed alongside each other without raising the lid of the pot. At the same time, she is dimly aware that she is growing into a new stage of existence; she accepts her responsibilities at home, is glad to be earning a few coins at the café, and cannot help feeling left out when some of her classmates ride off on the back of boys' motorbikes.

The power of the film derives largely from Bresson's mature mastery of montage. "To edit a film," he told Georges Sadoul, "is to link people with glances."[9] As Michel Mortier wrote,

> In fact, we can look at *Mouchette* as a film that pays attention to nothing except the exchange of glances. First, there are those of Arsène on the lookout for game, and of Mathieu watching Arsène. There are Mouchette's fearful glances at her teacher, her admiring look at the boy when she is riding the bumper-car, the loving and protective glances at Arsène during his epileptic fit, her imploring look at her mother who is already dead, the scorn she directs at the grocer's wife and the old lady who watches over the dead, and the pleading with which she looks at the peasant a few minutes before she drowns herself.[10]

Monteverdi's "Magnificat" is used only at the opening and the close. Though powerful and appropriate, it marks Bresson's last use of background music. The danger is that its accompanying text, Mary's response to the greeting of her cousin Elizabeth, has become such a cliché that we no longer recognize the boldness of its assertions—taken from different books of the Hebrew Bible—or the implications of their association with Mouchette:

My soul proclaims the greatness of the Lord,
and my spirit exults in God my savior;
because he has looked upon his lowly handmaid.
Yes, from this day forward all generations shall call me blessed,
for the Almighty has done great things for me. . . .
He has shown the power of his arm,
he has routed the proud of heart.
He has pulled down princes from their thrones and exalted the lowly,
The hungry he has filled with good things, the rich sent empty away. . . .

(Luke 1:46–52)

Inevitably, commentators have given special attention to Mouchette's "suicide," a few even speculating naively that such an ending indicates a weakening of Bresson's Catholicism. Most critics were able to recognize, however, that her act was carried out under duress, with some reluctance, and while she was still under the influence of the old woman who seemed so familiar with the dead. Michel Estève, an authority on both Bernanos and Bresson, says:

> Bresson's poetic realism imposes on us the certitude of (Mouchette's) liberation, but does not let us sense the deep motivation that the supernatural realism of Bernanos would suggest. . . . The novelist makes us feel a dreamlike and supernatural dimension of events . . . at the very heart of the suffering linked to the deepest misery. . . . Mouchette's dream also transmits the appeal of eternity. The suicide of Mouchette affirms itself, beyond despair and the temptation of Satan, as a quest for super-terrestrial value that would alone be capable of making one attain another life.[11]

It would be wrong, of course, to use the choice of Monteverdi to flatten out Bresson's ending into explicitly Christian terms, especially since he was increasingly inclined to leave his conclusions open-ended. The imagery is endlessly suggestive, especially the fact that the robe the old lady gives her can easily be seen as a wedding garment, and that Mouchette's gesture to the peasant on the tractor apparently went unnoticed. In any case, it is only fair to claim that *Mouchette* is accessible to audiences of all backgrounds. To those who see only the film's pain and darkness, Georges Sadoul's response should prove helpful: "For me, this cry of horror, this sublime dance of death, is not a 'song of despair,' but above all a hymn of 'resistance to atrocity.' Are not both those who believe in heaven and those who do not able in this case to find themselves in unreserved agreement as brothers in a 'Capital of pain?'"[12] Tilliette's insight is also worth recording: "In the universal connivance with evil and temptation, Mouchette has in some way been spared. Wild, stubborn, tormented, she is a savage who has been softened, a pale light reflected on her face. . . . Bresson has let himself be guided by the limpid spontaneity of his young interpreter; he who demands so much docility of his models is in turn infinitely attentive to their interior truth."[13]

Mortier is surely right in arguing against those critics who reject the film because they see in it an unhealthy Christian praise of resignation:

> Mouchette is not resigned; she too is in revolt. She could very well not be Christian. Is she? How many sisters does she have in all latitudes and in all religions and "non-religions"? Her revolt is pathetic. If all the Mouchettes of the world disappeared, wouldn't society secrete new ones? But before all those who suffer take efficacious means to eliminate the causes of their suffering, they must understand their situation. And Mouchette can help them.[14]

NOTES

1. Georges Bernanos, *Oeuvres romanesques*, Bibliothèque de la Pléiade (Paris: Gallimard, 1961), 1852. Interestingly, Bernanos had begun with sympathy for the Nationalists, but was profoundly shocked by the atrocities he witnessed at Majorca. He was moved to write a powerful denunciation, *Les grands cimitières sous la lune*, 1937 (*Diary of My Times*), which was a major break with earlier Catholic support for Franco.

Bernanos called his novella *Nouvelle histoire de Mouchette* because there had also been a Mouchette in his first novel, *Under the Sun of Satan*. "Both girls try in vain to break the circle of their solitude by giving themselves to a man. The failure of their effort on the human level leads them to voluntary death. But if the first suicide is a gift to Satan, the second represents the aspiration to divine Love" (*Oeuvres romanesques*, 1853). See Michel Estève, *Les sens de l'amour dans les romans de Bernanos* (Paris: M. J. Minard, Lettres Modernes, 1961).

2. Georges Bernanos, *Mouchette* (New York: Holt, Rinehart & Winston, 1966), 118.

3. Robert Bresson, interview in *Le Monde*, March 14, 1967.

4. Jean Sémolué, *Bresson ou l'acte pur des Métamorphoses* (Paris: Flammarion, 1993), 36.

5. Interview in *Cahiers du cinéma* no. 178 (May 1966).

6. Robert Bresson, response to a questionnaire, *L'Avant-scène cinéma*, no. 80 (April 1968).

7. Robert Bresson, interview in *Le Monde*, March 14, 1967.

8. Interview in *Cahiers du cinéma* no. 178 (May 1966).

9. *Lettres françaises*, March 16, 1967.

10. Michel Mortier, fiche filmographique, *Télé-ciné* no. 134 (August–September 1967): 30.

11. Estève, *Les sens de l'amour*, 37–38.

12. Georges Sadoul, in *Robert Bresson: Éloge* (Paris: Cinémathèque française, 1997), 51.

13. Xavier Tilliette, review of *Mouchette*, *Études* (May 1967): 428.

14. Mortier, fiche filmographique, *Télé-ciné* no. 134 (August–September 1967), 37.

9

Marriage without Communication

A Gentle Woman

AT FIRST GLANCE IT WOULD SEEM SURPRISING THAT DOSTOEVSKY was one of Bresson's favorite authors. The Russian's multiplicity of plots, the rapid mood swings of his characters, and the long, passionate dialogues between them seem alien to the ascetic French filmmaker, who aimed at formal perfection and warned his models against theatrical declamation. Given Bresson's reservations about excessive dialogue, one can understand the impatient response of Molly Haskell: "To take characters from Dostoevsky, whose very being is shaped and revealed by the exercise of speech, is the height of perversity."[1] Asked by Yvonne Baby, the film critic of *Le Monde,* about Dostoevsky's appeal for him, Bresson's reply is too brief: "He deals with feelings and I believe in feelings."[2] Nevertheless, the influence is clear; we have already noticed the borrowings from *Crime and Punishment* in *Pickpocket,* and many thematic parallels with Dostoevsky's work could be pointed out in Bresson's other movies.[3] Now, at the height of his powers, he drew on Dostoevsky's novella *A Gentle Woman* as the source for the next film (1969), and then adapted the story "White Nights," for *Four Nights of a Dreamer* (1971).

In the novella, an almost fifty-year-old pawnbroker-narrator stands over the body of the "gentle woman," his young wife, who has just committed suicide; he wants to understand why and how she could have come to such an end. He is speaking directly to us, justifying and abusing himself in turn, explaining what he understands of the different stages of his marriage, and offering a few clues to his wife's brief existence. Bresson's narrator, in contrast, is probably only thirty and is speaking directly to the servant Anna as they stand or sit observing the body on the bed. Their exchange of glances at the end of each sequence seems to catch every modulation of the tragedy that has unfolded.

The film opens with long shots outside the couple's apartment, the air filled with the noise of dense traffic and the flashing of colored signs. In contrast, there follows a shot of a French window, suggesting the silence of a middle-class apartment. Anna opens the window. On the balcony outside, a table and a rocking chair have been overturned, and the noise of the city fills the screen. A long white scarf floats gently through the air. There follows a tight shot of several cars bumping into each other, accompanied by the screeching of brakes. The body of a very young woman lies on the sidewalk with her head bleeding; passers-by stop short to look. Immediately we shift to a shot inside the apartment, of the bed where the dead woman has been laid out. Her feet extend a few inches beyond the end of the bed; the servant kneels in a chair at its side. The legs of a man can be seen going back and forth between the bed and the camera. He can be heard speaking to the servant: "She seemed to be only sixteen years old, Anna, do you remember?"

A Gentle Woman is Bresson's study of a marriage that had been lived almost totally without communication. The situation is especially pathetic because the couple were young, enjoyed good health, and had the benefit of all the superficial advantages of today's society. They even seemed to have had a mutually satisfying sexual life, but it never overflowed into expressions of gratitude and joy or really broke the silence between them. Like Dostoevsky's husband, the husband was happy to find a wife who was poor, young, and very attractive, and assumed she would be totally submissive. He did not think of himself as unkind when he laid down very definite rules for their life together.

Neither in Dostoevsky nor Bresson is any character named except the servant. She is called Lukeria in the novella; in the movie she is Anna and is present at the moment the gentle woman jumps from the balcony. In Dostoevsky, the husband/narrator speaks directly to the reader; in Bresson, he tells the story to Anna, with whom he interacts to some degree. It is important to keep in mind, as Lindley Hanlon has written, that

> restructuring by Bresson . . . shifts the emphasis of the narrative away from the husband's psychic tensions and perspective . . . to a focus on the mysterious character of the woman. . . . Although the events of the narrative are represented in the film as the husband's choices to illustrate his theories, the camera betrays him. Even when placed at an angle to mimic the husband's point of view in reverse-angle setups, the camera reveals aspects of his character to us in the reverse field that we realize he perceives falsely, if at all.[4]

In addition, Bresson changed the locale from an earlier St. Petersburg to contemporary Paris; this has prompted some to ask whether the young woman would be as totally dependent as she could be assumed to be in nineteenth-century Russia. In both novella and film the wife is dead from the outset, but because Bresson opens with the shocking images of her suicide, not only do viewers constantly ask themselves why, but the question is sharpened because the rest of the film continues to alternate between past scenes and brief moments in the present.

A Gentle Woman is notable in Bresson's career as his first film in color, with ivory, gold, wine, and pale blue predominating. It was also the screen debut of Dominique Sanda, the "model" for the central character, who, unlike almost everyone else who appeared in his movies, went on to a successful film career. Sanda had been a professional model, and Bresson had seen a picture of her in a fashion magazine. Unlike Dostoevsky's story, the movie extends beyond the husband's pawnshop and the couple's apartment into a variety of Paris backgrounds, providing a host of opportunities for Ghislain Cloquet, the cameraman, to present various combinations of colors and forms. As with the use of other formal elements, however, Bresson is careful not to allow color to become a distraction for the spectator, and he avoided extreme contrasts.

Jean Sémolué remarks that often, when a director first uses color, the action in his film slows down; "Bresson," however, "avoids this risk by the rapidity of his rhythm, the diversity of its registers. Color permits him to treat clothes and objects as actors in the drama, to show that our daily environment is insignificant only in appearance—which is a constant point in his work."[5] As in his black-and-white films, of course, Bresson wasn't trying to produce beautiful pictures that could be detached and put up on the wall.

He doesn't cheat with reality: his characters . . . live in an ordinary framework, their clothes remain ordinary, the objects around them are often ugly. How does he give a style, a soul, to that banal ensemble? To begin with, by means of a remarkable sense of materials. A painter knows that every fabric, every material, calls for a different treatment. In the bedroom, the Persian rug, the green velvet curtains, the Chinese screen with its shiny blacks and reds become familiar to us. The grayish white dressing gown, strewn with purple storks, the soft green of a gleaming raincoat momentarily matching the brilliance of a gold scale, the dull whiteness of a woolen shawl, help express states of soul, to the degree that they are linked to what is unique in the instant that is being depicted. The flashes of color on a bath towel as it falls to the floor to unveil a body, or a night shirt suddenly discarded to reveal the nudity of a breast reinforce the attractive value of the nudity that is revealed.[6]

Some reviewers, confusing Bresson's instinctive sense of restraint with prudishness, were surprised at the inclusion of the rape scene in *Mouchette*; they also inclined to overemphasize the nude shots—in fact, quite discreet—in *A Gentle Woman*. Bresson's positive and healthy attitude to the subject is summarized by his quotation of Valéry, "In the area of nudity, all that is not handsome is obscene."[7] Instead of the sexual gymnastics that have become a cinematic cliché, Bresson employs modest shots conveying the couple's sexual activity, which never seems to be accompanied by any expression of genuine affection. From the beginning the husband appears to reject any possible union of bodies and souls.

AFTER THE OPENING SEQUENCE OF THE WIFE'S SUICIDE, WE SEE the husband and Anna watching over the wife's dead body as it lies on a narrow bed. Anna kneels on a chair at the side; the husband walks back and forth nervously. The husband's story essentially makes up the rest of the film; scenes from the past between husband and wife are linked by his voice-offs, with a constant return to the room where he and the servant are watching. The first link in the chain of his memories shows the future husband in his shop; a sign reads "purchase of precious objects of all kinds." The "gentle woman" comes in and offers an old camera, which produces only an ironic dismissal. She comes back with a cigarette lighter, for which he pays what he considers a generous price: "I am doing this just for you," he says. Her identity card is examined by Anna, who keeps a record of transactions. As the young woman pockets the money, the pawnbroker says to himself, "I knew that she would come again." Her destiny is sealed: again we have a glimpse of the dead body on the bed.

When the young woman returns to the shop, they begin to speak to each other; she tells him that ever since her parents died, her aunts have been using her as a servant. He helps her rewrite a "situation wanted" notice she intends to put in a newspaper. After she offers to sell an ivory Christ set on a golden cross, they go upstairs to weigh the gold. He is willing to detach the Christ figure (which has no monetary value, since it is not metal) and return it to her, but she is prepared to surrender the whole piece. When he passes over considerably more money than she expected, she hands some of the bills back, leading him to say that she shouldn't scorn what another offers. He even quotes Mephistopheles in Goethe's *Faust*, "I am part of that force which sometimes wants to do harm, and sometimes does good." His interest in her increases when she recognizes the quotation. "As soon as she left," he says, "my decision was taken."

In the next scene he picks her up at the lycée where she still attends classes and takes her to the Botanical Gardens. They talk of love and he puts his arm around her shoulders: "Say yes; I promise you happiness." The young woman is hesitant: "You don't want love; you just want me to agree to marry you." She even admits that the idea of marriage bores her. When he takes the young woman back to where she is living, he follows her up the stairway; if she marries him, he argues, she could leave a place where she is miserable.

There is a dissolve to the office of the marriage clerk: "I now pronounce you man and wife." They sign the register and have a meal together; they are both wearing rings. When they return home (an apartment above the store), she drags him up the stairs, turns on the television—which is showing an auto race—and goes into the bathroom. She emerges with a towel wrapped around her, which falls as she turns off the television and jumps into bed. There are sounds of delight underneath a white sheet, followed by the voice-over of the husband the next morning, "I threw cold water on this exhilaration." He quickly lays out the ground rules of their marriage: they must live frugally in order to build up a nest egg; they will go to movies, but can't afford the theater or to get new furniture. When she insists that she doesn't care about money, he answers coldly, "I must broaden your outlook."

In a brief return to the present, the husband moans, "Why, from the beginning, did we adopt the habit of silence?"

They do go to the movies; we even see a fragment of *Benjamin,* a film directed by Michel Deville. In the dark of the theater another man sits next to the wife and puts his hand on her knee; she and her husband change places. As they leave the theater, she kisses him impulsively. The voice-off comments, "I was certain then of her love. She loved me, or wanted to love me," as we again see the image of the dead woman lying on the bed. Looking back on the past, however, the husband remembers that he soon began to be suspicious: "During that whole period I never stopped being jealous."

The wife comes back to the shop with books and records she has bought, and sits in a corner of the room listening to both pop and classical music on her record-player. She looks up excitedly from a book and suggests that they go to the Museum of Natural History. A quick transition takes her from the illustrated pages of an art book to the Louvre. There they look together at some paintings of nudes, which, he recognizes, encourage him to "see a woman as an instrument of pleasure."

On a Sunday drive out of the city, the wife has gathered some white daisies to make a bouquet. She then notices an affectionate young couple with a similar bouquet, and says, "We too constitute a couple, on the same model." Abruptly, she throws her flowers out the window. As they drive back they look at each other nervously through the rear-view mirror.

Their first open quarrel takes place in the shop when she pays a woman more for her pledge than it is worth. When the husband insists that "it's my money," she protests angrily: "Don't try to rule me with money!" They exchange insults—"Idiot!" "Coward!"—and she leaves. He waits all day for her return, especially disturbed because someone has given him tickets for a performance of *Hamlet.* When she returns, she gets dressed without giving an account of her absence; they don't look at each other, but exchange glances via her mirror.

At the theater, she sits absorbed during the performance of the climax—the duel between Hamlet and Laertes, Gertrude drinking from the poisoned cup Claudius intended for Hamlet, and the deaths of all four—but does not join in the applause. When she gets back to the apartment, she checks her text of Shakespeare to see if her suspicion is correct: yes, the production omitted the lines of Hamlet's advice to the players, "in order that they could bellow."

An erotic scene follows. The wife takes a bath, during which a bar of soap falls to the floor. As the husband bends down to give the soap back, we see her thighs above the water. His voice-over provides a disturbing commentary: "That night they took great pleasure in each other. But she has not changed her attitude and I was only seeking to possess her body."

Subsequently, he remembers what he endured because of his jealousy; "Do you know what it is like to suffer, Anna, when one has a wife who is so gentle and beautiful?" In the store he observes her talking to a stranger. When she leaves shortly after and fails to return, he looks for her in vain all over the Saint-Germain-des-Prés neighborhood. Back at the apartment, they share a painful meal that underlines their isolation: he breathes heavily over each spoonful of soup before putting it in his mouth. Later, she reads by herself in silence.

Voice-over: "Everything was a pretext for quarreling." The appearance of flowers brings the husband to ask his wife who gave them to her. Angry, she starts to leave; when he insists she stay, she only replies, "It isn't possible now." He watches a TV documentary on the Royal Air Force while waiting for her. When she returns, she again offers no explanation, but in bed she removes the top of her night dress and offers herself to him.

By this time she has begun to use the impersonal "vous" when speaking to him; he continues to use the intimate "tu" with her. In a morning discussion she says she has obtained information about his past. Apparently he had previously been director of a bank; we are left unclear as to whether he committed some impropriety or was blamed for something of which he was not guilty. Jealousy impels him to take a revolver and look for her in various neighborhoods. At night he finally finds her by chance—sitting with a man in an automobile on the boulevard Lannes. After hearing her say a few words which assure him she has rejected the advances of the stranger, the husband tells her to get out of the car. On the way home he wonders if she had seen him in the rear-view mirror before he opened the automobile door.

Instead of being satisfied that she has not betrayed him, the tormented man is convinced that his wife does not love him and is simply trying to provoke him. After they return to the apartment, he places the pistol on the table in full view of his wife and throws himself on the bed; she remains sitting in an armchair. A close shot reveals the wife holding the gun behind her back. She advances to the bed where her husband pretends to be sleeping and places the pistol close to his cheek. Finally, she hesitates and does not pull the trigger. She lowers her arm, puts the gun back on the table, and leaves in total confusion. The next thing we see is Anna's hand as she draws the window curtains, announcing morning, and the wife begins to pour the breakfast coffee.

The husband visits a furniture store, buys a camp bed and a mattress, and has them brought up the stairs; Anna places a sheet and a blanket over it. A voice-off declares: "the bed makes clear to her that I was not asleep." The revolver, however, remains on the table; as he watches her that night, she becomes delirious. His attitude immediately changes: rapid images refer to six weeks of illness, during which he tries to care for her and hires a nurse. Walking around the cadaver, he says he was happy to have spent a great deal of money to help her recover. As he sits at the feet of the dead woman, he cries out: "What is needed is prayer, but I can only think."

In the past again, we see the wife reading quietly in bed, a convalescent; winter passes, they walk past swans. He takes her to the Museum of Natural History, where she repeats a phrase used earlier, "the same original matter for all things," which Hanlon suggests may be a reaction to the thought of Teilhard de Chardin.[8] At the Museum of Modern Art, she shows an interest in an exhibit of turning machines, but her husband can't accept them as art. Back in the apartment she listens to records while he does crossword puzzles. In the present, he tells Anna he performed some charitable acts in the store at that time for his wife's benefit, and remembers how pale and thin she had become.

A doctor comes to the apartment, and after examining the wife, encourages the husband to take her to the mountains or the seashore. The young woman insists that she feels well, which makes him say to himself, "She is ashamed because I care for her like a husband." Some time later, however, while working in the store, he hears her upstairs singing very softly. Deeply troubled, he asks himself, "Has she forgotten I exist?" The husband goes out to stand at a railway bridge watching the trains pass below. The voice-off refers to a state of unspeakable enthusiasm: "No one will understand my emotion." When he comes back, she is listening to a record, which she turns off as he approaches.

For the first time, the husband seems to break down and profess genuine emotion. He confesses he was wrong, admitting that he had wanted to take everything and give nothing. Promising a total change, he embraces her feet: "I want to believe in you . . . I love you." Overwhelmed, she collapses in tears in her armchair. He kisses her and carries her curled-up body to bed. He talks excitedly of going away on a vacation together. She sobs, "And I thought you were going to leave me."

He doesn't understand her reaction and admits later that he did not pay enough attention to her fears. In the middle of their exchange, she begins reading aloud from a book on the singing of birds. When he repeats his hope of starting again from zero, she merely says, "But we—we will not be new. Is it possible to change?" His assurances are too automatic, and she can only blurt out impassively, "I want something else." She takes up her reading again; finally she bursts into tears, hides her face between the pages, and throws the book down. A long shot shows it on the rug before the husband bends down to pick it up.

Next morning, however, she presides at breakfast, making the toast and handing him his coffee. There seems reason for hope when she says, "I will be a faithful wife to you. I will respect you." He kisses her madly—"like a husband after a long separation," the voice-off declares—and rushes to a travel office to buy plane tickets.

At the apartment, Anna observes the young woman from the inner door; she is looking at the ivory Christ that is lying in a drawer. Anna comes in, pleased with the signs she has seen of the couple's reconciliation. "Are you happy?" she asks. "Yes," is the answer. Left alone, however, the gentle woman smiles at her image in the mirror and pulls out a white scarf from another drawer. There is a long shot at the balcony window. She opens the window, then closes it again and leans her back against it, turned toward the room.

Anna watches her from behind the glazed door. The gentle woman looks at herself in the mirror with a sad smile. In an extreme close-up, she reopens the French window of the balcony. As at the outset, we see the table and the rocking chair thrown over, then the scarf—finally, the shroud, which is also white. The husband lifts up the dead body, crying desperately, "Open your eyes for a second, just a second," then places it back in the casket. In a tight shot, three nails are carefully screwed into the lid of the casket.

———THE FILM ENDS WITH A PAINFUL SENSE OF INEVITABILITY, ALONG with some troubling questions. When we reflect, it becomes obvious that, as usual, Bresson has left the backgrounds of his characters murky, with many psychological developments unclear. Although our sympathy is clearly with the gentle woman, the husband has suffered as well; the woman, perhaps instinctively, has found ways to torture him, undermining his need to dominate, attacking his system of values. She has made it clear that she will not be controlled by money, and though she has not become wanton, the process that brought her to a stranger's car on the boulevard Lannes is ambiguous. In the Dostoevsky story, we learn that the husband had been an army officer who left the service under a cloud because he had refused to fight a duel, and later had a hard time surviving in the city. In Bresson it is unclear what led him to open up a pawnshop, but his past experience has clearly left him so intent on control that he has kept whatever real affection he might have for his wife completely hidden. He "needed" to possess her physically, whereas she was hungry for the genuine intimacy she had been denied when growing up.

Though it visits many places in and around Paris, *A Gentle Woman* also contains echoes of the prison themes of earlier Bresson films. As Keith Reader remarks, despite the "comparative breadth of topographical reference, it is still characteristically Bressonian in being a very claustrophobic work. The arid neatness of the couple's flat, which the wife disrupts with loud music, makes it something like a prison, an impression which is intensified by her financial dependence on her husband and his business. The determinedly non-reverberant voices in which the couple speak also contribute to the claustrophobic atmosphere."[9] Though the film is shot in a very up-to-date Paris there are no echoes of the student revolts and near chaos of 1968.

As so often in Bresson, the appetite for money destroys the possibility of genuine human interaction. The future husband's sense of values is indicated in the early scene in which he offers to buy the golden cross and let the young woman retain the Christ-figure that rests on it. The day after they are married the husband establishes the ground rules for their life together, in which the concern for money is dominant. Their day-to-day quarrels emerge principally from her instinctive generosity to the patrons of her husband's pawnshop. Lindley Hanlon reminds us that the golden cross was the last thing the wife pawned.[10]

On a first viewing, some may question the inevitability of the tragedy: hadn't the husband confessed he was wrong and offered the possibility of starting over? Further reflection, however, should make it clear that the very suddenness with which he embraced this "new life" had been more frightening to his wife than reassuring. She found little reason to be convinced that he had overcome his need to dominate, and immediately returns to her book on bird song. The "reconciliation" the following morning is also ambiguous: she promises to be "faithful" and "respect" him, but he has not yet taken any real steps to establish the spontaneity and intimacy that had been missing in their relationship.

Avarice had already been a dominating motif in *Au hasard Balthsar*. René Prédal points out that the first two shots of *A Gentle Woman* establish the film's aesthetic pattern,

> which is effectively based on matter. Things are going to control the story because they condition people. . . . the hardness of matter will prevail over the gentleness of the movie's heroine, as is underlined on two occasions by the husband's voice-offs. His occupation as pawnbroker emphasizes this insistence on the perpetual exchanges of objects for money which punctuate the whole film, and look ahead to Bresson's last movie, *L'Argent.* Money and things acquire a constant presence in the imagery that compete with and considerably reduce that of beings.[11]

A Gentle Woman is another example of the way Bresson combines fidelity to his literary source with a confident sense of independence. Concerned as always with questions of structure, he exhibits complete mastery in moving from present to past and in transitions from one scene to the next. "Say yes, say yes," the pawnbroker insists to the young girl when he brings her home after visiting the zoo. Even as she is closing the door, we already hear the background sounds in the city hall where they both sign the marriage contract. Later, we move seamlessly from the wife looking at reproductions in an art book to a visit to the Louvre, then to a scene in which they drive from Paris into the countryside.

Bresson's special concern for the soundtrack is evident from the start, when we hear the shock of Paris traffic brought to a halt as the wife's body lies bleeding on the sidewalk. Moments of silence during the movie make us more conscious of footsteps on the stairway and the servant opening the shades; we strain to hear the voice of the gentle woman when Anna tells the husband his wife is singing to herself. In the couple's apartment, the imposed quiet drives her to listen to records all day—the jazz of Jean Wiener alternating with a sonata of Mozart and the songs of Purcell. Far more jarring are the frequent fragments of television, projecting the noise of racing cars and warfare, the latter via a documentary about the British Air Force in World War II.

The wife's recognition that, in the performance of *Hamlet* she and her husband attended, Hamlet's advice to the players had been omitted becomes the occasion for a Bressonian lesson:

> Hamlet urges the players to speak the lines as he had pronounced them, to imitate his diction; Bresson has his actors repeat after him, again and again, until they have mastered his intonation, his rhythm, even the quality of his voice. In the version adopted for *La femme douce*, "trippingly on the tongue" is translated by "au bout des lèvres," the very idiom that serves Bresson to describe an ideal diction (and that Pascal had used to define the mechanics of prayer).[12]

Some critics have made too much of Bresson's not following Dostoevsky literally by having the gentle woman jump while clinging to her icon. In part, the change is one from nineteenth-century St. Petersburg to late-twentieth-century Paris; perhaps even more it is the difference between the flamboyance of the novelist and the restraint of the cinematographer. The latter's discretion is thoughtfully analyzed by Lindley Hanlon as she points out how the wife opens her dresser drawer a moment before moving out to the balcony. "She lifts it [the crucifix] out carefully, thinking she is alone and free from surveillance, and touches it gently, staring at it. The action seems to suggest that it is to regain the world of the spirit that she commits suicide."[13]

Since Bresson's constant concern for complete control of his films has probably been the aspect of his work that has led to the greatest incomprehension, it is especially valuable to have the insightful testimony of Dominique Sanda:

> I was a young girl of sixteen at the time of *A Gentle Woman*. Bresson told journalists that he had chosen me for my voice, which he had first heard on the telephone.
>
> According to Bresson, his protagonists are neither actors nor interpreters. "They are beings whom I approach like precious treasures. I ask them not to appear as characters, but as they are themselves. I adapt myself to them and they to me. There is an exchange, a secret understanding that has nothing in common with the direction of actors."
>
> I remember an anecdote during the shooting of *A Gentle Woman* when she goes to the pawnbroker's shop to give him a crucifix in gold that held an ivory Christ. We had been there in the store all morning, and there had been a large number of takes, perhaps twelve, and I thought that was enough. Since I had heard that was part of Bresson's method and that he was in the process

of carrying it out—shooting so many takes that the model was driven crazy (and also the producer!), I simply took off the raincoat that was part of my costume and said that I was going out to have a drink at the café next door. A few seconds after I had sat down on the bar stool my "master" came to sit down next to me and we had a glass together. I believe he liked the rebellious side of my personality. "I always tell actors that they should not think about what they are saying, but what they are doing. That they should be themselves when saying their lines."

He often gave one simple direction: not to look one's partner in the eye but rather to look at his right ear. It was a remarkable school for obtaining what was the most important thing for the actor: presence.

When we postsynchronized the film, Bresson did not want my partner Guy Frangin or myself to see the images; he made us speak our lines in the emptiness of the auditorium. Until the public showing of the movie at a theater on the Champs Elysées, I had never seen an image of the picture. Nevertheless, that night I discovered that I knew exactly what I was going to see. I did not experience any uneasiness, undoubtedly because I had remained myself during the whole course of my experience.[14]

These recollections of Dominique Sanda make it clear that she, at least, found it easy to follow Bresson's counsels in *Notes of a Cinematographer*:

To Your Models: "Speak as if you were speaking to yourselves." MONOLOGUE INSTEAD OF DIALOGUE. Models. Their way of being the people of your film is by being themselves, by remaining what they are. (*Even in contradiction with what you imagined.*[15]

A Gentle Woman is a frightening demonstration of the way in which the desire to dominate is a tragic obstacle to genuine dialogue. As usual, however, Bresson's approach is not didactic, but one that employs the means of cinematography. The scenes in which husband and wife are shown pursuing their activities in isolation are as telling as they are understated. It is not just that they never look directly at each other; even the objects have been carefully chosen to suggest contrasts. They occupy very separate spaces, a fact that becomes as significant as their different attitudes to money. Even in the one highly dramatic moment—borrowed directly from Dostoevsky— when the gentle woman places the gun at her husband's temple, Bresson's camera offers the same steady gaze, which serves to heighten the spectator's emotional tension. A second viewing of the film will only increase one's awareness of the emotional depth of each moment that is presented.

NOTES

1. Molly Haskell, *Village Voice*, November 4, 1971.

2. Interview in *Le Monde*, November 11, 1971.

3. Mireille Latil Le Dantec, "Bresson, Dostoevsky," in *Robert Bresson*, ed. James Quandt (Toronto: Cinematheque Ontario, 1998).

4. Lindley Hanlon, *Fragments* (Cranberry, N.J.: Associated University Press, 1982), 39–42.

5. Jean Sémolué, *Bresson ou l'acte pur des Métamorphoses* (Paris: Flammarion, 1993), 178.

6. Ibid., 178–79.

7. Quoted in Michele Estève, *Robert Bresson* (Paris: Editions Albatros, 1983), 63.

8. Hanlon, *Fragments*, 52.

9. Keith Reader, *Robert Bresson* (Manchester: Manchester University Press, 2000), 102.

10. Hanlon, *Fragments*, 49.

11. René Prédal, "Robert Bresson: L'aventure intérieure," *L'Avant-scène cinéma* (January-February 1992): 94.

12. Mirella Jona Affron, "Bresson and Pascal: Rhetorical Affinities," in *Robert Bresson*, ed. James Quandt (Toronto: Cinematheque Ontario, 1998), 178.

13. Hanlon, *Fragments*, 49.

14. *Le Cinématographie de Robert Bresson* (Tokyo: Tokyo International Foundation for Promotion of Screen Image Culture, 1999), 74.

15. Robert Bresson, *Notes of a Cinematographer* (Los Angeles: Sun and Moon Press, 1988), 84 and 86.

10

The Education of a Romantic

Four Nights of a Dreamer

BRESSON RETURNED TO DOSTOEVSKY FOR THE SOURCE OF his next film, *Four Nights of a Dreamer*, this time choosing "White Nights," a short story very different in tone from *A Gentle Woman*. The latter was published in 1876, in his *Diary of a Writer*, after he had written his major novels, whereas "White Nights" came early in his career, in 1848.

Four Nights of a Dreamer was completed very rapidly and released in 1971, which suggests that with reasonable financial backing Bresson's overall productivity would have been far greater than it was. It is the least tragic of his films, one that indicates close and sympathetic observation of Paris and of French young people of that time, including their clothes, and it borrows indiscriminately from several quite different styles. "The story treats the loves of young people," Bresson said. "This love and youth of Dostoevsky seem very contemporary to me . . . nevertheless these feelings seem to have, in a certain sense, become more complex for today's young people."[1]

The main character, Jacques, a lonely observer of the scene around him, is constantly using his tape recorder to set down what he thinks and to play back his reflections as he wanders through the city. Marthe, the young woman in Bresson's story, is initially so overwrought that she is contemplating suicide. Jacques gets her to abandon this idea, and the following night she confesses that she is desperate because the young man to whom she considers herself engaged, and who has been away for a year, is back in Paris but has not yet come to see her.

The situation in Dostoevsky, an encounter between two young people who nurse unfulfilled longings, reflects the international dimensions of nineteenth-century romanticism and provides a pretext for bravura passages reflecting the inner state of the young man, who is also the narrator.

Dostoevsky's subtitle, "A Sentimental Story from the Diary of a Dreamer," fits in perfectly with his narrator's early observation that the approach of spring reminds him of "a frail, consumptive girl [who] . . . in one instant suddenly becomes, as though by chance, inexplicably lovely and exquisite."[2]

Because it was not one of Dostoevsky's major works, Bresson felt free to modify it:

> Written too quickly, it's a very muddled story, so I allowed myself to make use of it. I made an adaptation in a few days. . . . Dostoevsky is a painter of the interior. He discovers without explaining. What is boring about psychological writers is that they explain what they discover. . . . People have reproached me for not explaining. But in real life people don't explain themselves. . . . I don't believe that we directors *realize* anything at all. We take the real as it is; we don't have to demonstrate anything but should try to find, to go to the depth of beings, to the soul of a human being, which neither poetry, drama or painting—in fact, nothing—has yet succeeded in rendering. I believe that the camera and tape-recorder are depth instruments; that is their destiny, and it's not at all a matter of taking actors and having them perform a show and photographing them.[3]

In addition to moving the story from St. Petersburg to Paris, Bresson introduced some slight modifications of the two main characters in order to make them somewhat more credible as late-twentieth-century Parisians. Jacques's inflamed monologues are drastically reduced; Marthe may still be a young woman who lives at home, but she is not, as in Dostoevsky, pinned to the dress of a blind grandmother so that she cannot get away. *Four Nights of a Dreamer* is not as sentimental either as Visconti's 1957 movie *White Nights* or the Russian original; the dreamlike atmosphere is retained, but it coexists with a relatively realistic presentation. As Jacques and Marthe walk along the Seine and later in the St. Germaine-de-Prés area, the clothes of the people they encounter, the constant presence of automobiles and telephones, and the overall atmosphere, fit in quite well with the Paris of the 1970s. Music again plays a large part in establishing the mood; no major composition is used as a leitmotif, as in *A Man Escaped* and *Au hasard Balthasar,* but strolling musicians, a Brazilian orchestra on one of the festively lighted *bateau-mouches,* guitar music during the credits, and a handful of contemporary pop tunes are scattered through the film.

As in *A Gentle Woman,* Bresson does not use the possibilities of color for shots that call attention to themselves. Jacques's apartment is almost bare, so that the small spots of color on his canvases have extra impact. Outside, the young women that Jacques observes on the street are wearing a variety of stylish outfits; even Isabelle Weingarten, who plays Marthe, has several changes of costume. In daytime scenes clear, cold colors dominate, while in the evening a variety of blues, browns, and tans stand out.

Structurally, Bresson's most significant change is that Jacques is not, as in Dostoevsky, the narrator, although the story reflects his point of view. Equally important is the fact that Jacques is not remembering a romantic encounter he had fifteen years previously, but interacts with Marthe in the present. Younger than the character in the story, who is twenty-six, he is an aspiring artist, not some low-level employee. He first meets the young woman after she takes off her shoes and climbs over the parapet of the Pont-Neuf, the oldest bridge in Paris. Jacques is worried that she might be about to jump into the river. The situation in Dostoevsky is less dramatic: the narrator merely offers Nastenka protection when she bursts into tears because a gentleman is following her.

Bresson divides the narrative into its four days by opening each section with a formal card announcing "First Night," etc., a procedure that Jean-Luc Godard had made familiar in the 1960s. In addition, the "Second Night" is interrupted by "Jacques's story" and "Marthe's story," in which the account of their lives that the two young people give to each other is presented in brief, elliptical fragments. Another departure from its nineteenth-century source is the movie's reflection of today's more relaxed sexual standards. Although there had been no direct relationship between Marthe and the stranger who was staying as a boarder in her mother's home, and hardly any conversation between them, the night before he is to leave she goes into his room and asks him to take her with him. Unlike the situation in Dostoevsky, they proceed to make love. In both the novel and the movie, he promises to come back to her in a year; if she still loves him, he promises, they will get married.

━━ AT THE OPENING OF *FOUR NIGHTS OF A DREAMER*, JACQUES HAS BEEN hitchhiking in the direction of Normandy. He is a tall, handsome young man with large eyes and a dreamy, ascetic look. It is a spring day: he enjoys the countryside, sings to himself, and even turns a cartwheel. At night, he finds a ride back to Paris and gets out of the car just as the credits come on, accompanied by shots of traffic lights and the sounds of guitar music.

First Night. On the Pont-Neuf, Jacques notices a young woman (Marthe) who seems distraught and climbs over the parapet. A passing car stops in alarm and a police car pulls up just before Jacques succeeds in getting Marthe back on the bridge. After the traffic starts up again, Jacques walks

Marthe home. When he gets to her house, he tells her he will be at the bridge at the same time the following night, standing under the statue of Henri IV.

Second Night. Jacques, arriving early, has just left a café when Marthe arrives for their rendezvous, wearing a long black cloak. Impressed by the young man's kindness and intelligence the previous evening, she asks him to tell her his story.

Jacques's story: After he gives his address, there is no further commentary, but a visual presentation of Jacques's typical activities. He enters his house, which features a number of canvases in varying states of completion, and sets down a bag of groceries. Later, on the street he notices a young woman in a clothing store. They exchange glances, and he follows her, but is soon distracted by a blond walking in the opposite direction. Obviously, he is a bashful but inveterate voyeur, who has "fallen in love" in this manner many times, to no avail. He has been in love with an ideal; Marthe tells him flatly that this behavior is stupid. "I know," Jacques agrees. "And God has sent me his angel to tell this to me. To reconcile me with myself."

During Jacques's ongoing account, an elegant couple get out of a car, and he follows them to the entrance of their building. Back home, he dictates the whole story into his tape recorder: "a pure and innocent love unites him with the lady of the manor, despite her elderly husband. . . . In the garden they walk hand in hand." The woman is held captive in an ancient castle, but when they meet again in Venice, she is free. Jacques begins to apply patches of color—black, blue, and red—to a few canvases that he has placed on the floor. He then listens to what he has dictated and stretches out on his bed. The bell rings; he tries to put things in order and places his canvases against the wall, so that only their backs are visible. Finally, he opens the door: it is a former fellow student from art school. Jacques seems not to know what to do with his visitor, who announces his abstract theories about art in rather pretentious terms. Although Jacques finally brings out wine, his acquaintance leaves abruptly.

This lonely and somewhat absurd existence seems to sum up Jacques's overall life, but he declares, "I was happy yesterday." Marthe, more down to earth, tells Jacques he should stop looking for pity and give her some needed advice.

Marthe's story: Marthe explains that her father is dead and she lives with her mother. Since he did not leave them enough money to live on, her mother takes in a boarder. As with Jacques's story, the remainder of the sequence tells its story in the present. Marthe is curious about the new lodger; she only sees his back when he returns to his room. She notices some books on the kitchen table, which her mother says were lent them by the lodger; they seem to be erotic novels. On one occasion, when Marthe is in the elevator going down, the boarder jams the mechanism so that it cannot move, and invites her—through the closed door—to go to the movies with him without telling her mother.[4] She refuses, but the next scene shows Marthe and her mother at the opening night of *When Love Possesses Us,* thanks to tickets from the lodger. The movie is a heavy-handed example of the gangster genre, exploiting the kind of overheated emotion Bresson's whole career was attempting to undermine. At the end, the dying gangster gazes fondly at the photo of his girlfriend while music swells up around him. Marthe tells her mother they should leave the theater; they have fallen into a trap. The boarder wanted to punish them because she had refused his earlier invitation.

While making tea, Marthe tells her mother she has never seen the boarder, whose footsteps they can hear in the corridor. That night, she takes off her clothes and looks at herself naked in the mirror—a "sequence," as Roger Greenspun comments, "of unembarrassed gravity that is rare in modern movies."[5] Her radio is playing dance music; suddenly there is a knock on her wall. Michel Estève points out that "[e]roticism is born here from both sound and image, arousing a dialectic between her glance and that of the spectator, with the montage both fragmenting and recomposing the naked body reflected in the mirror."[6] She puts on a wrap and goes out into the corridor; at the lodger's door, she looks in through the keyhole. When the light goes out in the young man's room, she rushes back to her own. He thereupon leaves his room, and goes to her door. Marthe stands still for a moment, her hands over her heart, before going to bed.

In the next scene Marthe's mother, just before she goes out to do the shopping, tells her daughter that their lodger is going away. Marthe quickly pulls some clothes together, throws them in a bag, and comes into the young man's room. She tells him she is fed up with her present life and asks him to take her away with him. The boarder explains that it is impossible— he is about to go to the United States; he has won a fellowship to Yale but has no money. As Mireille Latil Le Dantec says,

> Despite Marthe's tender affection for her mother, one has never seen such a power of transgression as that conveyed by a splendid parallel montage: in the locked room the tenant undresses Marthe while the footsteps of the mother resound through the tiny apartment. Onto the naked, standing bodies of the two young people falls a "Marthe, my dear" that echoes the "Marie, Marie" of the poor father looking for his daughter lying in the hay with Gérard [in *Au Hasard Balthasar*].[7]

After the couple make love, the young man promises that he will be back in exactly one year; if she is still in love with him, they will get married. As he gets into a taxi to go to the airport, he insists that he will look for her on the Pont-Neuf at night.

There is a last shot of the young man on the escalator at the airport before the film returns to Jacques and Marthe in the present time. A year has passed, but the boarder, who arrived three days ago, still has not appeared. Unselfish, Jacques tries to think about how he can be helpful. He volunteers to go to see the young man, and even improvises the kind of letter she should write to him. It deliberately avoids any effort at coercion: "I would not blame you for forgetting me." Young strolling musicians pass by, playing the song "Mystery Gal." Marthe is pleased with Jacques's response because she has already written a letter along the lines he has described. She asks him to carry it to friends, who will make sure it reaches the former lodger, and who will ask for a reply. Jacques will bring her back the answer the following night. "If it rains . . . but it won't rain."

In a minor reversal typical of Bresson, the sound of rain awakens Jacques the next morning. After a shower, he takes a bus to the address of Marthe's friends. Passengers look at him oddly as he listens to his tape recorder, which keeps repeating Marthe's name in his own voice. He goes up the stairs of a house and leaves Marthe's letter before returning to his own place. He then spends the rest of the day painting, listening to the tape recorder, and lying in bed.

Third Night. When Jacques and Marthe meet again, he tells her he has delivered her letter. She is understandably downcast, since there has been no reply, but she tries to show her gratitude. "I love you because you haven't fallen in love with me," Marthe tells Jacques; she loves him as a brother. The developing relationship between the two young people is played out against a highly romantic background: "Fantastically lighted *bateau-mouches* glide along the river like fabulous spaceships, on excursion from some distant galaxy."[8] We hear Brazilian music as a boat drifts past them. Jacques volunteers to go back to Marthe's friends the next day and find out what has happened. This brings Marthe to reflect aloud on the contrast between Jacques and the man she has been waiting for: "Why can't he be you? Why is he not made like you?" This outburst is used by Le Dantec as an example of the way in which young women in Bresson "are aware that they do not love 'as they are supposed to love.' . . . With Bresson, the wounding of the ego, the sensual love, is far deeper than with Dostoevsky."[9]

In the morning Jacques is again listening to his tape recorder as it keeps repeating Marthe's name. At the door of Marthe's friends he receives only an indefinite response: "Perhaps tomorrow." He sees Marthe's name in a shop window, on the prow of a barge, on the Pont des Arts. The dream atmosphere still envelopes him as he wanders into a public garden: two young couples are embracing, and pigeons are cooing amorously. Jacques even tapes their warbling.

Fourth Night. When Jacques finds Marthe again at the statue of Henri IV, he asks if her young man has come to see her. The answer, obviously, is no, and Marthe has abandoned hope: "He can do what he wants. I'm fed up." She goes down the stairs toward the river, continuing to voice her disappointment at the attitude of the ex-boarder. Jacques moves off in another direction; when she notices this, she asks if something is the matter. "I love you," he declares, "that's what's the matter." There is a pause as they both listen to a singer performing for a group of hippies. Marthe tells Jacques that he deserves to be loved more than the ex-lodger. When they go to a café, she asks him to help her forget the young man she has loved for a whole year. Perhaps she had been drawn to him simply because she wanted to get away from her mother.

Afterwards, they go to a drug store where Jacques buys Marthe a red scarf; she suggests that he rent the empty room in her house. Delighted, he calls her attention to the moonlit sky, but suddenly, in the midst of the passers-by and musicians around them, she recognizes her young man. "It's him," she says with joyful surprise. In response, the young man asks, "Is it you, Marthe?" She runs over and holds him in her arms. Then she comes back to Jacques and kisses him warmly on both cheeks. Finally, she goes off with her young man, leaving Jacques behind; "her red scarf, which disappears into the crowd, symbolizes an impossible love, just as in *The Gentle Woman* the heroine's white scarf was linked to suicide."[10]

Back in his studio, Jacques speaks into his tape recorder: "She sees me from a distance, she flies to meet me. . . . O Marthe, what force makes your eyes gleam with such a flame, and lights up your face with such a smile? Thank you for your love. Be blessed for the happiness you bring me." He listens to the whole monologue while beginning to paint. When it is finished, the only sound to be heard is that of his brush on the canvas.

▬ ALTHOUGH *FOUR NIGHTS OF A DREAMER* IS OBVIOUSLY NOT ONE OF Bresson's major films, it is hard to account for its cool reception by both critics and the general public. In the *New York Times* Roger Greenspun found the movie unique in the director's career "for its opulence, its lyricism, its ordinary ways of feeling and behavior." He recognizes the familiar

Bressonian imagery of imprisonment in the film, but "this time an impris-onment involved with being in love."[11] Nevertheless, it would seem that some reviewers refused to accept Bresson in a less-than-tragic mode; the fact that relatively little has been written about the movie may also be due to the fact that it has been less available. Without making exaggerated claims for *Four Nights*, it's hard to see why it wouldn't give pleasure to anyone who would enjoy walking around Paris at night. The city is more of a presence than in any other movie of Bresson's, with the possible exception of *The Devil Probably* (1977).

Four Nights of a Dreamer is a refreshing contrast to the pseudo-sophisti-cation of so much contemporary cinema. Despite the lack of probability in several aspects of its narrative—especially in the character of the boarder—the idealism implicit in its overall atmosphere could well prove attractive to many young people who may have never heard of Bresson but sense the shal-lowness of contemporary relationships. Many young women, moreover, may respond to Marthe's "Why couldn't he be you?" when the latter complains about the young man who has not returned to claim her, since Guillaume des Forêts (Jacques) is so much handsomer.

There is a wealth of humorous observation as well as careful concentra-tion in Bresson's presentation of his two main characters, as seen particu-larly in Jacques's story and Marthe's story. Jacques certainly can't be called a womanizer, but he is constantly looking for chances to exchange glances with attractive young women. It is entertaining to watch him hunting out his opportunities, especially since he is so easily distracted by a good-looking alternative. This combination of boldness and shyness, both arising from an introspective uneasiness with everyday sociability, also make the scene with his former classmate from art school almost worthy of *Le Misanthrope*. His visitor is so full of himself that he makes no real effort to communicate with his host; meanwhile, Jacques can hardly fathom the pretentious flow of his friend's discussion of art. Though Jacques makes a social effort, and finally offers a bottle of wine, both are happy to make the interview a brief one.

The closed world of Jacques's room is an obvious contrast to the open-air Paris scenes through which he is constantly walking. The tape recorder is the bridge between them. But as Le Dantec notes, "The mastery offered by this talisman is illusory: that of a space without gravity, freedom without obstacle. . . . His monologue in the room, a shell in which the dreamer retreats from the world, is the perfect equivalent of the closed space in which Dostoevsky's dreamer encloses himself."[12] She also refers to Bresson's masterly use of objects and concrete details, which can become so identified with a character as almost to define him:

passers-by, lovers in the square, pigeons, the blaze of the *bateau-mouches*, the close-up of no. 14 on a building, the noise an electric bolt makes, an opening or closing door, together form a universe of desires, one of anxiety and happiness combined, in harmony with the state of mind of the narrator in "White Nights."[13]

For Jean Sémolué, *Four Nights of a Dreamer* concludes with "an opening on the future. Perhaps the sound of the paintbrush, which can be heard after the tape recorder has finished repeating its monologue of love and gratitude, signifies the passage from the dreams of adolescence to the age of creation. Is it Jacques's first adult gesture?" The critic also quotes from an interview in which Bresson declared: "For me, this ending is pessimistic; not sad but bitter. . . . This work, encouraged by illusions, creates an ambiguous ending."[14] Although Bresson never flattens out the meaning of his films, Sémolué's comments are extremely suggestive: "Jacques's almost childish reticence seems sublime at the end. In his ultimate monologue he assimilates himself to the other young man by imagining Marthe coming to him; he reconstructs his relations with the young woman, accepting her union with the other while realizing that she has given him a form of happiness that may be more decisive."[15]

Jonathan Rosenbaum, who was able to observe the director at work while serving as an extra on the film, reports that Bresson "uses non-actors effectively. They speak their thought simply without any facial emotion, which gives them greater impact, enhanced by the fluid pacing, the telling dialogue, and the extra technical knowhow that is never intrusive or used for its own sake."[16] However, the broader appeal of *Four Nights of a Dreamer* is perhaps best summarized in Pierre Marcabru's review in *Elle*: "Young people have rarely been described so well—stubborn, unsure of themselves, vulnerable; the fragility of beings has rarely been presented so powerfully. . . . *Four Nights of a Dreamer* is bewitching yet true, outside of time yet in the real world, a crazy movie that Bresson signs just as a painter signs his canvas."[17]

NOTES

1. Interview in *Le Monde*, November 11, 1971.

2. Fyodor Dostoevsky, "White Nights," in *The Short Stories of Dostoevsky*, ed. William Phillips (New York: Dial Press, 1946), 305.

3. Robert Bresson, *Amis du film et de la télévision* no. 185 (October 1971).

4. The scene reminds Jean Sémolué of the episode in *The Ladies of the Bois de Boulogne*, in which Hélène, rushing down the stairs, pursues Jean, who is in the

closed cage of a descending elevator (*Bresson ou l'acte pur des Métamorphoses* [Paris: Flammarion, 1993], 193).

5. Roger Greenspun, *New York Times*, November 26, 1972.

6. Michel Estève, *Robert Bresson* (Paris: Editions Albatros, 1983), 71.

7. Mireille Latil Le Dantec, "Bresson, Dostoevsky," in *Robert Bresson*, ed. James Quandt (Toronto: Cinematheque Ontario, 1998), 330.

8. Greenspun, *New York Times*, November 26, 1972.

9. Estève, *Robert Bresson*, 72.

10. Le Dantec, "Bresson, Dostoevsky," 330.

11. Greenspun, *New York Times*, November 26, 1972.

12. Mireille Latil Le Dantec, "Une nouvelle et deux films," third cycle thesis, defended at the University of Paris X, 1982, 19, as cited by Estève, *Robert Bresson*, 69.

13. Le Dantec, "Bresson, Dostoevsky," 333.

14. Jean Sémolué, *Bresson ou l'acte pur des Métamorphoses* (Paris: Flammarion, 1993), 201.

15. Ibid., 199.

16. Jonathan Rosenbaum, *Village Voice*, June 17, 1971.

17. Pierre Macabru, *Elle*, February 21, 1972, in *Robert Bresson: Éloge* (Paris: Cinémathèque français, 1997), 54.

11

The End of Knighthood

Lancelot of the Lake

LANCELOT OF THE LAKE WAS A PROJECT BRESSON HAD LONG dreamed of; he first hoped to work on it even before *A Man Escaped*. It is a purely speculative question as to how different the movie would have been if he had made it in the mid-1950s; the only thing that can be said for sure is that it would have been in black and white. Successive delays in acquiring financial support for his proposal to deal with the Arthurian legend at least meant that Bresson had the opportunity to become experienced in working with color. He was probably glad to interrupt the adaptation of the work of others and develop his own scenario without worrying about questions of "fidelity." Bresson was undoubtedly familiar with Chrétien de Troyes's *Lancelot, ou le chevalier de la charrette* and *Le roman de Perceval ou le conte de Graal*, as well as *La Mort du Roi Artur*, composed around 1230 by an unknown author. He could also assume a general knowledge of the Grail legend, the idea of the Round Table, and the love between Lancelot and Guinevere. As Jeff Rider suggests, however, Arthurian legend plays a different role in France than in England or the United States. "A French audience today associates the Arthurian legend with artistic greatness rather than with the thwarted imperial destiny of a pseudo-historical king."[1]

King Arthur and his knights have, of course, been part of the western European imagination since the thirteenth century. They were figures of a misty past from the beginning, since the real Arthur is supposed to have lived at the end of the fifth or the beginning of the sixth century. As with *The Trial of Joan of Arc*, although he wished to suggest the spirit of an earlier age, Bresson was not aiming at historical accuracy. Nor had he ever intended to draw on the spectacular or fairy-tale elements of his material; "I am going to try to transpose this fairy-tale aspect into the domain of feelings—that is, to show how feelings modify the very air we breathe."[2] The result reinforces the comments of Michel Estève:

> Stripped of the dross of false realism, the Middle Ages presented to us [in *Lancelot*] is in accord with our time, and a dialectic of the temporal (the time of legend) and the a-temporal (our own age, and the one to come), or past and present, gives to the testimony of the author a character that is both universal and exemplary. On the level of customs or costumes (the fighting dress of the knights, the duels, the preparation and unfolding of the tournament, even the way of mounting a horse), the spiritual and psychological climate (fear of God, union of mystical and carnal love, obsession with the woman, courtly love) of the age, *Lancelot* revives the chivalry of the thirteenth century, but in many ways the mentalities presented and the quest pursued are also our own.[3]

This means that there is no effort to make sure that the clothes, the knights' tents, or even the Round Table are authentically of the period. An atmosphere is established by shields and banners, the music of drums and fifes, and men in full armor riding splendid horses; studio sets are avoided in favor of real backgrounds at Noirmoutier, a forest near the abbey of Grainetière, in the area of western France called the Vendée. Most anachronisms, like the chess game Mordred plays with one of his followers, present no problems. On the other hand, armor, which seems a requirement of the material, has disadvantages as well as advantages. It provides the opportunity for some striking images of knights on horseback, and the opening and closing of visors, but it also makes clanking noises that make the action seem somewhat ridiculous when supposedly wounded knights fall off their horses and pile up on the ground in a heap.

Understandably, the Arthurian material has extra appeal for those who lament the crassness and limitations of modernity; Chrétien de Troyes's version even tries to enhance the attractiveness of feudalism. Whatever appeal these stories may have held for Bresson as a boy, the most striking thing about *Lancelot* is that it presents the age of knighthood without its patina of glamour, at the very moment it is coming to an end. In *Positif*, a journal often resistant to Bresson's approach to film, Barthélemy Amengual recognized the special suitability of the material for the director:

> The painter recognizes in medieval illumination. . . the very form of his art. Doesn't illumination, like Bresson, excel in signifying, in arousing more by less? Through the elimination, conciseness, and elliptical violence customary with him, Bresson revives in its physical status a culture and an obscure world that is manipulated by mystery and the invisible. . . . Bresson insists on flattening this marvelous quest, with its lyrical combats and adventurous

challenges, into exercises, ritual, interior debate, and exalted gestures, almost formalities. But here this formalism is inspired, since it blends with the fundamental formalism of chivalry. . . . A game of chess and a tournament—indeed, the entire film, is conceived as an ordered and moral game, a bullfight, a judgment of God.[4]

One could easily maintain that the age of chivalry has ended even before the beginning of the film: the very first shots of *Lancelot* offer a succession of destructive images. The knights are killing each other. Heads are cut off, bodies hang from trees; sacred objects are swept off an altar, and blood seems to gush everywhere. It is not simply a matter of the knights having met with some disaster; they have abandoned their vocation, which involved the search for the Grail. The Grail was the magic cup, preserved in an obscure castle in Brittany, in which Joseph of Arimathea had preserved the blood of Christ. Hence it was linked with the mystery of both the incarnation and the redemption. A text at the very beginning of the film, before the credits, summarizes the essentials of this legend:

> After a series of adventures which draw on the marvelous and in which Lancelot of the Lake was the hero, the knights of King Arthur, known as "the knights of the Round Table," set out in pursuit of the Grail. . . . Merlin the enchanter, before dying, vowed the knights to this holy adventure. . . . Two years have passed. The knights return to the castle of King Arthur and Queen Guinevere, decimated and without having found the Grail.

This prologue is spelled out in letters of blood red, unfolding on the image of a chalice, and accompanied by the music of fife and drum. The action to follow will show the collapse of the knightly ideal; we are left to speculate as to the reasons for its failure.

━━━AFTER THE PROLOGUE WE HEAR THE STEPS OF A HORSE. A PEASANT woman tells a little girl that the man whose steps we are about to hear will soon be dead. A knight appears; he says he has lost his way. The woman informs him that he has come to Escalot. A close-up of a horse's eye precedes a shot of the peasant hovel, which remains in the background of the credits, and the music returns.

Night has fallen when the knight arrives back at the castle. He raises his visor and is recognized as Lancelot by Gawain, a nephew of the king and Lancelot's greatest admirer. King Arthur joins them, and welcomes Lancelot with the reversal of the biblical tag: "The first is the last to arrive." A horse whinnies; once again there is an unnerving close-up of his eye. As the knights put their belongings away in the tents, there is a commotion in the stables. Lancelot sadly acknowledges to Arthur that he has not brought back the Grail; the king instructs an aide to tell the queen that her knight has returned.

Bells ring, horses are drinking. When Lancelot emerges from his tent to ask if the signal for mass has been given, he is told the three knocks have not yet sounded. He enters a small barnlike building in the nearby wood and kneels before Guinevere. As she kisses him, she declares, "Nothing shall take you from me again." She asks for his hand and notices with dismay that he is no longer wearing the ring she had given him. He tries to tell her of an experience during his search for the Grail: a voice had challenged him, accusing him of deceit and treachery. Chastened, he swore no longer to be her lover. In response, she reminds him of another vow, one that ties him to her. "Free me from that vow," he implores. Later, when Lancelot kneels at mass in the chapel, Guinevere is present, wearing her crown and observing him closely.

Afterwards, King Arthur meets with his knights. He tells them he has decided to dismantle the Round Table; they will not meet again as a formal group. Although the king does not assign individual blame for the failure to find the Grail, he tells them that "we have provoked God . . . he has forsaken us." The knights are unsure about how to proceed: What if God no longer guides us? Arthur's counsel is for them to remain united: "Discipline yourselves; perfect yourselves." Back in their tents, Gawain indicates his impatience with such counsel. He is further dismayed that Lancelot speaks of trying to disarm the hostility of Mordred, another nephew of the king, for whom Gawain has only contempt.

Encountering the queen in the castle, Gawain tells her Lancelot has become a saint. Later, when he begs the king, "Give us a purpose," he is frustrated by simply being instructed to pray.

In a second meeting with Lancelot, Guinevere is still unsuccessful in winning him back. "God does not ask us to forswear the vows we have pronounced," she reminds him, as he walks back and forth restlessly. "I am the one created to help you," she pleads, "is it my fault that I cannot live without you?" She accuses him of remaining shut up in his pride and insists that God cannot separate them. Guinevere is quite aware that the knights have not lived up to their ideals—they have pillaged, set fires, even murdered—and uncovers the fundamental fallacy in their quest: "God is not a trophy to bring home." As they leave, there is a shot of the hay on the floor of the barn where they have been speaking, and we notice that she has left her scarf on the bench.

Outside, many of the knights are looking up at Guinevere's window, the moon appears, and the clouds retreat. Lancelot goes to Mordred's tent, where the queen's scarf is visible, though he does not notice it. Lancelot tries to speak healing words and even offers his right hand as a gesture of reconciliation, but Mordred does not accept it. Back in Lancelot's tent, Gawain does not understand how his friend can put up with Mordred's insolence and worries that his brother Agravain and some other knights have come to support their enemy. Appreciative of his loyalty, Lancelot gives Gawain his favorite harness. In the midst of his interior struggle, he goes into the chapel to pray: "Do not forsake us."

A new center of interest emerges: knights come riding through the trees, bearing the flag of Escalot. They offer a challenge to Arthur, Gawain, and Lancelot: a tournament will take place in two weeks. The process of preparation is shown in detail: training in using a spear, target practice with a dummy, and so on. Lancelot notices that Gawain, like the other knights, watches the high window of the queen. "Guinevere is our only woman, our sun," his young friend answers.

The queen calls Lancelot to a third meeting, again in the loft of the lodge. "I know everything is over but I wanted to see you one last time and then leave you." Lancelot lets his arms and armor fall to the ground and they embrace. "Take this forbidden body," the queen declares, "revive it." Through the window they hear the sounds of Mordred and his confederates drawing close, then withdrawing. Lancelot's response is simply to say he is unafraid; he must stand his ground. Guinevere, however, warns him not to go to the tournament; he should avoid danger and use the occasion to join her in her room. A sense of imminent crisis arises as, close to the queen's quarters, Mordred shows some of his followers where they can hide in order to surprise Lancelot and kill him.

As the knights are about to leave for the tournament, Lancelot has not yet arrived, causing considerable comment. He suddenly appears and announces that he is not taking part, disappointing Gawain and eliciting Mordred's sarcasm. The camera focuses on visors closing and the movement of horses' legs as Arthur and his men mount and leave for the tournament. Mordred's followers, who are on the lookout for Lancelot, see Guinevere's serving women enter the queen's room. The servants bathe her while the queen looks at herself in a small mirror.

At night in his tent, Lancelot takes the queen's ring and kisses it; he then orders his squire to prepare his white shield and saddle his chestnut horse. "Pardon, my love," he murmurs, "it is necessary." A shot of the light shining in Guinevere's room as the servants brush her hair is followed by the sound of Lancelot's horse galloping to the tournament. In the forest, as Arthur and his knights are en route to the tournament, Mordred accuses Lancelot of loving the queen. Gawain replies angrily that he is a liar.

At Escalot, Arthur and Gawain observe the jousting. We see the strength of the horses' legs and hear the fife music. Then an unknown white knight arrives who knocks all his adversaries to the ground, including Mordred. Impressed by this feat, Gawain is sure the white knight who has suddenly departed is Lancelot. In the forest, meanwhile, we see Lancelot fall from his horse, bleeding.

When they return from the tournament, Arthur and his knights are still unsure about the unidentified combatant: "Was it Lancelot?" Back at the castle, Gawain runs to tell the queen that Lancelot was the victor at the games, but that Lionel fears he is wounded. Some of the knights go out to look for Lancelot, but do not find him. "Some force is manipulating us," they complain. The wind and the rain shake the door of Guinevere's room, where she lies in bed, weeping.

The next morning many of the knights are afraid that Lancelot is dead. Mordred is playing chess in his tent; Gawain comes in and accuses him of cheating. Somehow a fight between them is avoided, although Mordred refuses to back down. Gawain goes to Guinevere in her lodge and returns her scarf, which he had found in Mordred's tent. He reports that Mordred accuses her of returning to the lodge because it reminds her of her criminal love. She is indifferent to the accusation; she admits she loves Lancelot and senses that he is still alive. The king arrives with some of his knights, but Gawain begs him not to judge Guinevere.

Three knights set out to search again for Lancelot; they come across the old woman who had seen him at the opening of the film but she refuses to answer their questions. She has been nursing Lancelot in her hut and warns him that if he leaves he will die. He is unmoved; the little girl who helps him get ready kisses the ground when he gallops away. Arriving at the castle where the queen is now held prisoner, Lancelot breaks through the doors. Covered with blood, he takes Guinevere in his arms, and they go off together on horseback.

Lancelot learns that while rescuing the queen he has killed Agravain, the brother of Gawain. Feeling that he must attack anyone who approaches, he strikes out blindly, and without knowing it wounds Gawain himself, his most faithful follower. When the king comes to Gawain's bedside as he is dying, however, the loyal friend insists that Lancelot is not to blame and begs Arthur not to judge the queen.

Back in his own castle, Lancelot learns that Gawain is dead and that the king is willing to take Guinevere back if Lancelot will bring her to him. The queen exhorts her knight to submit: "We have a great deal to atone for." This time it is Lancelot's turn to insist on the vows they had sworn: How can it be said that "the woman that was made for me is not made for me?" What Guinevere asks may be right but "right is not justice." He tries to sum up the meaning of his life: "I crave the impossible." Finally, however, he consents to take Guinevere back to Arthur under a white flag of truce. "I will look neither to the right nor the left," Guinevere says, and they make the long walk, hand in hand, to the royal tent. Halfway there, she leaves Lancelot and continues alone, places her hand on that of Arthur, and enters the king's tent with her husband.

When he returns to his castle and learns that Mordred has launched a rebellion against the king, Lancelot rallies his followers: "For Arthur, against Mordred!" High above the woods, columns of smoke appear. Among the trees, a riderless horse gallops aimlessly past wounded knights. The same horse passes again and again, and the music that had been heard during the credits is repeated. Archers positioned in the trees take deadly aim at the knights and their horses, and both men and animals are quickly revealed as easy targets. Men in armor pile up on the ground, including the king. One of the knights manages to get up after a great effort—it is Lancelot, who cries, "Guinevere," and falls down again, In the sky a bird wheels high above the heap of armor lying on the ground, and the film ends in silence.

▬— ALTHOUGH *LANCELOT* DISPLAYS THE TOTAL COLLAPSE OF A PROUDLY proclaimed ideal—and indeed of a whole civilization—it is not simply a cry of despair. Its sheer physical beauty hardly needs demonstration. Emmanuel Machuel, who was the film's assistant photographer—and also worked on *Balthasar, Mouchette, A Gentle Woman,* and *L'Argent*—said that he would give it first place for photography among all of Bresson's films.[5] The colors are so dark that it may take a while to realize that the film is in color; the browns and blacks are found in every shade, making the queen's long blue robe all the more striking. Machuel observes that while Bresson had always been concerned to avoid lighting effects, working in color made this effort easier. "*Lancelot* shows especially well this total absence of effects due to color; there is no backlighting and faces are lit with exemplary sobriety. Lamps and projects were employed with great delicacy. It was necessary to eliminate everything that was artificial."[6]

Rider describes the lighting as "simultaneously naturalistic and significant. It is generally low-key (dim and subdued) and diffused. The only high-key scenes in the film (scenes with bright even lighting) are those in the tournament sequence, and this contrast makes these rounds of civil violence in the sun the visual opposite of the dark forest in which the knights meet their fated end."[7] As Bresson always insisted, it is a matter of seeing images in relation to each other; a shot-by-shot analysis would be needed to show in detail what he and his director of photography, Pasqualo De Sanctis, accomplished.

The film's visual subtleties are always in the service of its tragic theme, announced from the beginning, in which the demands of love-passion, an insistence on loyalty, and a search for the impossible combine to make death inevitable. Of course, many commentators rightly point to the sudden and unexplained appearance of the archers as confirming the inadequacy of the older warrior ideal, but Lancelot is doomed long before that. Although the film can be used to support the conventional characterization of Bresson as austere, this should not be understood to mean that *Lancelot of the Lake* is simply bleak and cynical. The love of Guinevere and Lancelot is genuine and profound. Lancelot, who feels responsible for the failure of the knights' quest, at first resists the queen's reminders of his earlier vow to her and calls on God's help to give him the strength to leave her. At the end, after accepting the painful necessity of bringing Guinevere back to the king, he responds instantaneously to the uprising against Arthur, a final proof of generosity and loyalty. Guinevere, too, is a figure of poignancy; despite her youth, she shows dignity and an adult sense of her own value. (From the evidence presented in the film, we cannot judge whether or not she is justified in her disdain for the king.) Finally, there is Gawain, Lancelot's faithful ally, who tells the king not to judge his wife and refuses to blame his friend for the fatal sword-thrust that costs him his life. Imperfect and hotheaded, he nevertheless embodies much of what was best about the Round Table, especially its sense of genuine fellowship.

Connecting the story of Lancelot and Guinevere with that of Tristan and Isolde, Estève emphasizes that its pattern is in conformity with the reality of courtly love studied in Denis De Rougemont's *Love in the Western World*: "The fundamental rule of courtly love is opposed to having such a love become reality–i.e., to end up in full possession of the lady. . . . he and Guinevere act like Tristan and Isolde, as if they had understood that everything that is opposed to love consecrates it in their heart and exalts it in that instant of absolute obedience which is death."[8]

Lancelot may be Bresson's most complete demonstration of the deliberate elimination of excess and ornamentation that governed his approach to film. Julien Gracq praises his refusal to load his work with second-rate medieval antiquities, simultaneously preserving just what a Hollywood spectacle would have eliminated:

> What survives of this massacre, strangely, or what surges from it new and never before seen, is what the novels about the Round Table themselves never show. Blood. Wounds. Fatigue. Mud. The brutality of the clash. . . . And floating about the Round Table an air of rugged and ruined nobility that remains verdant despite the imminent ruin. Not the great hall with its tapestries, the cathedrals, the trumpets and the banners, but a tent the rain goes through, the hay barn, the wobbly ladder, Guinevere's peasant room littered with straw, whose latch shakes and where the wind blows through cracks in the wall. One of the extraordinary things about the film—and a good part of its impact on the spectator—is there, in what we don't dare to call—since the two words protest being placed side by side—its arthurian realism: the materialization, without any connivance with magic, almost poor in its lack of ornamentation, of a story that has never had a model or real locality, which since its birth has never had any other climate than that of myth, nor any dwelling place but the wings of imagination.[9]

As usual, the soundtrack merits extended study; Jeff Rider's comments support Gracq's paradoxical claim:

> Many of the sound effects have an unnatural quality, yet Bresson uses them in ways that pretend to invoke a naturalistic ambience. This technique gives the illusion of a natural setting: the audience hears horses whinny and gallop, hears the knights' armor clanking as they walk, hears an earthenware vessel being emptied. Some of these sounds are anchored visually; others are not. The sounds have been so elaborately constructed and enriched, however, that they take on a life and significance of their own when the audience hears them, bold and alone, on the soundtrack. The whinnies that one hears, off screen, for example, are not intended to make us believe in the presence of off-screen horses. They are hyper-real intrusions that create a sense of anxiety and hidden meaning, both because one cannot attach them to anything in the film and because their peculiar quality undermines their credibility. The clanking cacophony of armor similarly serves to enhance this impression.[10]

As for the dialogues between Lancelot and Guinevere, which constitute the heart of the film, they are worthy of high tragedy. The vocabulary is as simple as that of Racine; the carefully balanced lines recall the thrust and riposte of Sophoclean *stichomythia*. Pronounced in a near monotone by Bresson's models, these exchanges—at least for those who can follow the French —communicate with far greater power than the histrionic love scenes found in most plays and movies.

All this supports René Prédal's emphasis on *Lancelot* as a poem. He emphasizes its plastic and sonorous leitmotifs,

> such as blood, gestures, lances, the changing reflections from armor (whether in darkness, candles, or daylight), the groaning of horses (their eyes, hind-quarters, and nostrils). In order to find a modern equivalent to the richness of the original texts Bresson dissociates the meaning from the aesthetic, the soundtrack from the image, "verses" and "rimes" no longer being (as in Eric Rohmer's *Perceval*) in the text but in the resonant and visual material of cinematographic language, appearing, for example, in the dazzling image of blood sweating from the interstices of the iron armor: the inspired visualization of the human death of an order.[11]

Estève points out the paradoxical position of *Lancelot* in comparison with Bresson's other films containing explicitly religious subject matter:

> *Lancelot* is the one in which the presence of God is least felt. The fundamental project of the hero, the prayers and oaths of Lancelot and Arthur, the conversations of the knights, the evocation of Mass, Lancelot's offer of reconciliation to Mordred . . . all suggest a Christian vision of the world. But to evoke the celebrated search for the Grail, Bresson opens the story with shots of duels and the sacking of a church altar which show more iconoclastic violence than mystical aspiration. Invoked, prayed to, supplicated, God never responds.[12]

But this is by no means to say that the film leaves us in a mood of total pessimism. Bresson ignores the pious endings of *La Mort du Roi Artur*, in which Guinevere becomes a nun after Arthur is killed, and Lancelot a priest after the death of the queen. Instead, he gives us Gawain's last words of affection for Lancelot and the royal couple and emphasizes that Lancelot carries out the vow that the queen had reminded him of in the grange, "For you, I prefer death to life." As Jean Sémolué concludes, "The voyage to the end of disaster does not lead the hero to deny what he holds as most dear."[13] We should recall that when the knights are looking in vain for Lancelot, they say, "Some force is manipulating us," a line that prefigures the theme of Bresson's next movie, *The Devil Probably*. But although there is little sense of liberation and God does not work a miracle to prevent the victory of the archers over an older civilization, it is worth recalling Bresson's cautionary response to parallel concerns voiced after *Au hasard Balthasar*: "If I succeed through the means of cinematography, in representing a human being . . . someone who is not a marionette who wriggles, if there is a human presence, there is a divine presence."

NOTES

1. Jeff Rider, *Cinema Arthurian: Essays on Arthurian Film* (New York: Garland, 1991), 43.
2. Interview with Jean-Luc Godard and Michel Delahaye, *Cahiers du cinéma* no. 178 (May 1966).
3. Michel Estève, *Robert Bresson* (Paris: Editions Albatros, 1983), 78.
4. Barthélemy Amengual, *Positif* (October 1974): 55.
5. See the interview with Emmanuel Machuel at the conclusion of the book by Philippe Arnaud, *Robert Bresson* (Paris: Cahiers du Cinéma, 1986).
6. Emmanuel Machuel, "Ce que l'on voit dans le caméra," *Cahiers du cinéma,* "Hommage à Bresson" (January 2000): 16.
7. Rider, *Cinema Arthurian,* 48.
8. Estève, *Robert Bresson,* 77.
9. Julien Gracq, "Un compagnonnage d'exception," *Les nouvelles littéraires,* September 23, 1974.
10. Rider, *Cinema Arthurian,* 45.
11. René Prédal, "Robert Bresson: L'aventure intérieure," *L'Avant-scène cinéma* (January-February 1992): 105.
12. Estève, *Robert Bresson,* 78.
13. Jean Sémolué, *Bresson ou l'acte pur des Métamorphoses* (Paris: Flammarion, 1993), 226.

12

Apocalypse Now

The Devil Probably

"OF ALL MY FILMS," BRESSON CONCEDES, *THE DEVIL PROBABLY* (1977) is "the most ghastly. But none of them are despairing."[1] A courageous indictment of the forces in contemporary society that are hastening the destruction of humanity—and indeed, of the universe—the movie begins with two contradictory newspaper accounts of the suicide of its central figure, Charles. The next ninety-five minutes are a flashback covering the previous six months, during which Charles sees no reason to continue living and is looking for a way to end his life.

In making the majority of his movies, Bresson adapted literary texts with imagination and growing independence; such a starting point left him free to concentrate on the relation of narrative structure to the needs of cinematography. Prior to *The Devil Probably*, his only original screenplays had been for *Angels of Sin*, in which the dialogue was by Jean Giraudoux; *Pickpocket*, which contained some parallels with *Crime and Punishment*; *Au hasard Balthasar*, perhaps his most personal work; and *Lancelot of the Lake*, which drew on medieval sources.

In composing *The Devil Probably* Bresson shows a profound concern about the deadly, ongoing pollution of the entire world. In one sequence Charles's closest friend, a young ecologist named Michel, at a meeting sponsored by the Association for the Safeguard of Humanity and the Environment, presents powerful film footage, accompanied by alarming statistics, that reveals what a dangerous direction humanity has taken. A television program announces that new "superior" weapons of mass destruction are being developed, and we discover that Charles's wealthy father is a contractor employed in the destruction of forests.

Although we assume that Charles's despair is confirmed by his awareness of these developments, his sense of total alienation seems to exist independently of such factors, almost as a given of his personality and destiny; no external cause seems adequate to account for it. Early in the film he attends a meeting of young people, where the speakers appeal for violence. This could be interpreted as a darkly humorous critique of the lack of a serious political opposition to the status quo in France (and elsewhere) at that time, but despite the sympathetic presentation of Michel, one gets no sense that group political action has any meaning. To the extent that Bresson is successful in reminding his audience of the desperate problems being raised, he is also implicitly critical of his young main characters, who are, after all, privileged members of the upper middle class. Since the director always emphasized the importance of the voices of those he chose as models, several critics understandably complained that the accents of the chief interpreters in *The Devil Probably* reveal their comfortable backgrounds in Paris's wealthy sixteenth *arrondissement*.

Nevertheless, Bresson's criticism of the direction of contemporary society possesses considerable power. If the radicals at the political meeting early in the movie seem largely caricatures, the emptiness of the attempt to communicate the Gospel message during the succeeding scene in church is almost painfully convincing. Of course, Bresson is deliberately offering "a fragment," not a carefully researched survey of the subjects touched on; the sample is insufficient for us to decide whether this proclamation of a "contemporary Christianity" is merely the voice of clerical pseudo-intellectualism or is meant to suggest the overall superficiality of post–Vatican II rhetoric.[2]

None of this should suggest that Bresson's angle of vision in *The Devil Probably* is that of a crank looking back sentimentally at "the good old days." Instead, we are reminded of the fondness with which Bresson regards young people, already evident in *Balthasar, Mouchette,* and *Four Nights of a Dreamer.* The long-haired, aristocratic Charles, a brilliant university dropout, is an object of desire to good-looking young women in great part because of the purity with which he rejects the world. In contrast, parents are absent from the film and seemingly indifferent; as presented here, the major institutions for social stability and renewal—family, government, and religion—have essentially abandoned the new generation.

The title of the movie repeats the phrase heard on a bus taken by Charles and Michel, during which complaining passengers ask who is controlling our actions without our knowledge. Recalling Bresson's fondness for Dostoevsky, it is worth repeating a few lines of Ivan's exchange with his father in *The Brothers Karamazov,* which come just after Ivan has insisted that there is no God:

> "Then who is laughing at mankind, Ivan?"
> "Must be the devil," Ivan smirked.
> "And is there a devil?"
> "No, there is no devil, either."[3]

It hardly needs to be said that Ivan does not represent Bresson's point of view or that the movie's "devil" does not emerge from fundamentalist nightmares about the end of the world. What may seem surprising is that there are no obviously evil characters in the film, like Mordred in *Lancelot* or Gérard in *Au hasard Balthasar.* Charles says he is not attracted by death; he simply sees no reason to go on living. In many of his criticisms of modern life he is presenting a more absolutist version of what seem like Bresson's views; in his session with the psychoanalyst late in the film, he does not deny God but simply says he does not expect to be blamed for "not comprehending the incomprehensible."

One needs to remember, in any case, that though Bresson made the movie as a warning against dangerous directions in contemporary society, he is not arguing a thesis or presenting an alternate plan of action. He remains, above all, an artist continuing his research on what cinematography can express in a way that no other art can. *The Devil Probably* emerges out of darkness and closes in the same way; its sounds and images, the blank glances of its main characters, all reinforce an atmosphere in which its themes can reverberate with power. J. Hoberman points out that the movie "maintains its formal rigor through Bresson's geometric interest in fragmenting his actors—isolating their feet or truncating their gestures. The close-ups of hands trafficking in drugs by the Seine affords the sort of transaction he revels in."[4] In Michel Estève's judgment, it is "a film of emptiness, cold, and gloom. We see bare walls, smooth objects and surfaces; the dominant tonality is that of night."[5] It would appear that Bresson has deliberately chosen a different kind of narrative strategy for this film. Jean Sémolué describes its construction as

> more a medley than a strict sequence; more a juxtaposition than an interlacing of situations. . . . The system put in place is less a tragic process of contradictory decisions that produce a fatal result than an alternation of equivalent and interchangeable decisions.
>
>   In the composition of *The Devil Probably* there is neither the straight line created by the undertaking of the protagonist and establishing its continuity through the ellipses themselves . . . nor the vortex that either brings the characters together or violently separates them.[6]

There is no line of inevitable development: Charles doesn't come to some climactic disillusionment, but is oriented to suicide from the outset. Since Bresson doesn't clearly identify the physical locale of the scenes he is shooting, and the shifts between the fragments he includes are so abrupt as to often seem arbitrary, the following summary of the action may be fully comprehensible only after viewing the film.

━━ WE SEE LIGHTS ON THE DARK WATER—PRESUMABLY OF THE SEINE— and a *bateau-mouche* moves from left to right. Then, after the credits, the previously mentioned newspaper stories about Charles's death appear on the screen. A title intervenes: "Six months earlier," followed by brief segments highlighting widespread desperation and the apparent impossibility of finding any significant response to the problems presented.

The opening scene shows young people along the Seine conducting a comically earnest conversation about the best way to walk. The action then shifts to a political meeting at which the speaker is roundly cheered as he calls for acts of destruction. Unmoved, Charles mutters an insult and leaves. Finally, at a gathering of the Association for the Safeguard of Humanity and the Environment, Michel and two ecologist collaborators show a frightening film documentary, with shots of tankers leaking effluvients, seals being butchered, and so on, which add up to a strong indictment of "the destruction of entire species for profit."

After thus establishing the movie's underlying mood, Bresson pursues the central story of Charles and his friends, including two young women, Alberte and Edwige, both of whom are ready to offer him needed emotional support. As Alberte leaves her apartment, Michel, who is in love with her, pleads with her not to go: "You are going to break your parents' hearts." Alberte feels she can't help it: she loves Michel but "he [Charles] asked me to be here at five o'clock and I am." Edwige and Charles arrive in a car, and Alberte goes off with them. Edwige, who is also in love with Charles, drops him and Alberte off at his building. They climb the stairs, walk through a rundown apartment full of empty bottles, and collapse in bed laughing.

Bresson then takes us to a meeting at the church of St. Eustache, undermining its seriousness by including the competing sounds of a vacuum cleaner and the organ that is being tuned. It is hard to understand the motives of the young people in attendance, but the discussion consists mostly of tag-lines of tired religious discourse. The statement that the Christianity of the future will be one without religion may suggest that the group has a sympathy for "the option for the poor," an objective popularized by the Latin American liberation theology of that era. Someone quotes Victor

Hugo to the effect that God disappears as soon as priests appear; the clerical speaker advocates the presentation of a more logical Christianity, only to be told that all religions are illogical. The inconclusive rhetoric and competing sounds suggest that Bresson finds the church discourse little better than the earlier political meeting; in any case, Charles and his friends soon leave.

The world of contemporary sophistication is presented in equally depressing terms. At an intellectual bookstore Charles reproaches the self-satisfied owner for using Edwige as a model for pornographic pictures—which have already been seen in publications sold at St. Eustache. He waits outside as Edwige has a session with the bookseller, who is shown reading *Le Monde*. As she leaves, Edwige tells the man there is something ridiculous about him. The sequence, far from being shocking, emphasizes the tired quality of much fashionable intellectualism.

Back at Charles's place, Alberte shows Michel a container of cyanide she has found there. She has also run across a page on which he had copied a citation from *The Brothers Karamazov*: "When will I kill myself, if not now?"[7] On Charles's return, however, he simply takes her in his arms.

At the Pont-Neuf Charles gives some quick advice on mathematics to a lycée student but rejects the idea of offering paid lessons. Encountering Michel, Charles asks him, "Who do I love more—Edwige or Alberte?" At the apartment, Alberte asks Michel to stop intervening. When Michel takes Charles for a drive, they encounter another ecological horror—some huge ancient trees are being systematically cut down.

Back in Paris Michel and his assistants make a presentation of images of destruction due to pollution. Michel, who still sees a reason to go on living, tells Charles that "he wants to be exceptional in an exceptional world," but the latter says he just wants to enjoy things like a brute, and joins a young woman hailing him from a passing car.

Charles's fixation on death is reemphasized when he is shown stepping out of a bathtub after an unsuccessful attempt at suicide. Opening the door to the young woman who was knocking, he says, "You can't put your head at the bottom of the water and just wait." After handing him his clothes and a box of chocolates, she pushes him out on the landing, crying "Imbecile."

Walking along the quai de la Seine, Charles shows the box of chocolates to Michel. The latter goes to Charles's place, where Alberte tells him she has the keys to her parents' apartment and is going there for what she needs. She says that Charles wants to live with Edwige in the absence of the latter's parents. When Alberte shows Michel the chocolates Charles brought her, Michel throws the box out the window, and cars run over it.

In the bookstore there is a display of Michel's book on ecology. He tells Alberte this is because the owner wants to please her. He waits for her in front of her parents' apartment while she cleans out the refrigerator.

At night on the quai de la Seine Charles's preoccupation with death is again highlighted when he wanders off with a revolver that a hippie tells him is for sale. When the latter goes to look for him, however, Charles is firing harmlessly into the water.

Charles tells Michel he is going to marry Alberte. The illogic of personal relations is paralleled by the blindness of a university lecturer who assures his audience that nuclear energy presents no dangers. Afterwards, Charles and Michel get on a bus and continue their conversation. As previously noted, it is during this bus ride that one of the other passengers asks, "Who, then, is maneuvering us on the sly?" After the answer—echoing the movie's title, "The devil probably"—the bus collides noisily with another vehicle and the scene ends abruptly.

Edwige and Alberte are still unsure what Charles is going to decide. When the book-seller/pornographer tries to involve Alberte, she flatly rejects him: "To hell with your money."

Valentin, who turns out to be someone Charles had known earlier, steals some fruit and begins to run away. Charles and Edwige, who happen to be driving by, pick him up and take him to Edwige's. He is broke and on drugs; after they make him eat, he goes to sleep. Later, Charles and Valentin gather together the pieces of a high fidelity set, sleeping bags, and a disk; before they leave the apartment, Valentin shoots up. They go to the church of St. Eustache , where they play a recording of Monteverdi's "Ego Dormio" in the nave while stretched out on their sleeping bags. Valentin, however, gets up, succeeds in breaking open a few offertory boxes, and disappears after filling his pockets. Police soon arrive, and Charles is brought to the police station for questioning.

At Edwige's, Charles seems especially depressed. She speaks to Michel about a well-known psychoanalyst, Dr. Mime, whom she believes represents a last-ditch hope of curing their friend. After Alberte and Michel leave, the former breaks down, acknowledging her long-suppressed affection. "Can you ever pardon me?" she asks Michel. They embrace.

In a well-furnished office, Charles answers the analyst's questions. There is dark humor in his discussion of present-day society and its trivialized menu of available pleasures. (By calling the office during the appointment, Edwige confirms the fact that Charles is there, and informs Alberte and Michel.) Charles tells the doctor he has found it difficult to do away with himself. The analyst, who seems mostly a caricature, asks him about spankings he may have been given as a child. Charles, who has noticed the wad of bank notes in the analyst's drawer, insists he does not desire to die; he "detests death as much as life." The doctor informs him that Romans dealt with Charles's problem by asking a slave or one of their friends to kill them, and tells his patient that the fee for the session is 300 francs. (At this point, a little too neatly, Edwige again calls her friends, "He is saved!")

All that remains is for Charles to carry out the analyst's suggestion. After taking some bills from a desk in Edwige's apartment, he gives the money to a young man at the quai de la Seine to purchase a revolver. With the revolver, he goes and wakes up Valentin, offering him a considerable sum of money if "you will do me a service." In the Metro the map lights up the way to the station at Père-Lachaise, a cemetery where many famous figures of French history are buried. They get off the train and go to a café, where Charles has a cognac. Back on the street, through an open window, one can see a lighted television set; a few bars of Mozart can be heard on the piano.

Charles and Valentin climb over the cemetery wall, and walk ahead single file before stopping. "At such a solemn moment," Charles says, "I thought I'd have sublime thoughts, but what I'm actually thinking about is—" Valentin doesn't let him complete the sentence but shoots twice before placing the revolver in Charles's outstretched hand. He then takes some money from Charles and puts it in his pocket. We hear his footsteps walking away before a final blackout.

▬▬ IT IS WORTH KEEPING IN MIND THAT THE FILM WAS SHOT IN THE summer of 1976. By this time the extravagant hopes of French youth, stimulated by the near-revolution of 1968, had been thoroughly extinguished, and Charles's rejection of society might well have been shared—in a less extreme form—by many of the student generation. Because of fears that it might make suicide all too "reasonable" to the young, *The Devil Probably* was originally authorized to be shown in France only to those over eighteen years of age.

Audience resistance to the pessimism of the movie is understandable, but some thoughtful critics give it a high place in the Bresson canon. Richard Roud, of *Film Comment*, for example, considers it his best film since *Pickpocket* and no more a downer than *King Lear* or *Oedipus*:

> Pollution implies that there was something pure in the first place to be polluted, and this is one of the reasons why the film, which sounds as if it ought to be depressing, is not.
>
> It is not the only reason, however. Bresson has achieved such a degree of emotional involvement with his characters, and his artistic control has

created such a perfectly realized film, that one comes away from the film uplifted. . . . When a civilization can produce a work as exalting as this one, it is hard to believe that there is no hope.[8]

Roud refers to such effective touches as the moment when Charles, walking to his death, pauses in front of an open window to hear a minuet of Mozart. At the end, when Charles admits he has no sublime thoughts, Roud suggests that Bresson may be expressing a preference for emotion over abstraction. The critic also offers insightful comments about the scene on the bus that produces the movie's title:

> On the one hand, such a sequence is "pure cinema," on the other it is a paradigm of the film itself. The mechanical gestures, with their mechanical responses, correspond to the mechanistic view of life which Bresson believes prevails today. And the conversations, which aren't really conversations but alternating monologues, are emblematic of the life of his characters, who never seem to be talking to each other but rather *at* or *away from* each other, as is the contrast between the almost desultory rhythm of these various remarks and the dynamic workings of the bus and its gadgets.[9]

It should hardly be necessary to repeat that Bresson did not make *The Devil Probably* to argue some abstract proposition. The director Louis Malle, a former assistant to Bresson, says that it is extremely naive to treat the subject of the movie as ecology, or to reduce it to Bresson's vision of the world: "When he deals with the news, it's foolish. . . . What is fascinating about the film is that it looks like Pascal—it's all about grace, about people with a gift for life, which is something divine. . . . It's a completely mystical film."[10]

Even though Charles says that his problem is that he sees too clearly, and neither the psychoanalyst nor his friends are his equals in debate, we are also made sympathetic with Michel, who finally bursts out, "I want to live even if it's illogical." And after he shoots Charles, the camera is on Valentin: "Sick and gaunt, Valentin is a negative image of the other characters, a wretched zombie who scorns charity and cares for nothing but his next score of smack. Yet he, too, wants to live, even if it's illogical."[11]

Despite the film's bleak picture of the modern world, François Truffaut provides an important corrective note when he emphasizes the beauty of the four young people at the center of the movie:

> I insist on their beauty because it is in part the subject of the film: a beauty that has been wasted, a youth that has been spoiled. Bresson distributes these four young people like figures in a game of cards, while controlling variations. Of course, he often begins scenes by filming door knobs and waists . . . but isn't this just to economize, to make us wait, to make us desire, and finally to

show the face at the moment . . . when this handsome intelligent face speaks with gentle gravity, as if the person were speaking to himself? Obviously, for Bresson as for Valéry's *Monsieur Teste,* it's a matter of killing the marionette and showing the person at his best, at his truest moment of emotion and expression. . . . In a film of Bresson, it's less a matter of showing than of hiding. Ecology, the modern church, drugs, psychiatry, suicide? No . . . the true subject of *The Devil Probably* is the intelligence, the seriousness, and the beauty of today's adolescents, and of the four among them of whom one could say with Cocteau that "the air that they breathe is lighter than air."[12]

Perhaps some further insight into Bresson's intentions can be found in his 1976 interview with film critic-screenwriter-director Paul Schrader, whose *Transcendental Style in Film* (1972) was one of the first serious analyses of Bresson's work. Bresson was about to start shooting *The Devil Probably* and Schrader, informed of its plot, asked him about suicide. "For myself," Bresson said,

> there is something which makes suicide possible—not just possible but even necessary: it is the vision of void, the feeling of void which is impossible to bear. You want anything to stop your life. . . . this way of wanting to die is many things: it is a disgust with life, with people around you, with living only for money. To see everything which is good to live for disappear, when you see that you cannot fall in love with people, not only with a woman, but all the people around you, you find yourself alone with people. I can imagine living in disgust with so many things which are against you around you, and then you feel like suicide.[13]

A little later in the interview Bresson talked of Charles as looking for something, even going to church to seek it, but not finding it. He quotes the line, "When you come in a church, or in a cathedral, God is there, but if a priest happens to come, God is not there anymore," and called it "the line of his death."

Schrader claims that from *Diary of a Country Priest* to *Balthasar* Bresson was working from a given theology, whereas he was now taking a different path, but the director protests:

> No, because the more life is what it is—ordinary, simple—without pronouncing the word "God," the more I see the presence of God in that. . . . I don't want to shoot something in which God would be too transparent. So, you see, my first films are a bit naive, too simple. . . . The further I go on in my work . . . the more careful I am to do something without too much ideology. . . . I want to make people who see the film feel the presence of God in ordinary life, like *Une femme douce* in front of death. I think back to the five minutes before she is going to kill herself. There is something there ideological.

That death is there and mystery is there, as in *Mouchette,* the way she kills herself, you can feel there is something, which, of course, I don't want to show or talk about. There is a presence of something which I call God, but I don't want to show it too much. I prefer to make people feel it.[14]

Mireille Latil Le Dantec and Pierre Jouvet's moving essay in *Cinématographe* is the strongest possible case for the aesthetic and moral power of *The Devil Probably.* They recognize that the film traces those moments of hope in *A Man Escaped* and *Pickpocket* in the opposite direction. Since Bresson has solemnly banned the use of music, there can be no equivalent to the introduction of Monteverdi's "Magnificat" in *Mouchette,* and no sense of some final spiritual rehabilitation.

> Nothing appears on Charles's face. Hardly a word is exchanged with his executioner who is in a hurry to get back to sleep. . . . An anonymous hand serving a cognac in a café that is already closed would be his last contact with life if Charles didn't stop for a minute in front of an unknown window from which the sweetness of a few piano notes filters. . . . But the sacred nevertheless returns as an absence, a nostalgia, in a way that is both strong and subtle, like a faraway rime. The face of Charles lying on his back, his hair falling free, has now—like the "gentle woman"—the calm beauty of statues. It is the echo of the shot in which he slept in an empty church to the sounds of the psalm from Monteverdi's *Canticle of Canticles:* "Ego dormio, cor meum vigilat." And what are the words of the psalm that Bresson has chosen to hear mount tirelessly under the vaults? . . . "Immaculata mea columba"—my dove without stain.[15]

Bresson says that Charles commits suicide both for personal reasons—he has experienced what the director calls "the void"—and because he wants to make the world better. The film itself, however, does not seem to unite these reasons convincingly. It is hard to believe that Charles ever really listened to Michel's protest against ecological destruction (though he was too intelligent not to agree with it); his sense of the void appears to have left him almost completely isolated.

Whatever may be one's response to Charles's death, *The Devil Probably* provides convincing evidence that Bresson's mastery of his medium has continued to grow. As René Prédal observes,

> the economy of means is drastic. . . . The ways in which the film proceeds from one shot to the next are very simple, reduced to the minimum; the locales are extremely bare (an end of a quai, a corner of a table), the framings thwarted by what they eliminate. . . . The objects themselves are extremely banal and Bresson does not hesitate to use similar components several times. Charles's bag hangs in his apartment and he also has it with him when he is

outside. Alberte will extract the cyanide from it, the woman with the Mercedes will take it with his clothes, and he will draw the box of chocolates out of it which he will later show to Michel. Finally, the hippy will have an almost identical bag from which he will take the revolver.[16]

As Prédal points out, this object has a presence as strong as the characters. With such an emphasis, Bresson, perhaps unconsciously, is looking ahead to his last movie, *L'Argent,* in which a counterfeit bank note, passing from hand to hand, becomes a relentless agent of tragedy.

NOTES

1. Robert Bresson, *Cinématographie,* no. 29 (July–August 1977).

2. Ibid.

3. Fyodor Dostoevsky, *The Brothers Karamazov,* trans. Richard Pevear and Larissa Volokhonsky (New York: Vintage Classics, 1990), 134.

4. J. Hoberman, *Village Voice,* November 17, 1994.

5. Michel Estève, *Robert Bresson* (Paris: Editions Albatros, 1983), 73.

6. Jean Sémolué, *Bresson ou l'acte pur des Métamorphoses* (Paris: Flammarion, 1993), 235–36.

7. Dostoevsky, *Brothers Karamazov,* part 3, book 8, ch. 8.

8. Richard Roud, "The Devil Probably: The Redemption of Despair," *Film Comment* (1977), reprinted in *Robert Bresson,* ed. James Quandt (Toronto: Cinematheque Ontario, 1998), 404.

9. Ibid.

10. Jonathan Cott, "Fires Within Us: The Chaste Sensuality of Director Louis Malle" (interview), *Rolling Stone,* April 6, 1978.

11. Michael Dempsey, "Despair Abounding: The Recent Films of Robert Bresson," *Film Quarterly* 34, no. 1 (1980): 12.

12. François Truffaut, *Pariscope,* June 21, 1977.

13. Paul Schrader, "Robert Bresson, Possibly," *Film Comment* 13, no. 5 (1977).

14. Ibid.

15. Mireille Latil Le Dantec and Pierre Jouvet, "*Le diable, probablement,*" in *Cinématographe* (September 1977).

16. René Prédal, "Robert Bresson: L'aventure intérieure," *L'Avant-scène cinéma* (January-February 1992): 121.

13

A Murderous Rage for Money

L'Argent

THOUGH BRESSON IS NOT A POLITICAL ARTIST, AND HIS FILMS do not mirror the lives of the poor or of the many immigrants who have settled in Paris in recent years, the deadly centrality of money in contemporary culture is a constant theme in his work. Already in *Ladies of the Bois de Boulogne*, two different worlds are summed up by the contrast between the elegance of Hélène's dress, apartment, and belongings and the spare simplicity of Agnès's surroundings. The fascination of the betting windows at the racetrack during the opening of *Pickpocket*, the idealism of the country priest forced into humiliating dealings with callous merchants and the haughty count, the miserable coins earned by Mouchette for helping out in the village café, the terrible pride of the father in *Au hasard Balthasar*, who refuses to contest legal proceedings that will ruin him financially, the pawnbroker's willingness to return the Christ-figure to the "gentle woman" since it is only the gold cross on which it is mounted that has any value—these are central images in Bresson's films that show the deadly power of money.

L'Argent (1983) is a triumphant and appropriate conclusion to Bresson's career, a film for which he adapted a relatively minor work of Tolstoy, *The False Coupon* (1904). The movie shows how a dishonest means of acquiring money—passing on a counterfeit bill—leads to unjust accusations against a young oil delivery worker, setting in motion a chain of ill fortune. The worker is arrested when he uses the bill to pay for a meal, loses his job, and rashly involves himself in an attempted bank holdup, for which he is imprisoned. This in turn leads to the breakup of his marriage, a failed attempt at suicide, and an outbreak of murderous rage.

Bresson shows a great deal of independence in his treatment of the original, not only moving the action from Russia to contemporary Paris, but making many cuts and changes. Tolstoy's story takes place over fifteen years and has a huge cast; most importantly, its second half follows its main character through a complex process of atonement. Bresson was attracted by the Russian's account of how the desire for money is the motor for the spread of evil, but he eliminates the presentation of Tolstoy's ethical-religious convictions, which had become so combative that he was excommunicated from the Orthodox church in 1901.

Tolstoy's story moves with quick, masterful strokes; for his part, Bresson shows how perfectly he has come to understand the special needs of cinematography. As Michel Estève explains,

> The action develops over several years, but the structure, resting constantly on ellipsis, is so dense and tight that the story seems to enroll in a few weeks. The tempo is very rapid, without a pause, almost without respite. The author holds our attention without a break, sometimes deliberately inverting established logic between facts and their causes. The fact presented is revealed as itself the effect of the cause for a given instant still unknown to us. . . . For example, when Yvon [the central figure in the story], just out of prison, goes to the inn, we wonder: to do what? After ellipsis, we observe him in the bathroom; as he washes his hands, we see the blood.[1]

It is ironically appropriate that Bresson should have experienced even more difficulty than usual in getting the financing needed to make a movie about the evil influence of money. Refused help by the commission that sometimes provided an advance against future receipts, he was able to go ahead only with the direct aid of the minister of culture. The marvel is that at age eighty-two Bresson worked with the confidence and high spirits of a young man; his assistants on the film speak of the speed with which he worked and the evident pleasure he had in making the film. Jean François Naudon, who edited *L'Argent*, said, "What is remarkable is the youth and boldness of Bresson: he doesn't hesitate. But his work isn't gratuitous, he's not trying to do something chic or fancy."[2] Bresson himself said, "I worked in a manner that was both more strenuous and more casual; I felt freer, more impulsive."[3] Shot in the summer of 1982, *L'Argent* shared the Special Jury Prize at Cannes with Tarkovsky's *Nostalgia* in 1983. The decision, booed by some of the fashionable festival-goers who believed that Bresson was passé, was particularly appropriate in view of the special esteem Tarkovsky had for his work.

Jean Sémolué remarks that its "rhythms and narrative processes make *L'Argent* the most boldly experimental of Bresson's films. . . . Its movements are more rapid, and there are far more characters."[4] He also notes the emphasis on chance; commenting on the movie, Bresson himself says, "Life is almost entirely made up of random events."[5]

Another departure in *L'Argent* is that its central figure, Yvon Targe, is a worker. The model used was Christian Patey, an athletically built young man who conveys the impression of being instinctive rather than reflective. Yvon is not asked to narrate his story, like Fontaine in *A Man Escaped*, nor does he keep a journal like the curé d'Ambricourt or *Pickpocket*'s Michel.

━━APPROPRIATELY ENOUGH, *L'ARGENT* OPENS WITH A SHOT OF A CASH machine. Its metal doors close as the credits begin to roll; there has just been a transaction. The action proper begins when Norbert, a young lycée student, knocks on the door to his father's study to ask for his monthly allowance. The father, an unwelcoming bourgeois, coldly doles out the money—Bresson shoots the bills in close-up—but when his son asks for an advance to meet a loan, he curtly refuses. Norbert goes next to his stylish mother, who is sympathetic but says she cannot help at this time. Kent Jones observes pertinently, "Anyone who comments about the lack of acting in Bresson should take careful note of such a scene, in which a whole family dynamic is described within seconds, with a minimum of screen time and detail."[6]

Norbert immediately gets on the phone to his classmate Martial and hops on his motorbike. He is prepared to pawn his watch in order to pay off his loan, but the more sophisticated Martial tells him that is unnecessary. Martial hands Norbert a counterfeit five-hundred-franc note, saying it will be easy to pass it on. As they are leaving, Norbert looks through an art book, mostly reproductions of nudes; Martial comments, "The body is beautiful."

The two ride off to a business street and stop in front of a photography shop. Martial tells the proprietress that they are looking for a cheap frame and confidently reassures her when she looks suspiciously at the bill offered in payment. The students have hardly taken the change and gone off on their mopeds when we hear the angry insult, "Imbecile!" The husband has returned to the shop; the camera shows his hands as he examines the counterfeit bill. The wife retaliates by reminding him that he had accepted two fake bills not long before, but he effectively damps down the animosity by confidently announcing, "I'll pass them on."

There is an immediate cut to the red-gloved hands of Yvon Targe, who is delivering oil to the store. Yvon goes in, hands the invoice for the oil to the shop assistant (Lucien), and receives payment (in counterfeit money) from the proprietor. He then drives to a nearby café, and pays for his meal with the fake money. The waiter challenges Yvon and refuses to return the counterfeit bill, assuming that he is dealing with a common thief. Yvon grabs the waiter, who falls, knocking over the table. When the police arrive, Yvon, seeking vindication, leads them to the photography shop, but Lucien pretends never to have seen him before.

Returning home, Yvon is greeted by his little daughter. His wife Elise suggests that he seek advice, and a lawyer explains that what is important is to clear his name. In court, however, Lucien sticks to his story and the judge believes him. It is only after a plea by his lawyer that Yvon avoids jail and liability for court costs. The judge further infuriates him by saying he should be grateful for the clemency shown him. Relieved at the outcome, the owner of the photography shop hands Lucien an envelope and tells him to buy a suit that he has wanted. The latter accepts his reward but asks himself, "What's the penalty for perjury?"

Elise tells her husband that if he would explain things to his employers, they would give him back his job, but Yvon is stubborn: "I won't beg."

The machinery of deception grinds on. At the photography shop, Lucien changes the price of a camera, pocketing the difference for himself. Caught by the owner, he is fired, but not before acquiring a duplicate set of keys. The photographer's wife, however, who realizes justice has not been done, goes to the school where Martial and Norbert are students, and speaks to the chaplain: "It's about a boy whose name I don't know." This leads to a class discussion about forging checks, leaving Norbert sufficiently shamed that he confides in his mother. She, however, is only interested in protecting him from possible repercussions and advises him to deny everything. At the photography shop, there is a close-up of the mother's hand as she hands an envelope to the owner's wife, explaining that what is enclosed is intended to pay for the trouble the incident has caused her.

Norbert's father goes to see the religion instructor to make sure his son won't be in trouble. In the street we see his wife passing by Yvon, who is sitting outside at a café. An acquaintance joins him with a proposition: driving the getaway car for a bank robbery. He lays out a map of Paris and shows Yvon where he should wait in his car. Before leaving home, Yvon kisses his little girl good night, then goes down the stairway without speaking to Elise. "You don't like me to ask any questions," she says, "but I have the right to be worried."

The robbery sequence is brilliantly conceived. After following the reactions of a passerby on the street who is reading his newspaper, we notice Yvon sitting behind the wheel of a car. There is a disturbance, and we see a robber holding a woman hostage at gunpoint. Suddenly a gun is fired. Yvon finally starts his car, but there is an almost immediate collision, and he is arrested. The court proceedings that follow emphasize the ceremonial trappings of justice. Yvon gets a three-year sentence; when he glances toward Elise who is sitting in the gallery, she leaves the courtroom, picking up her daughter outside.

The scene moves quickly to the outside of a prison: a van stops, agents place bags on the ground, four men—including Yvon—get out, each takes his belongings, goes up the steps, and passes into a corridor as a heavy door closes behind them.

Back at the photography shop, the owners find the safe empty. Lucien and his confederates are immediately seen walking down the steps of a metro station.

We hear echoing footsteps in a prison corridor; a guard tells Yvon he has a visitor. Bresson crosscuts between Elise and Yvon, their heads separated by a plastic partition. "We'll make a new life, the three of us," he tells her, but she is clearly unconvinced.

On the sidewalk, an unknown man goes to a cash machine which is out of order; he can't get his card back and leaves. Lucien sees what has happened, and manages to get the card unblocked, explaining the process to his confederates. Since he had also observed the code number, he is able to use it and pocket the money.

The mail truck arrives at prison and women employees go through the inmates' mail. There is a letter from Elise: when she had visited the prison, she did not have the strength to tell Yvon of the illness and death of Yvette, their little daughter. Yvon is seen lying prostrate on a bed in his cell, Elise's letter on the floor. His cellmates pick up the letter, read it, and put it back before having a drink together. One says, "Death frightens us because we love life."

At the photography shop the owners are explaining to a friend their financial difficulties ever since Lucien robbed them. Suddenly the mail arrives with a letter from Lucien, along with a check repaying what he has taken.

Meanwhile Yvon's letters to Elise have been returned to the prison. In the dining hall Yvon becomes enraged after some of the prisoners start talking about his wife; he has to be restrained and is given forty days of solitary confinement.

Another letter from Elise says goodbye; she wants to start a new life. A guard administers pills to Yvon, who is still in solitary; he spits them into a paper where he has been storing them up. Some prisoners notice an ambulance that has come into the prison yard (for Yvon); one of them falls to his knees: "Excuse me: I always pray for suicides." In the intensive care unit a nurse leans over to see how Yvon is doing; Elise's letter is alongside his bed.

The action then shifts to a courtroom, where Lucien boldly defies the authority of the law. He arrives at prison with two other men at the same time that Yvon comes back from the hospital. Yvon is given a well-intentioned but somewhat pretentious cellmate, who denounces the absurdity of society against the background noise of a vacuum cleaner. "Money, our visible God," he orates, "what is there that you don't make us do?" From behind a door a voice addresses Yvon: "A man named Lucien . . . hopes to see Yvon at mass in the chapel."

Out of curiosity, Yvon goes to the chapel, where mass is being said in Latin; shots of the prisoners' hands reveal a steady exchange of black market goods. Lucien says he has prepared an escape and encourages Yvon to accompany him. "I'd rather kill you than go with you," Yvon responds.

In the cell, Yvon and his cellmate hear an alert; Lucien has been caught. The cellmate believes the news will satisfy Yvon's need for revenge, but the latter shows him Elise's letter and says, "I have neither a parent, friend, nor wife."

Abruptly, Yvon receives his release papers and passes through the prison doors. He proceeds to another door, that of the Hotel Moderne. We next see him going downstairs past a body and into a lavatory. As Yvon washes his hands, the water in the sink turns red. He empties the cash drawer, unbolts the door, and leaves.

On the street he exchanges glances with a gray-haired woman who is going to the post office to cash a money order. On her way home she passes over a footbridge, where a large dog is waiting for her. She looks back; the dog growls when the stranger follows her in. Yvon takes a seat while the woman looks at him closely. After closing the door of one room where her father is sitting, she takes care of a sick boy in another room, and returns to the kitchen. Sensing what has taken place, she asks Yvon, "Why did you kill them?"

Yvon, sitting down at the table to eat, tries to recall details, but offers no real answer: he just couldn't stand their looks. The woman tries to assure him that he will be pardoned; "If I were God, I would pardon everybody." There is a noise: the woman's brother and sister-in-law enter by a different door and go to bed upstairs. As he pets the dog, Yvon says, "I know you won't turn me in."

In the morning the old woman pours coffee into a bowl and carries it outside. Her father, who is in the garden, is so angry with her for letting Yvon stay that he slaps her, but she holds onto the bowl, and puts it down next to where Yvon has been sleeping. The latter wakes up, drinks a little coffee, then notices an axe.

The woman is busy ironing clothes while Yvon plays with the dog. In the drawing room the father, who has been playing Bach's "Fantasie chromatique," places his glass of wine on the right arm of the piano. When the glass falls, the woman goes in to pick up the pieces. She explains to Yvon that her father began to drink and lose his piano students after her husband died. She goes out to dig up some potatoes, and Yvon brings a basket of them into the kitchen. When she leaves to do some shopping, however, he goes upstairs to look for money, searching through drawers, under a pillow, and so on. At the bakery, the woman passes two policemen who have just bought some bread.

After she walks back, she immediately starts scrubbing clothes, prompting Yvon to call her a slave. "Are you expecting a miracle?" he asks, unable to understand her spirit of acceptance. "I expect nothing," she says. Yvon picks some hazelnuts and they work together hanging the washing on the clothes line.

A shot of the axe interrupts this lyrical moment; apparently it is hours later, and a lantern moves up the stairs past a body, and from room to room. In the woman's room, Yvon asks, "Where's the money?" She simply looks at him. Another shot of the axe, followed by a streak of blood on the wallpaper, then darkness, and the sound of the axe being thrown in the water.

Yvon then walks to a nearby café, an indifferent cop behind him. He orders a drink, downs it quickly, and walks over to the cop's table. Calmly, he confesses to all the murders: "It is I who killed the hotel keeper and his wife in order to steal from them, and I have just assassinated a whole family." The waiter in the next room and the customers quickly gather to see what is going on. "In a strangely appropriate final image, the café patrons remain massed before the door through which Yvon and the police have penetrated. They represent the audience in the theater which is watching the screen. How," asks Jean Sémolué, "could Bresson's cinematography have ended more appropriately?"[7]

──AS THE SCREEN TURNS TO BLACK, WE UNDERSTAND THAT THE handcuffed Yvon is truly free for the first time, but the ending remains devastating. Bresson deliberately eliminated the whole second half of Tolstoy's novella, which describes a lengthy and complex redemptive process. "I am sorry," he said, "that in *L'Argent* I was unable to linger on Yvon's redemption . . . but the rhythm of the film, at that stage, would not stand for it."[8]

In Tolstoy the original victim of the false bank note was Ivan Mironov, who received it when he delivered wood to a photography shop. His trial is decided by the false testimony of Vassili, the photographer's assistant, an exact equivalent of the action in *L'Argent*. Released from jail, Ivan becomes a horse thief; when he takes Stefan's horses, however, the latter kills him and is himself condemned. The subsequent parallels in the narrative are between Yvon and Stefan. The latter's wife dies while he is in prison, and his sentence is increased after he tries to kill the prison cook. When Stefan gets out of jail, he is as enraged as Yvon, and kills two hotel keepers with an axe. He then encounters Maria Semionovna, a widow, just as she is receiving her pension. Stefan kills her sister and brother-in-law; Maria, who has worn herself out caring for her family, offers no resistance, but tells him he is losing his soul. After asking her where her money is, he cuts her throat.

Tolstoy's part 2 begins with Stefan haunted by the memory of Maria's words and the look on her face. After confessing to a police officer, he finds himself in jail with Vassili, whose perjury had sent Ivan to prison early in the story and who had subsequently become a successful thief. Tolstoy twists his material into a tale of inspiration when a cellmate reads key texts from the New Testament to both men. The novelist even shows Makhine, the former student who originally passed the false bank note and is now a judge, becoming deeply touched by Stefan's spiritual transformation. Tolstoy's novella ends in the gold mines of Siberia ten years later, where the influence of the holy convict Stefan leads the engineer Mitya to change his life and be reconciled with his father.

Contemporary audiences would be apt to find the latter half of Tolstoy's story pietistic and unconvincing; Bresson's abrupt conclusion is aesthetically superior. Tolstoy's Stefan is so haunted by the look on Maria's face that he can't sleep at night until he changes his life, but there is no genuine meeting between them. In contrast, the final long sequence of *L'Argent* is a complex and powerfully moving encounter between Yvon and the old woman, one of the high points of Bresson's career. Sylvie Van Den Elsen avoids any trace of sentimentality while helping us see the woman's profound gentleness; only a false sophistication would interpret her acceptance of death as sadomasochism. Though Yvon completes his explosion of violence by murdering her and her family, we are understandably convinced that her image will remain embedded in his memory. The lyrical moments they share—not only the woman's words assuring him of forgiveness but hanging the wash on the clothesline together, and Yvon picking hazelnuts for her—recall the signals of grace found in *A Man Escaped* and *Pickpocket*. The fact that Yvon kills her even after such sharing makes *L'Argent* more terrifying than those earlier movies, but is also a strong reason to take his confession seriously.

Bresson's subtle mastery is also demonstrated by his ability to convey the pernicious domination of money over so many lives without falling into didacticism. For example, when Yvon's cellmate denounces "money, our invisible God," the director succeeds in distancing the audience from the rhetoric of the speech, even though its convictions are close to his own. The film also shows the way in which a working-class character like Yvon is almost automatically treated with suspicion, as is shown when he innocently uses the counterfeit bill to pay for his meal in the restaurant. A similar class prejudice obviously lies behind the condescension with which the handsomely robed judge addresses Yvon after the latter's case has been determined by Lucien's perjured testimony.

The same kind of economy in conveying moral judgment is evident in the way Norbert—who used a counterfeit bill to pay back his loan—is counseled by his parents when his conscience has begun to bother him. As Kent Jones says, "they are acting in their own self-interest." Similarly, when the shopkeeper coaches Lucien, Bresson is "showing us the formation of cynicism in a young mind . . . unconsciously, strictly through action . . . a turning point in his adolescent study of everyday adult life. In its own way, the scene is just as hurtful as the violence that will follow. Only here, the violence is done silently, to a young soul."[9]

Bresson establishes and completes each scene as a self-contained unity, treating them almost like separate musical units. Keith Reader suggests that the sequence in which Yvon is positioned as the getaway driver is like some in Jean-Luc Godard's *Breathless*; it "could not be further from conventional action filming, for what counts is the effect of the fragmented units we see and hear rather than any drama inherent in them."[10] To encounter the robbery in process by following a stranger on the street who is absorbed in his newspaper adds a comic touch to proceedings that will have disastrous consequences for Yvon, whose car collides with another when he tries to get away. "The next shot is that of his wife waiting at the police station. When they tell her Yvon has been jailed and that she will not be able to see him until his trial, Bresson cuts and immediately starts again with a shot of the red-sleeved judges returning to deliver the sentence. In this way ellipsis dictates the overall conception of the story but is also present between each shot which often constitutes only the connection between facts."[11]

Not surprisingly, *L'Argent* has several echoes of Dostoevsky; many commentators have referred to *The False Coupon* as the most Dostoevskyan of Tolstoy's narratives. Sémolué reminds us that Yvon's confession at the end is very similar to that of Roskolnikov in *Crime and Punishment* and that "the old woman's key sentence to Yvon the previous night repeats a line of Grushenka in *The Brothers Karamazov*." He recalls, however, that Grushenka was delirious after drinking with Dmitri, which is hardly the case for the woman in *L'Argent* who "removes all pride from her line by adding, 'If it were only up to me.'"[12]

Kent Jones points out that Bresson presents "one action at a time, every-thing happening at eye level, the time frame resolutely human . . . for Bres-son the compulsion to murder merits its own exploration. The rejection of life against the acceptance of life: that is the opposition at the core of the final scenes of *L'Argent*."[13] Starting from the difference between Bresson's and Tolstoy's idea of the good, the novelist Alberto Moravia makes quite a different point:

> Bresson sees "the good" in the Attic basis of French civilization—that is, in its traditional mixture of rigor, restraint, and rationalism, the distinctive sign of its national genius. In other words, "the good" would be "style." This leads to the curious conclusion that evil exists in life, and good in the way that it is represented. The real axe, stained with blood, with which the assassin kills his victims is a baleful object; but the image of the axe is somehow beneficial. In brief, style exorcises evil.[14]

Even if one believes that Moravia's formula is too neat, he correctly reminds us that the director's primary interest is style rather than tradi-tional storytelling. But Bresson's concern is not that of fashionable aes-theticism; he wants us to look closely at things as well as people, and at the relations between them. Although there is violence in all the films of Bres-son it is never exploited for sensational effect, but is intended to help us see more clearly. As novelist Jean-Marie G. Le Clézio suggests, a new purity shines with greater clarity than in *A Man Escaped* or *Pickpocket*, a "purity of the glance that scrutinizes all the objects and actions of life" with "a harsh, true light" that gives them strength and precision:

> From the beginning Bresson's cinematography has been just that: to show us, to offer what eyes distracted by the mirages of life have not known how to see. It is a work of painting and architecture as well as philosophy, for its relentless research into the real is not an imitation of nature or its sacraliza-tion (the eternity of art, that delusion of human vanity!) but simply a way of helping us see. In *L'Argent* it is this purity and harshness that I sense from the start, like an exaltation of life, to which the violence of evil, of the desire for possession, is opposed.

The rage that money triggers in this film is comparable to that of Christ when he drove the money-changers out of the temple:

> In *L'Argent* money interposes itself between people, the false money of lying and false testimony divides them into winners and losers, and creates pun-ishments, bloodthirsty madness, and death. No one has expressed the hatred of money with more force and truth than Bresson, who is in complete revolt against such a venal and murderous world. But this idealism is not innocent.

In order to denounce this world of violence and murder, Bresson's film is composed of anger and revolt, it is a flash of lightning that frightens us and leaves us bruised, profoundly changing all those who pay attention to it. In this world dominated by violence and crime, where more than ever money seems the symbol of our greatest desires and of our vain search for happiness, the violence and purity of Bresson seem fierce and implacable.[15]

This prophetic revolt, flaming out in the eighty-two-year-old director's last film, is a powerful summary of earlier themes and an appropriate climax to his career. What is amazing is that he has composed his images with such speed and precision that, despite the horrors that are recorded, the audience, as in high tragedy, emerges both cleansed and renewed.

NOTES

1. Michel Estève, *Robert Bresson* (Paris: Editions Albatros, 1983), 86.

2. Interview with Philippe Arnaud, in *Robert Bresson* (Paris: Cahiers du Cinéma, 1986).

3. Interview with Serge Daney and Serge Toubiana, *Cahiers du cinéma* no. 348-9 (June/July 1983).

4. Jean Sémolué, *Bresson ou l'acte pur des Métamorphoses* (Paris: Flammarion, 1993), 251.

5. Interview with Jacques Drillon, *Le Nouvel Observateur*, May 6, 1983.

6. Kent Jones, *Robert Bresson's "L'Argent"* (London: British Film Institute, 1999), 40.

7. Sémolué, *Bresson ou l'acte pur des Métamorphoses*, 263.

8. Quoted in Michel Ciment, "I Seek Not Description but Vision: Robert Bresson on 'L'Argent,'" in *Robert Bresson*, ed. James Quandt (Toronto: Cinematheque Ontario, 1998), 507.

9. Jones, *Robert Bresson's "L'Argent,"* 55.

10. Keith Reader, *Robert Bresson* (Manchester: University of Manchester Press, 2001), 148.

11. René Prédal, "Robert Bresson: L'aventure intérieure," *L'Avant-scène cinéma* (January-February 1992): 125.

12. Sémolué, *Bresson ou l'acte pur des Métamorphoses*, 250.

13. Jones, *Robert Bresson's "L'Argent,"* 55.

14. Alberto Moravia, in *Robert Bresson: Éloge* (Paris: Cinémathèque française, 1997), 60–61.

15. Jean-Marie G. Le Clézio, "Le voyage initiatique," *Le Monde*, July 7, 1983.

14

Images in a Certain Order

NOW THAT WE HAVE LOOKED—HOWEVER BRIEFLY—AT BRESSON'S films, what remains except to urge you to see them, if possible more than once? You will probably discover many things I missed or failed to point out because I thought they were already clear. Perhaps you will also have difficulty at first with one or another element in them that may seem strange or even forbidding. What should be useful, if his work is to find the English-language audience it deserves, is to pinpoint the reasons for resistance to it and perhaps to think of ways to overcome them.

A brochure for a future Bresson retrospective in North America should not be afraid to concede that his work is demanding and that it contradicts the assumptions with which most of us were indoctrinated when we started going to the movies. It's not just that we went mostly for escape, to indulge in romantic illusion, to laugh at the farcical antics of comedians, or to be horrified by hair-raising images. Movies were a way of forgetting classroom or family discipline, identifying with Hollywood glamour, sharing the anarchy of the Marx Brothers, ogling Claudette Colbert in a Roman bathtub, or watching Fred Astaire dance. Of course, there is no need to feel guilty about enjoying such entertainments, but cinematography is a radically different way to think about film that can provide more liberating and enduring pleasures. David Thompson is right in saying that "to watch Bresson is to risk conversion away from the cinema. His meaning is so clearly inspirational, and his treatment so remorselessly interior, that he seems to shame the intrinsic glamour and extravagance of movies. For that reason alone, he is not an easy director to digest. To go beyond admiration might be too near surrender."[1]

The truth is that Bresson's movies do not fit into the established genres, and are constructed in a way that is quite different from most of those we have seen. It isn't that Bresson doesn't tell stories, but he doesn't build them with the usual dramatic blocks, creating an inevitable climax that grows out of a clearly established climax.

As P. Adams Sitney explains,

> One speaks of "narration" in discussing the films of Robert Bresson rather than "plot." He replaces the conventional outline of events with a sense of the process by which events are arranged on the screen. . . . Essentially, narrative becomes interesting in these works from which it almost disappears. It turns into a formal element when it diminishes as the focus of interest in a work.[2]

Lindley Hanlon applies this awareness to the discussion of *A Gentle Woman*. She points out that although most of the dialogue and character traits are taken from Dostoevsky's novella, "it is Bresson's selection, reduction, and arrangement of these widely dispersed fragments of material that distinguish his vision."[3] He begins the film, one recalls, with terrifying shots as a hand opens a French window, a rocking chair and table are upset, a young wife jumps from the terrace of her apartment, and a white scarf floats from the balcony. Bresson is showing the effect before we can have any idea of a cause. In a sense the whole movie is devoted to an inconclusive search for causes. The director implies that no psychological "explanation" can be adequate, but we are not limited, as in Dostoevsky, to the understanding of the narrator-husband: Bresson finds a way to show aspects of the wife's character even when the camera seems to emphasize the husband's point of view.[4]

Hanlon's argument doesn't mean that dramatic development in Bresson is arbitrary, but it does suggest that almost equal weight is given to a long series of brief scenes, with few clear indications of the time that may have passed between them. The result is that we have to pay closer attention to what is shown in each shot than we are accustomed to, and may initially feel baffled when we always seem to be watching characters ascending or descending stairs, or waiting in front of closed doors. The latter aspect of his movies should sharpen our sense of transitional space; we are so accustomed to moving from one place to another that we forget how strong a role chance plays in our everyday activities and go through much of our lives as little more than sleepwalkers. It is worth remembering that in *A Man Escaped* Bresson never gives an overall shot of the prison, or even of Fontaine's cell; after he has managed to remove the wooden slats of his door and left his cell, he still has to move cautiously through the hall in order to determine a possible escape route. This helps explain why Philippe Arnaud says, "In the

films of Bresson we may have the experience of what could be called a com-
pression of the real . . . each shot falls with the irreversible decision of an
assignation."[5]

Bresson speaks with such passion against "filmed theater" that one could
easily assume that his choice of subject was merely a pretext to find out what
could be accomplished by pursuing "cinematography." At the same time we
should keep in mind that he did not begin with theory, was always suspicious of abstract intellectualism, and never strained for some isolated aesthetic response—he was not interested in making stills to be reproduced on
picture postcards. That is why, even when one has memories of being deeply
moved by particular moments in one of his films, it is almost impossible to
explain them in isolation. The truth is that they cannot easily be detached;
their impact comes from their careful arrangement in a series of shots that
prepare and follow them. It is hard not to be impressed by such famous
sequences as Fontaine's escape from Fort Montluc, the balletlike performance of the pickpockets in the Gare de Lyon, the gentle woman's premar-
riage encounters with her husband-to-be pawnbroker, the sovereign
independence of Joan's replies to the judges during her trial, the death of
Balthasar surrounded by sheep, Lancelot walking Guinevere back to rejoin
Arthur, or the moments of peaceful collaboration between Yvon and the
gray-haired lady in *L'Argent*. But to explain properly why these scenes—and
many more—are so memorable would require us to review the whole film in
which they appear. After the kind of technical shot-by-shot analysis that
could probably be made only in a classroom, we would still need to look
closely at the relations between the characters and the objects around them,
the background sounds as well as the spoken dialogue, the hints contained
in each exchange of glances, and much that is revealed simply by the automatic movements of bodies in motion.

Nevertheless, the main barrier keeping the general public from Bresson's
work, and which also made it difficult to find producers to finance them, was
the absence of actors. We are so accustomed to watching actors' "interpretations" that we have ended up accepting them as the normal way of presenting human action on the screen. For Bresson, the idea of employing a
camera to photograph what is not reality but only role-playing is a fundamental contradiction. John Keegan reminds us:

> People in real life are not "actors." Still, real people will play roles and act.
> But even then they do not talk in the way that actors who are performing tend
> to do. Interpretation is not a premeditated part of our speaking. We simply
> speak—without always being consciously aware of the depth of what we are

saying. Bresson's method of filmmaking is an attempt to give expression to the "spiritual resources" beyond (within) human effort.[6]

In addition, the fact that Bresson was quickly labeled a "Catholic director" at the very outset of his career probably turned out to be a handicap to his finding the broad audience he deserves. It may also have been a contributing cause for why some commentators have found his later films—from *Balthasar* to *L'Argent*—"despairing." Apparently they misinterpreted Bazin's line on *Diary of a Country Priest*—"the only perceptible movements are those of the life of the spirit"—to imply that Bresson would unfailingly smooth out the anguish of human existence. Such an assumption, of course, would flatten the complexities consistently found in his work, which could never have properly been considered "pious" and resists any interpretative framework that would reduce it to ideology. Other critics want to account for the perceived darkening of his landscape by reminding us that, because of the difficulties he had in getting various projects financed, a somber film like *Lancelot of the Lake* was originally planned at least twenty years before it was actually made, and that the much discussed change in tone, therefore, may be more apparent than real. In any case, the implications of Bresson's concession, in an interview with Michel Ciment, that "[p]erhaps I do see the world more somberly than I used to, unintentionally,"[7] would seem to have been considerably exaggerated.

It would be more useful to reflect seriously on the comment of Mireille Latil Le Dantec: "We need to dispel the stereotyped image of an austere man, labeled once and for all with the tag 'jansenist.' As one of the characters in *L'Argent* says, 'People fear death because they love life.' It is the shiver of life, the aspiration of being to liberty, the fierce refusal of restraints, that should be seen as the motor of his films, including the most tragic."[8] Above all, we need to look at Bresson's "pessimism" in the light of his entire career. He was never a likely prospect to deliver the kind of syrupy romantic comedy that Hollywood used to be able to make with considerable success; the fact that grace seemed to enter the equation at the end of several of his early movies should never have been understood to mean that he was committed to offering his audiences easy reassurance.

An inner spiritual movement enlivens his very first movie, *Angels of Sin*, but Hollywood executives would hardly consider it to have a "happy ending." Its conclusion, after all, links a painful death for the exalted Anne-Marie with the acceptance of handcuffs by the long-resistant Thérèse, who will shortly be indicted for murdering her former lover in revenge. Such a plot resolution only makes sense if the inner destinies of these women are seen in the light of a mysterious sisterhood that allows the fruits of the spiritual victory gained by one to assist in the inner liberation of the other. A specifically religious context is absent from *The Ladies of the Bois de Boulogne* but Bresson has developed the character of Agnès in term of a comparable regeneration. "In her final confession," Jean Sémolué writes, "Élina Labourdette [who plays Agnès] already announces the curé of Ambricourt in agony at Dufréty's home during the conclusion of *Diary of a Country Priest*."[9]

The ending of *Diary*, of course, is deeper and more aesthetically realized, but the consolation suggested at the end calls for a wholehearted carrying of the cross. The young curé is a victim of stomach cancer who lives under a cloud of suspicion from his ecclesiastical superiors after failing to realize his own naive hopes for his parish. He even dies without the last sacraments, with no company except that of a renegade priest. But if we have attended to the inner revelations of the priest's soul, as revealed in the journal entries that are read aloud during the film, and to his climactic encounters with souls in torment, we can to some degree participate in his final words of acceptance: "What does it matter? All is grace."

Bresson's involvement with *A Man Escaped* confirmed his belief that providence makes use of the most random occasions: after all, it was only by chance that he happened to see André Devigny's story of his wartime adventures in *Le Figaro*, a "realistic" account that also breathes an atmosphere of spiritual deliverance. The movie is a profound expression of the human aspiration for liberation, a theme that recurs again and again in Bresson; it is also a testimony to the mysterious community of freedom in which we may encounter grace. Just as Anne-Marie's dedication and suffering give Thérèse the strength to accept the handcuffs of the police at the end of *Angels of Sin*, the once-despairing, elderly prisoner Blanchet comes to such understanding that he can remind Fontaine, "it was necessary that Orsini fail in order that you should succeed."

Pickpocket is so dominated by its ballet of hand motions and the sense of the almost uncontainable excitement of stealing on a person-to-person basis that we may at first be unprepared for the suddenness of its positive resolution. A second viewing, however, should reveal that Michel's change in orientation has been long prepared. He needed to play out his gesture of rebellion to the end, and the fact of being imprisoned after he had already decided to abandon crime and help support Jeanne's child is merely a paradoxical resolution of his deepest impulse. Sémolué usefully reminds us that Michel's famous last line—"What a strange path I had to take"—"is not spoken by Michel to his partner, though Jeanne is invoked, but as the commentary that he addresses to himself and to us: it is the conclusion of his story."[10]

It is evident from the outset that the liberation of Joan of Arc can take place only by her becoming a burnt offering, totally consumed by the executioner's fire. Nevertheless, Bresson's film manages to avoid both pious inflation and the temptations of dolorism; he offers only the "happy ending" of martyrdom, its cost almost unbearably high. Historically accurate without being encumbered with historicism, *The Trial of Joan of Arc* is all the stronger because the saint's fear of the flames is made real, her brief moment of recantation all too understandable. At the same time the movie is so inclusive that even the chief inquisitor Cauchon is seen in three-dimensional terms, allowing the "heretic" to receive communion although she has defied what he considers God's will by again putting on men's clothing.

In Bresson's first six films, therefore, a positive resolution of the central conflict is made available on some level. Although their developments can be accounted for in human terms, Amédée Ayfre's claim is justified: in them "all is grace . . . and simultaneously, all is freedom."[11] For whatever reason, such a pattern is far less clear in *Au hasard Balthasar* and the remaining films, but rather than emphasize a growing sense of despair, it might be wiser to attribute this to Bresson's increasing mastery of his art. Although the blows inflicted on the donkey in *Balthasar* are painful to observe, they are intended to reflect the result of perennial human vices through which suffering is visited on an innocent animal. Almost more difficult for the spectator is to follow the self-deceptions of Marie as she collaborates in her seduction by Gérard, though her devotion to the constantly observant Balthasar remains undiminished. Nevertheless, Bresson is right not to force his material into some consoling pattern. The audience's memories of Marie's close relation with the donkey in childhood, the shots near the end of his participation in a procession to a nearby shrine, as well as the sheep's bells calling out while Balthasar is dying—all serve to nourish the deepest aspirations of the audience even after the movie is over.

The pattern established in *Balthasar* is repeated in Bresson's later films. The first sequence of *Mouchette*, with the death of the trapped partridge, is an advance commentary on the fate of its heroine. But another partridge escapes, its painful flight into the sky offering a hint of liberation beyond death. Those who have read Bernanos's *Nouvelle histoire de Mouchette* may well find it easier to place the young girl's story squarely in a supernatural framework. As for Bresson, who reminds an interviewer that "[t]he domain of cinematography is the domain of the unsayable,"[12] he ends his film with an appropriate passage of Monteverdi, "Et exaltavit humiles" ("And he has exalted the humble").

As in so many of his movies, the use of sounds reveals the director's mastery: the struggling of the hunted animals, the slapping of Mouchette's clogs on the ground as she walks the village's muddy streets, the crackling of the wood fire in the cabin during the epilepsy sequence, the confident voice of the adolescent girl who is finally able to sing the words of hope they had tried to teach her in school, all combine to give a felt immediacy to the action. Bresson's handling of the rape scene should be studied by young directors as a lesson in the power of suggestion and restraint. As Hanlon points out, "the fugitive meeting of Mouchette and the half-drunk poacher has a beauty and richness that recall the deathwatch of Prince Myshkin and Rogoshin over the body of Natasha in Dostoevsky's *Idiot.*"[13]

In such late films as *Balthasar* and *Mouchette* we confront the extreme cruelty of reality; perhaps their most healing element is the absence of censure. "He [Bresson] never makes his intentions explicit . . . this would be imposing his point of view. . . . He respects the liberty and mystery of his characters *to the degree that they depend on him*; he does not arrogate to himself the point of view of God in order to judge them."[14]

In the final analysis, it would seem that Bresson's vision did not essentially change; he simply gained an increasing mastery of narrative structure. He had always been aware of the significance of silence; *A Gentle Woman* provides powerful reminders of this through moments of noncommunication between wife and husband. In addition, the servant Anna is left silent throughout the film, even though she is constantly present by the wife's corpse as the husband tries to explain—and inevitably, to justify—his conduct. As Hanlon says, "Bresson has mastered . . . the possibilities of representing silence through images of severe glances and through what he has termed the 'pessimism' of noises. The connective tissue of the narrative of *A Gentle Woman* is a series of hundreds of footsteps made by the man as he passes from silent room to silent room."[15] In addition, the many images of the corpse overwhelm the effect of the husband's continued "explanations."

The shocking but strangely beautiful opening of *A Gentle Woman*, including a close-up of the wife just before she jumps to her death, leaves its mark on the entire film, raising questions that only become more painful as it progresses. There is no way to eliminate the shock of such material, but Hanlon is perceptive in interpreting that close-up as suggesting "that her soul has already departed from her body, which would then be discarded, that contact has already been made with another life in which she finds solace."[16]

Bresson's repeated choice of heroines at precisely their point of development from girls to young women was more than a response to their charm. Joan of Arc, *Balthasar*'s Marie, Mouchette, and the gentle woman, each convey a sensitivity and passion for justice that is all too absent in their environment. Though they do not completely break with the limitations of their time and place, they all suggest inchoate longings for self-determination and love that precede the more recent findings of feminist psychologists. Marie's collaboration in her own destruction and the ambiguous suicides of Mouchette and the gentle woman should not blind us to their instinct for rebellion and sense of interior independence. If Joan offers the most poetic testimony in her responses to her judges, the others, too, find ways of expressing their rebellion against the roles in which society has tried to imprison them. In sum, Bresson's heroines are subtle educators who call our attention to the brutality that weighs on all of us, especially on young women moving through this crucial stage of early maturity.

Bresson's next film, *Four Nights of a Dreamer,* is in great part a meditation on the origin of an artistic vocation. After the success of his first movie in color, *A Gentle Woman,* he felt increasing confidence in using this new resource, and his pleasure is reflected in the many shots taken along the Seine at evening. Perhaps the movie reflects a more sympathetic observation of the world around him than in the majority of his movies, but Bresson's central preoccupation continued to be the distinctiveness of cinematography, how to refine what could uniquely be expressed in this art.

With *Lancelot of the Lake* he was finally able to carry out a project he had dreamed of for years; although the suppression of background information often leaves us unsure of time and place, it may nevertheless be his most beautiful film. Choosing to begin with a pitiless description of the collapse of the Arthurian ethos, Bresson gives powerful expression to the hiddenness of God, and the cry for human liberation becomes all the stronger. It is the end of an age, but the idealism of Gawain and fidelity of Lancelot, though severely tested, both survive.

After Bresson's insightful successes with such heroines as Joan, Mouchette, and the gentle woman, it was hardly a surprise that Bresson's Guinevere, Laura Duke Condominas, would be so young. All the knights, even Gawain, look up at her window, but she is more than a *femme fatale;* after insisting that Lancelot remain true to his vows to her, she criticizes him and his brother knights for misunderstanding the meaning of their search for the Grail: "God," she insists, "is not a trophy to be carried home."

Although *The Devil Probably* is generally considered Bresson's most dark and forbidding film, Bresson demonstrates a sympathetic understanding of his four main characters, all young and strikingly attractive. At the time the movie first appeared authorities worried that Charles's suicide would be seen as a model to be imitated, but it is presented very differently from those of Mouchette or the gentle woman, who immolate themselves in the name of an absolute. As Charles explains to the analyst, "I am not depressed. I only wish to enjoy the right to be what I am." What he wants to avoid is "to have false desires imposed on him, desires determined by means of statistics, opinion polls, and formulas. . . . I wish to be neither a slave nor a specialist." The entire film is a powerful repudiation of the empty rhetoric spoken by "experts" in science, religion, politics, psychoanalysis, and even ecology, since the truths each of these pretends to enunciate are seen to have been reduced to slogans and jargon.[17]

L'Argent is an appropriate final film for Bresson, because the chain of evil forged through the pursuit of money was a central theme during his whole career. It also reminds us that the "spiritual style" of his films does not depend on explicitly religious subject matter, but has to do with going beyond surface realism while observing the relation between persons and things as closely as possible. When Yvon offers some hazelnuts to the gray-haired lady and they work together hanging out her wash, all the details of the scene work together to create a moment of sublime harmony. What is terrible is that a further outburst of terror can find expression even after this; perhaps it is the only way that the poison of "Where is the money?" can be finally expelled.

Throughout his career Bresson retained a strong sense that our life is made up of a combination of predestination and chance, but he has no interest in demonstrating any theories. He sums up his intentions in *Notes of a Cinematographer*:

> Not to shoot a film in order to illustrate a thesis, or to display men and women confined to their external aspect, but to discover the matter they are made of. To attain that "heart of the heart" which does not let itself be caught either by poetry, or by philosophy, or by drama.[18]

Kent Jones said he was jolted in *L'Argent* "to see Bresson track the evolution of murder purely through unembellished action, the physical world all the while remaining vibrantly, thrillingly alive. . . . It's bracing to witness Bresson laying out the plain truths of the modern world by returning his medium to the level of pure action. . . . One action at a time, everything happening at eye level, the time frame resolutely human. . . . The rejection of life against acceptance of life: this is the opposition at the core of *L'Argent*.[19]

Bresson recognized that whereas in the Tolstoy novella he was adapting the whole second half had an evangelical tone, his film suggested the possibility of redemption only at the end. To a great extent this is a recognition of today's climate of unbelief, which may also cause Yvon's fellow-prisoner to apologize to his cellmate when he says, "I always pray for suicides." Bresson underlines the fact that when Yvon attends mass in prison, a number of prisoners, despite the surveillance of the guards, can be seen exchanging various contraband articles even as the chaplain recites the first prayers of the canon. Nevertheless, at the end of the sequence the celebrant says, "Snatch us from damnation and receive us among your elect." This might seem like empty formalism at the time, but it takes on extra resonance at the film's conclusion.

—ANDREY TARKOVSKY, THE GREAT RUSSIAN DIRECTOR WHO MADE *Andrey Rublyov, Stalker,* and *The Sacrifice,* rightly insisted that Bresson doesn't have a genre:

> He is a genre in himself. . . . Bresson is perhaps the only man in the cinema to have achieved the perfect fusion of the finished work with a project formulated beforehand. . . . His guiding principle was the elimination of what is known as 'expressiveness,' in the sense that he wanted to do away with the frontier between the image and actual life, to make life itself graphic and expressive. . . . The principle has something in common with Zen art where, in our perception, precise observation of life passes paradoxically into sublime artistic imagery.[20]

But perhaps Bresson's instinctive rebellion against the various forms of excess found in most commercial movies is adequately summarized in his wonderful bit of self-advice: "Not to use two violins when one is enough."[21]

One can only speculate as to what Bresson might have created in *Genesis,* a project he had been turning over in his mind since 1963, but it would obviously not have been a conventional "religious" movie. It was presumably to be based on the first eleven chapters of the Bible, from the creation to the building of the Tower of Babel. Philippe Arnaud believes that we should understand this long-standing project as

> the desire to create his absolute film, the one that underlies them all. If there is an obsession about origins in Bresson, we should certainly not understand it as a regression, a return to the beginning. It is a matter of something quite different: the world that he presents to us is seized at its origin—not that of the unattainable cause of causes, but in the moment when it comes to us. He has a extra interest in the first, brute matter, of a withdrawal which would detach it from the corrective and falsifying weight of habits, of forgotten filters. . . . That is why *Genesis* appears as his summa, the ultimate film, at once first and last, and which as ideal and impossible object is the cause of the others. . . . In this sense it would occupy the same place that for Dreyer was occupied by his film on Christ"[22] [—which also remained unmade].

Genesis is another reason why it is unwise to concentrate on Bresson's "pessimism"—a term, he points out, that is often used as a substitute for "lucidity." Better to recall Susan Sontag's emphasis: "Bresson is interested in the forms of spiritual action—in the physics, as it were, rather than in the psychology of souls. Why persons behave as they do is, ultimately, not to be understood."[23] She relates Bresson's intentions to key sentences in Simone Weil's *Gravity and Grace:*

> Grace fills empty spaces, but it can only enter where there is a void to receive it, and it is grace itself which makes this void. The imagination is continually at work filling up all the fissures through which grace might pass.[24]

Bresson refuses to cheat: he will not stage false miracles or bring on angelic voices to drown out the power of evil. He offers no recipe for a "spiritual style in film." Yet the desire to create such a style is present in his passion to suggest what William James described as the unfinished nature of the universe, our common struggle to break out of the prisons of society and self. But Bresson recognizes that such a struggle includes negative—in *L'Argent,* even murderous—aspects. "The true," he reminds us, "is not encrusted in the living persons and real objects you use. It is an air of truth that their images take on when you set them together in a certain order."[25]

The shocking sequence in *Au hasard Balthasar* that begins when a hungry and desperate Marie comes to the grain merchant's house at night should remind us of what that statement implies. Her wet clothes, the candle in the room, the pot of jam that Marie grabs, the money he offers her—which she rejects after his bold summary of his philosophy of greed—all work to create an atmosphere that deserves to be called infernal. In addition, Bresson's severe cutting links this and succeeding scenes with startling speed: suddenly Marie has her clothes back on and has rushed outside; her parents arrive; the merchant tells her father to take the donkey back; the latter refuses, but in the next shot Balthasar and the family are home.

"Living persons and real objects . . . are set together in a certain order"—but notice that this does not imply a positive resolution of the world's evils. Even after a moment of hope with Jacques—"I will love him"—Marie is subjected to further humiliations at the hands of Gérard and his gang, again returns home with the donkey, and mysteriously disappears. Next, her father dies just after his wife prays that he be spared. When Gérard comes to make use of Balthasar to bring illegal goods across the border, Marie's mother can only lament that he is all she has left: "He has worked a great deal. Besides, he is a saint." Indeed, the donkey is a witness or an important reminder of the pain of existence long before the sheep surround him during his own death agony. Bresson's "spiritual style in film" is no guarantee of edifying endings, but his austere, clear-eyed cinematography fosters a deep understanding of the grandeur and pain of our common humanity.

NOTES

1. David Thompson, *Biographical Dictionary of Film* (New York: 1994), 72.

2. P. Adams Sitney, "The Rhetoric of Robert Bresson," in *The Essential Cinema* (New York: New York University Press, 1975), 184–85.

3. Lindley Hanlon, *Fragments* (Cranberry, N.J.: Associated University Press, 1982), 27.

4. Ibid., 29–32.

5. Philippe Arnaud, *Robert Bresson* (Paris: Cahiers du Cinéma, 1986), 12.

6. John E. Keegan, "Film Style and Theological Vision in Robert Bresson," *Horizons* 8, no. 1 (1981): 89.

7. Michel Ciment, in *Robert Bresson*, ed. James Quandt (Toronto: Cinematheque Ontario, 1998), 507.

8. Mireille Latil Le Dantec, personal letter to the author, June 2001.

9. Jean Sémolué, *Bresson ou l'acte pur des Métamorphoses* (Paris: Flammarion, 1993), 53.

10. Ibid., 106.

11. Amédée Ayfre, "The Universe of Robert Bresson," in *The Films of Robert Bresson*, ed. Ian Cameron (New York: Praeger, 1970), 24.

12. *Le Monde*, March 14, 1967.

13. Michel Estève, *Robert Bresson* (Paris: Editions Albatros, 1983), 36.

14. Sémolué, *Bresson ou l'acte pur des Métamorphoses*, 164.

15. Hanlon, *Fragments*, 39.

16. Ibid., 45.

17. Luigi Bini, *Revista del Cinematografo* (December 2000): 63.

18. Robert Bresson, *Notes of a Cinematographer* (Los Angeles: Sun and Moon Press, 1988), 47.

19. Kent Jones, *Robert Bresson's "L'Argent"* (London: British Film Institute, 1999), 75–76.

20. Andrey Tarkovsky, *Sculpting in Time* (New York: Knopf, 1987), 150, 94–95.

21. Bresson, *Notes of a Cinematographer*, 26.

22. Arnaud, *Robert Bresson*, 152.

23. Susan Sontag, "Spiritual Style in the Films of Robert Bresson," in *Against Interpretation* (New York: Farrar, Straus and Giroux, 1966).

24. Simone Weil, *Gravity and Grace* (New York: G. P. Putnam, 1952), 55 and 62.

25. Robert Bresson, *Notes of a Cinematographer* (Los Angeles: Sun and Moon Press, 1988), 80–81.

Filmography

Angels of Sin (*Les Anges du péché*) 1943
  Production Company: Synops-Roland Tual
  Screenplay: Robert Bresson (based on an idea by R. P. Brückberger)
  Dialogue: Jean Giraudoux
  Cinematography: (black-and-white) Philippe Agostini
  Editor: Yvonne Martin
  Sound: René Longe
  Music: Jean-Jacques Grünewald
  Art Director: René Renoux
  Running time: 97 minutes
  Cast: Renée Faure (Anne-Marie); Jany Holt (Thérèse); Sylvie (the prioress); Mila Parély (Madeleine); Marie-Hélène Dasté (Mother Saint-Jean); Yolande Laffon (Anne-Marie's mother); Paula Dehelly (Mother Dominique); Sylvia Montfort (Agnès); Gilberte Terbois (Sister Marie-Joseph); Louis Regnier (Prison director)
  Date of filming: February 8–April 1943

The Ladies of the Bois de Boulogne (*Les Dames du Bois de Boulogne*) 1945
  Production Company: Les Films Raoul Ploquin
  Screenplay: Robert Bresson (based on *Jacques le fataliste et son maître* by Denis Diderot)
  Dialogue: Jean Cocteau
  Cinematography: (black-and-white) Philippe Agostini
  Editor: Jean Feyte
  Sound: René Louge
  Music: Jean-Jacques Grünewald

Art Director: Max Douy
Assistant director: Roger Spiri-Mercanton
Running time: 84 minutes
Cast: Maria Casarès (Hélène); Élina Labourdette (Agnès); Paul Bernard (Jean); Lucienne Bogaert (Agnès's mother); Jean Marchat (Jacques)
Date of filming: (frequently interrupted) May 3, 1944–February 10, 1945

Diary of a Country Priest (*Journal d'un curé de campagne*) 1951
Production company: Union Générale Cinématographique
Screenplay: Robert Bresson (based on the novel by Georges Bernanos)
Cinematography: (black-and-white) Léonce-Henri Burel
Sound: Jean Rieul
Music: Jean-Jacques Grünewald
Art director: Pierre Charbonnier
Assistant director: Guy Lefranc
Editor: Paulette Robert
Running time: 110 minutes
Cast: Claude Laydu (the curé d'Ambricourt); Jean Riveyre (the count); Armand Guibert (the curé of Torcy); Nicole Ladmiral (Chantal); Martine Lemaire (Seraphita); Nicole Maurrey (Mlle. Louise); Marie-Minique Arkell (the countess); Antoine Balpêtré (Dr. Delbende); Léon Arvel (Fabregard); Jean Danet (Olivier)
Date of filming: March 6–June 19, 1950

A Man Escaped (*Un condamné à mort s'est échappé, ou Le vent souffle où il veut*) 1956
Co-producers: Gaumont, Nouvelles Éditions de Films
Screenplay: Robert Bresson (based on the account by André Devigny)
Cinematography: (black-and-white) Léonce-Henri Burel
Sound: Pierre-André Bertrand
Music: Wolfgang Amadeus Mozart, *Kyrie* of Mass in C Minor
Art director: Pierre Charbonnier
Assistant directors: Michel Clément, Jacques Ballanche, Jean-Paul Clément, Louis Malle
Editor: Raymond Lamy
Running time: 100 minutes
Cast: François Leterrier (Fontaine); Charles Le Clainche (Jost); Maurice Beerblock (Blanchet); Roland Monod (the pastor); Jacques Ertaud (Orsini); Roger Tréherne (Terry)
Date of filming: May 15–August 2, 1956

Pickpocket (1959)

    Producer: Agnès Delahaie

    Screenplay: Robert Bresson

    Cinematography: (black-and-white) Léonce-Henri Burel

    Art director: Pierre Charbonnier

    Sound: Antoine Archimbaut

    Music: Jean-Baptiste Lully

    Assistant directors: Claude Clément, Michel Clément, Jacques Ballanche

    Editor: Raymond Lamy

    Running time: 75 minutes

    Cast: Martin Lasalle (Michel); Marika Green (Jeanne); Jean Péligri (the inspector); Dolly Scal (Michel's mother); Pierre Leymarie (Jacques); Kassagi (the first accomplice); Pierre Étaix (the second accomplice)

    Date of filming: June 22–September 12, 1959

The Trial of Joan of Arc (*Procès de Jeanne d'Arc*) 1962

    Producer: Agnès Delahaye

    Screenplay: Robert Bresson

    Cinematography: (black-and-white) Léonce-Henri Burel

    Art director: Pierre Charbonnier

    Sound: Antoine Archimbaut

    Music: Francis Seyrig

    Assistant directors: Serge Roullet, Marcel Ugols, Hugo Santiago, Alain Ferrari

    Editor: Germaine Artus

    Running time: 65 minutes

    Cast: Florence Delay (Joan of Arc); Jean-Claude Fourneau (Bishop Cauchon); Roger Honorat (Jean Beaupère); Marc Jacquier (Jean Lemaître); Jean Gillibert (Jean de Chatillon); Michel Heubel (Isambert); André Regnier (d'Estivet); André Brunet (Massieu); Marcel Darbaud (Nicolas de Houppeville); Philippe Dreux (Martin Ladvenu); Paul-Robert Nimet (Guillaume Erard); Richard Pratt (Warwick); Gérard Zingg (Jean Lohier); André Maurice (Tiphaine)

    Date of filming: July 17–September 15, 1961

Au hasard Balthasar (1966)

    Co-producers: Argos Films, Parc Film, Athos Films (France); Institut suédois du film; Svensk Filmindustri (Sweden)

    Screenplay: Robert Bresson

    Cinematography: (black-and-white) Ghislain Cloquet

    Art director: Pierre Charbonnier

    Sound: Antoine Archimbaut

Music: Franz Schubert, Sonata no. 20; Jean Wiener
Assistant directors: Jacques Kébedian, Sven Frostenson, Claude Miller
Editor: Raymond Lamy
Running time: 95 minutes
Cast: Anne Wiazemsky (Marie); Walter Green (Jacques); François Lafarge (Gérard); Jean-Claude Guilbert (Arnold); Philippe Asselin (Marie's father); Pierre Klossowkski (the grain merchant); Nathalie Joyaut (Marie's mother); Marie-Claie Frémont (the baker's wife); Jean-Joël Barbier (the curé); Jean Remignard (the lawyer); Guy Brejnac (the veternarian); Jacques Sorbets (the police captain); François Sullerot (the baker); Tord Paag (Louis), Sven Frostenson and Roger Fjellstrom (members of Gérard's gang); Rémy Brozeck (Marcel); Mylène Weyergens (nurse)
Date of filming: July 21, 1965–February 28, 1966

Mouchette (1967)
Co-producers: Argos Films and Parc Film
Screenplay: Robert Bresson (adapted from *Nouvelle histoire de Mouchette*, by Georges Bernanos)
Cinematography: (black-and-white) Ghislain Croquet
Art director: Pierre Guffroy
Sound: Séverin Frankiel and Jacques Carrère
Music: Claudio Monteverdi, Jean Wiener
Assistant directors: Jacques Kébadian and Mylène van der Mersch
Editor: Raymond Lamy
Running time: 82 minutes
Cast: Nadine Nortier (Mouchette); Jean-Claude Guilbert (Arsène); Paul Hébert (the father); Marie Cardinal (the mother); Jean Vimenet (Mathieu); Marie Susini (Mathieu's wife); Marie Trichet (Louisa); Liliane Princet (the teacher); Raymonde Chabrun (the grocer); Suzanne Huguenin (the old lady who watches over the dead)
Date of filming: September 12–November 17, 1966

A Gentle Woman (*Une femme douce*) 1969
Co-producers: Parc Film and Marianne Production
Screenplay: Robert Bresson (based on "A Gentle Woman," a story by Fyodor Dostoevsky)
Cinematography: (color) Ghislain Cloquet
Sound: Jacques Maumont, Jacques Lebreton, Urbain Loiseau
Music: Henry Purcell, Jean Wiener
Art director: Pierre Charbonnier
Assistant directors: Jacques Kébadian and Mylène van der Mersch

Editor: Raymond Lamy

Running time: 88 minutes

Cast: Dominique Sanda (She); Guy Frangin (He); Jane Lobre (the maid); Claude Ollier (the doctor)

Date of shooting: September 2–November 11, 1968

Four Nights of a Dreamer (*Quatre nuits d'un rêveur*) 1972

Co-producers: Albina Productions, i Film dell'Orso, Victoria Film, Gian Vittorio Baldi (Italy), and ORTF (France)

Screenplay: Robert Bresson (based on "White Nights," a story of Fyodor Dostoevsky)

Cinematography: (color) Pierre Lhomme (Ghislain Cloquet for the police film scene)

Sound: Roger Letellier

Art director: Pierre Charbonnier

Assistant director: Mylène van der Mersch

Editor: Raymond Lamy

Running time: 83 minutes

Cast: Isabelle Weingarten (Marthe); Guillaume des Forêts (Jacques); Jean-Maurice Monnoyer (the lodger); Jérome Massart (the visitor); Patrick Jouanné (the gangster); Lidia Biondi (Marthe's mother); Groupe Batuki (musicians on the *bateau-mouche*)

Dates of shooting: August 8–October 7, 1970

Lancelot of the Lake (*Lancelot du Lac*) 1974

Co-producers: Mara-Films, Laser-Production ORTF (France) and Gerico Sound (Italy)

Screenplay: Robert Bresson (adapted from "Le chevalier à la charrette," of Chrétien de Troyes)

Cinematography: (color) Pasqualo De Sanctis

Sound: Bernard Bats

Music: Philip Sarde

Scene design: Philippe Charbonnier

Assistant directors: Mylène van der Mersch, Bernard Cohn, and Robert Barody

Editor: Germaine Lamy

Running time: 93 minutes

Cast: Luc Simon (Lancelot); Laura Duke Condominas (Queen Guinevere); Humbert Balsan (Gawain); Vladimir Antolek (King Arthur); Patrick Bernard (Mordred); Arthur de Montalembert (Lionel); Marie-Louise Buffet (old peasant woman); Marie-Gabrielle Carton (young girl)

The Devil Probably (*Le Diable probablement*) 1977
    Co-producers: Sunchild G.M.F./M. Chanderli
    Screenplay: Robert Bresson
    Cinematography: (color) Pasqualino de Santis
    Sound: Georges Prat
    Music: Claudio Monteverdi, Wolfgang Amadeus Mozart
    Scene design: Eric Simon
    Assistant directors: Mylène van der Mersch; Thierry Bodin; Humbert Balsan; Éric Deroo, Mahant de Cordon
    Editor: Germaine Lamy
    Running time: 97 minutes
    Cast: Antoine Monnier (Charles); Tina Irissari (Alberte); Henri de Maublanc (Michel); Laetitia Carcano (Edwige); Nicolas Deguy (Valentin); Régis Hanrion (the psychoanalyst); Geoffroy Gaussen (the bookseller); Roger Honorat (the police officer)
    Dates of shooting: June 5–August 15, 1976

Money (*L'Argent*) 1983
    Co-producers: Marion's Films, FR3 (France), and Eos Films (Switzerland)
    Screenplay: Robert Bresson (adapted from the novella of Leo Tolstoy, "The False Coupon")
    Cinematography: (color) Pasqualino de Santis; Emmanuel Machuel
    Sound: Jean-Louis Ughetto and Jacques Maumont
    Music: Johann Sebastian Bach
    Scene design: Pierre Guffroy
    Assistant directors: Mylène van der Mersch, Thierry Bodin, and Pascal Bony
    Editor: Jean-François Naudon
    Running time: 85 minutes
    Cast: Christian Patey (Yvon); Vincent Risteruci (Lucien); Caroline Lang (Elise); Sylvie Van den Elsen (the woman with gray hair); Michel Briguet (her father); Béatrice Tabourin (woman in the photography shop); Didier Baussy (man in the photography shop); Marc-Ernest Fourneau (Norbert); Bruno Lapeyre (Martial); Jeanne Aptekman (Yvette); André Cler (Norbert's father); Claude Cler (Norbert's mother); François-Marie Banier (Yvon's cellmate)

Bibliography

Affron, Mireille Jona. "Bresson and Pascal: Rhetorical Affinities." In *Robert Bresson*, ed. James Quandt, 165–88. Toronto: Cinematheque Ontario, 1998.

Amengual, Barthélemy. In *Positif* (October 1974).

Amiel, Vincent. *Le corps au cinéma: Bresson, Keaton, Cassavetes*. Paris: Presses univérsitaires de France, 1997.

Andrews, Dudley. "Desperation and Meditation: Bresson's *Diary of a Country Priest*." In *Modern European Filmmakers and the Art of Adaptation*, ed. Andrew S. Horton and Joan Magretta. New York: Ungar, 1981.

Arnaud, Philippe. *Robert Bresson*. Paris: Cahiers du Cinéma, 1986.

Arts no. 574 (June 27–July 3, 1956).

Avant-scène no. 80 (July 1967).

Ayfre, Amédée. "The Universe of Robert Bresson." In *The Films of Robert Bresson*, ed. Ian Cameron. New York: Praeger, 1969.

Barthes, Roland. In *Robert Bresson: Éloge*. Paris: Cinémathèque française, 1997.

Baugh, Lloyd. *Imaging the Divine*. Kansas City, Mo.: Sheed & Ward, 1997.

Bazin, André. *What is Cinema?* Volume 1. Berkeley: University of California Press, 1967.

Ben-Gad, Schmuel. "To See the World Profoundly: The Films of Robert Bresson." *Cross Currents* (Summer 1997).

Bernanos, Georges. *Mouchette*. New York: Holt, Rinehart & Winston, 1966.

———. *Oeuvres romanesques*. Bibliothèque de la Pléiade. Paris: Gallimard, 1961.

Blue, James. Excerpts from an interview with Robert Bresson, June 1965, by the author.

Bongiovanni, Marco. "Robert Bresson: dalla non-violenza alla gratia." *Revista del Cinematografo* no. 9 (December 2000).

Bordwell, David, and Kristin Thompson. *Film Art: An Introduction*. 6th edition. New York: McGraw Hill, 2001.

Bresson, Robert. Interview in *Cahiers du Cinéma* no. 178 (May 1966).

———. Interview in *Cahiers du Cinéma* no. 180 (July 1966).

———. Interview with Yvonne Baby, *Le Monde*, May 26, 1966.

———. *Notes of a Cinematographer.* Los Angeles: Sun and Moon Press, 1988.

Robert Bresson: Éloge. Paris: Cinémathèque française, 1997.

Briot, René. *Robert Bresson.* Paris: Éditions du Cerf, 1957.

Cameron, Ian, ed. *The Films of Robert Bresson.* New York: Praeger, 1970.

Ciment, Michel. "I Seek Not Description but Vision: Robert Bresson on 'L'Argent.'" In *Robert Bresson*, ed. James Quandt. Toronto: Cinematheque Ontario, 1998.

Collet, Jean. "Le drôle de chemin de Bresson à Balthasar." *Études* (July–August 1966).

———. In *Télé-ciné* no. 88 (March–April 1960).

Cott, Jonathan. "Fires Within Us: The Chaste Sensuality of Director Louis Malle." *Rolling Stone*, April 6, 1978.

Daney, Serge, and Serge Toubiana. Interview with Robert Bresson, *Cahiers du cinéma* no. 348–349 (June–July 1983).

Dempsey, Michael. "Despair Abounding: The Recent Films of Robert Bresson." In *Robert Bresson*, ed. James Quandt. Toronto: Cinematheque Ontario, 1998.

Dostoevsky, Fyodor. *The Brothers Karamazov.* New York: Vintage Classics, 1990.

———. *The Short Stories of Dostoevsky.* Edited by William Phillips. New York: Dial Press, 1946.

Drillion, Jacques. Interview with Robert Bresson, *Le Nouvel Observateur*, May 6, 1983.

Durgnat, Raymond. "Le Journal d'un Curé de Campagne." In *The Films of Robert Bresson*, ed. Ian Cameron. New York: Praeger, 1969.

Endo, Shûsaku. In *Le Cinématographie de Robert Bresson.* Tokyo: Tokyo International Foundation for the Promotion of Screen Image Culture, 1999.

Estève, Michel. *Robert Bresson.* Paris: Editions Albatros, 1983.

———. *Le sens de l'amour dans les romans de Bernanos.* Paris: M. J. Minard, Lettres Modernes, 1961.

Fantuzzi, Virgilio. "L'anima nella prigione: osservazioni sul cinema di Robert Bresson." In "Robert Bresson," *Revista del Cinematografo* no. 9 (December 2000).

Godard, Jean-Luc, and Michel Delahaye. Interview with Robert Bresson in *Cahiers du Cinéma* no. 178 (May 1966).

Gracq, Julien. "Un compagnonnage d'exception." *Les nouvelles littéraires*, September 23, 1974.

Greenspun, Roger. *New York Times*, February 20, 1970.

———. *New York Times*, November 26, 1972.

Guth, Paul. *Autour des "Dames du Bois de Boulogne," journal d'un film.* Paris: Julliard/Sequana, 1945.

Hanlon, Lindley. *Fragments.* Cranberry, N.J.: Associated University Press, 1982.

Haskell, Molly. In *Village Voice*, November 4, 1971.

Hoberman, J. In *Village Voice*, November 17, 1994.

Jones, Kent. *Robert Bresson's 'L'Argent.* London: British Film Institute, 1999.

Keegan, John E. "Film Style and Theological Vision in Robert Bresson." *Horizons* 8, no. 1 (1981).

Labourdette, Élena. In *Le Cinématographie de Robert Bresson.* Tokyo: Tokyo International Foundation for the Promotion of Screen Image Culture, 1999.

Lanzoni, Rémi Fournier. *French Cinema: From Its Beginnings to the Present.* New York: Continuum International, 2002.

Le Dantec, Mireille Latil. "Bresson, Dostoevsky." In *Robert Bresson,* ed. James Quandt. Toronto: Cinematheque Ontario, 1998.

————. "Une nouvelle et deux films." Thesis of the third cycle, defended at the University of Paris X, 1982.

————, and Pierre Jouvet. "*Le diable, probablement.*" *Cinématographe* (September 1977).

Le Clézio, Jean-Marie G. "Le voyage initiatique" *Le Monde,* July 7, 1983.

Macabru, Pierre. In *Robert Bresson: Éloge.* Paris: Cinémathèque française, 1997.

Mathews, Thomas F. *The Clash of Gods: A Reinterpretation of Christian Art.* Princeton, N.J.: Princeton University Press, 1993.

Maurice, René. "De Lucifer à Balthasar, en suivant Robert Bresson." *Lumière et vie* no. 78 (1966).

Moravia, Alberto. In *Robert Bresson: Éloge.* Paris: Cinématheque française, 1997.

Mortier, Michel. In *Télé-ciné* no. 134 (August–September 1967).

Pipolo, Tony. "Rules of the Game: On Bresson's *Les anges du péché.*" In *Robert Bresson,* ed. James Quandt. Toronto: Cinematheque Ontario, 1998.

Prédal, René. "Robert Bresson: L'aventure intérieure." *L'Avant-scène cinéma* (January–February 1992).

Quandt, James, ed. *Robert Bresson.* Toronto: Cinematheque Ontario, 1998.

Radio-Télévision-Cinéma no. 426, March 16, 1958.

Rahner, Karl, ed. *Encyclopedia of Theology.* New York: Seabury Press, 1975.

Reader, Keith. *Robert Bresson.* Manchester: Manchester University Press, 2000.

Rider, Jeff. *Cinema Arthurian: Essays on Arthurian Film.* New York: Garland, 1991.

Rohmer, Eric. In *Cahiers du cinéma* no. 65 (December 1956).

Rosenbaum, Jonathan. "The Last Filmmaker: A Local Interim Report." In *Robert Bresson,* ed. James Quandt. Toronto: Cinematheque Ontario, 1998.

————. In *Village Voice,* June 17, 1971.

Roud, Richard. "The Devil Probably: The Redemption of Despair." In *Robert Bresson,* ed. James Quandt. Toronto: Cinematheque Ontario, 1998.

Sadoul, Georges. In *Robert Bresson, Éloge.* Paris: Cinémathèque français, 1997.

Samuels, Charles T. *Encountering Directors.* New York: G. P. Putnam & Sons, 1972.

Sarris, Andrew. *The Primal Screen.* New York: Simon & Schuster, 1973.

Schrader, Paul. "Robert Bresson, Possibly." In *Robert Bresson,* ed. James Quandt. Toronto: Cinematheque Ontario, 1998.

————. *Transcendental Style in Film: Ozu, Bresson, Dreyer.* Berkeley: University of California Press, 1972.

Sémolué, Jean. *Bresson ou l'acte pur des Métamorphoses.* Paris: Flammarion, 1993.

Sontag, Susan. "Spiritual Style in the Films of Robert Bresson." In *Against Interpretation*. New York: Farrar, Straus and Giroux, 1966.

Stéphane, Roger. Interview with Robert Bresson, *Télé-ciné* no. 173 (March–April 1967).

Tarkovsky, Andrei. *Sculpting in Time*. New York: Knopf, 1987.

Thiher, Allen. "Bresson's *Un condamné à mort*: The Semiotics of Grace." In *Robert Bresson*, ed. James Quandt. Toronto: Cinematheque Ontario, 1998.

Tilliette, Xavier. "Des ânes et des hommes." *Études* (June 1966).

Truffaut, François. *The Films in My Life*. New York: Simon & Schuster, 1978.

———. In *Pariscope*, June 21, 1977.

Wiazemsky, Anne. "400 Japonais en larmes." *Cahiers du Cinéma* (February 2000).

Bresson Films in America

1. New Yorker Films (85 5th Avenue, New York, NY 10011) has the following 35mm films for sale or rental:
>
> *L'Argent*
> *Lancelot du Lac*
> *The Devil Probably*
> *A Gentle Woman*
> *The Ladies of the Bois de Boulogne*

They are planning to issue DVDs of *A Man Escaped* and *Lancelot du Lac* in 2003.

2. Facets Multi-Media (1517 West Fullerton, Chicago, IL 60614) has the following videos available for rental:
>
> *Diary of a Country Priest*
> *A Man Escaped*
> *Pickpocket*
> *L'Argent*
> *A Gentle Woman*
> *The Devil Probably*
> *Mouchette*
> *Ladies of the Bois de Boulogne*
> *Lancelot du Lac*

3. Criterion is planning to issue DVDs of *Diary of a Country Priest* and *Ladies of the Bois de Boulogne*.